Advanced Mathematical Applications in Data Science

Edited by

Biswadip Basu Mallik
Department of Basic Science and Humanities
Institute of Engineering & Management, Kolkata
West Bengal, India

Kirti Verma
Department of Engineering Mathematics
Lakshmi Narain College of Technology, Jabalpur
Madhya Pradesh, India

Rahul Kar
Department of Mathematics
Kalyani Mahavidyalaya, Kalyani
West Bengal, India

Ashok Kumar Shaw
Department of Basic Sciences and Humanities
Budge Budge Institute of Technology
Budge Budge, Kolkata
West Bengal, India

&

Sardar M. N. Islam (Naz)
ISILC, Victoria University
Melbourne, Australia

Advanced Mathematical Applications in Data Science

Editors: Biswadip Basu Mallik, Kirti Verma, Rahul Kar, Ashok Kumar Shaw
& Sardar M. N. Islam (Naz)

ISBN (Online): 978-981-5124-84-2

ISBN (Print):978-981-5124-85-9

ISBN (Paperback): 978-981-5124-86-6

need for a court order if at any point you breach any terms of this License Agreement. In no event will any delay or failure by Bentham Science Publishers in enforcing your compliance with this License Agreement constitute a waiver of any of its rights.

3. You acknowledge that you have read this License Agreement, and agree to be bound by its terms and conditions. To the extent that any other terms and conditions presented on any website of Bentham Science Publishers conflict with, or are inconsistent with, the terms and conditions set out in this License Agreement, you acknowledge that the terms and conditions set out in this License Agreement shall prevail.

Bentham Science Publishers Pte. Ltd.
80 Robinson Road #02-00
Singapore 068898
Singapore
Email: subscriptions@benthamscience.net

BENTHAM SCIENCE

CONTENTS

FOREWORD i

PREFACE ii

LIST OF CONTRIBUTORS iii

CHAPTER 1 THE ROLE OF MATHEMATICS IN DATA SCIENCE: METHODS, ALGORITHMS, AND COMPUTER PROGRAMS 1
Rashmi Singh, Neha Bhardwaj and *Sardar M. N. Islam (Naz)*
INTRODUCTION 1
DATA SCIENCE 2
MAIN MATHEMATICAL PRINCIPLES AND METHODS IMPORTANT FOR DATA SCIENCE 3
 Linear Algebra 3
  Matrices 3
  System of Linear Equation 4
  The Number of Solutions 5
  Vectors 5
  Loss Function 6
  Regularization 7
  Support Vector Machine Classification 7
 Statistics 8
  Probability Theory 8
  Normal Distribution 8
  Z Scores 10
  The Central Limit Theorem 11
  Some Other Statistical Methods 11
  Skewness 11
  Kurtosis 12
 Applications of Statistics in Data Science through Machine Learning Algorithms 13
  Regression 13
 Machine Learning Using Principal Component Analysis to Reduce Dimensionality 14
 Mathematical Basis of PCA 15
 Classification 16
  K-Nearest Neighbor 16
  Naive Bayes 17
 Calculus 17
 Optimization or Operational Research Methods 18
  Dynamic Optimization Model 19
  Stochastic Optimization Methods 19
 Some Other Methods 21
 Computer Programs 21
 CONCLUDING REMARKS 21
 REFERENCES 21

CHAPTER 2 KALMAN FILTER: DATA MODELLING AND PREDICTION 24
Arnob Sarkar and *Meetu Luthra*
INTRODUCTION 24
 Why Kalman Filter? 24
UNDERSTANDING THE KALMAN FILTER 25
 What is Kalman Filter? 25

State Space Approach 26
    Mean Squared Error 26
KALMAN FILTER EQUATIONS 27
GENERAL APPLICATIONS OF KALMAN FILTER 33
KALMAN FILTER EQUATIONS IN ONE DIMENSION 33
EXAMPLE 1: FINDING THE TRUE VALUE OF TEMPERATURE 35
   First Iteration 36
   Second Iteration 36
EXAMPLE 2: FINDING THE TRUE VALUE OF ACCELERATION DUE TO GRAVITY 37
EXAMPLE 3: VERIFYING HUBBLE'S LAW 41
LIMITATIONS OF KALMAN FILTER 45
OTHER FILTERS 46
FUTURE PROSPECTS 46
CONCLUDING REMARKS- KALMAN FILTER IN A NUTSHELL 47
APPENDIX – BASIC CONCEPTS 47
   A.1. LINEAR DYNAMIC SYSTEMS 47
   A.2. ERROR COVARIANCE MATRIX 48
   A.3. TULLY FISHER RELATION 49
   A.4. RED SHIFTS AND RECESSIONAL VELOCITY 49
REFERENCES 50

CHAPTER 3 THE ROLE OF MATHEMATICS AND STATISTICS IN THE FIELD OF DATA SCIENCE AND ITS APPLICATION 51
Sathiyapriya Murali and *Priya Panneer*
INTRODUCTION 51
   Data Science 51
DATA SCIENCE IN MATHEMATICS 52
MATH AND DATA SCIENCE IN EDUCATION 52
TYPES OF DATA SCIENCE IN MATH 53
   Linear Algebra 53
APPLICATION OF LINEAR ALGEBRA IN DATA SCIENCE 53
   Loss Function 53
   Mean Squared Error 53
MEAN ABSOLUTE ERROR 54
COMPUTER VISION 54
CALCULUS 54
CALCULUS IN MACHINE LEARNING 54
APPLICATIONS IN MEDICAL SCIENCE 55
APPLICATION IN ENGINEERING 55
APPLICATIONS IN RESEARCH ANALYSIS 55
APPLICATIONS IN PHYSICS 55
STATISTICS 55
   Types of Statistics in Data Science 56
     Descriptive Statistics 56
     Inferential Statistics 56
   Application of Statistics in the Field of Study 57
VITAL STATISTICS IDEAS OBTAINING STARTED 57
DISTRIBUTION OF DATA POINT 57
APPLIED MATH EXPERIMENTS AND SIGNIFICANCE TESTING 57
NONPARAMETRIC STATISTICAL METHODS 58

APPLICATION OF STATISTICS IN DATA SCIENCE ANALYZING AND
CATEGORIZING DATA 58
NUMERIC DATA & CATEGORICAL DATA 58
EXPLORATORY KNOWLEDGE ANALYSIS 58
SIGNIFICANCE TESTS 58
    Null Hypotheses 59
    Alternative Hypotheses 59
CHI-SQUARED CHECK 59
STUDENT'S T-TEST 59
ANALYSIS OF VARIANCE CHECK (ANOVA) 59
    Unidirectional 60
    Two-ways 60
RESERVATION AND PREDICTION 60
    Linear Regression 60
    Logistic Regression 60
CLASSIFICATION OF KNOWLEDGE SCIENCE IN STATISTICS 60
    Naive Mathematician 61
    K-nearest Neighbors 61
PROBABILITY 61
FREQUENCY TABLES 61
HISTOGRAM 62
CONTINUOUS RANDOM VARIABLES 63
SKEWNESS DISTRIBUTION 63
RIGHT SKEW DISTRIBUTION 63
LEFT SKEW DISTRIBUTION 63
NORMAL DISTRIBUTION 63
EXPONENTIAL DISTRIBUTION 64
UNIFORM DISTRIBUTION 64
POISSON DISTRIBUTION 64
IMPORTANT OF INFORMATION SCIENCE 64
DATA WHILE NOT KNOWLEDGE SCIENCE 65
DATA CAN PRODUCE HIGHER CLIENT EXPERTISE 65
DATA USED ACROSS VERTICALS 65
POWER OF INFORMATION SCIENCE 65
FUTURE OF INFORMATION SCIENCE 65
DATA SCIENCE IN TRADE 66
BENEFITS OF KNOWLEDGE SCIENCE 66
STATISTICAL INFORMATION 66
DATA SCIENCE IS VERY IMPORTANT IN THE MODERN WORLD 66
DATA INDIVIDUAL 66
DATA SCIENCE WORKS 67
CONCLUDING REMARKS 67
REFERENCES 67

CHAPTER 4 BAG OF VISUAL WORDS MODEL - A MATHEMATICAL APPROACH 68
    Maheswari
INTRODUCTION 68
HISTOGRAM REWEIGHTING – TF – IDF APPROACH 69
COST MATRIX GENERATION 69
EUCLIDEAN DISTANCE AND COSINE DISTANCE 70
MODEL DESCRIPTION 71

Histogram Generation for Image 71
Computation of Cost Matrix 71
Reweighting of Histogram using TF – IDF 72
Visualization of Original Euclidean, Reweighted Euclidean 72
Normalization of Original Histogram 74
Checking for Similarity of the Normalized Histogram 74
Visual Comparison of Histograms 76
CONCLUSION 78
REFERENCES 78

**CHAPTER 5 A GLANCE REVIEW ON DATA SCIENCE AND ITS TEACHING:
CHALLENGES AND SOLUTIONS** 80
Srinivasa Rao Gundu, Charanarur Panem and *J. Vijaylaxmi*
INTRODUCTION 80
THE IMPACT OF DATA SCIENCE ON THE SOCIETY 83
EDUCATIONAL GOALS OF DATA SCIENCE 83
DATA SCIENCE IN PRACTICE AS A PROBLEM SOLVING 84
LITERATURE REVIEW 85
**DEMANDS OF THE DATA SCIENCE INDUSTRY AND THE DATA SCIENCE
CURRICULUM** 86
INHERENT PROBLEMS IN DATA SCIENCE CURRICULA DEVELOPMENT 88
TEACHING DATA SCIENCE 89
CONCLUDING REMARKS 90
REFERENCES 90

**CHAPTER 6 OPTIMIZATION OF VARIOUS COSTS IN INVENTORY MANAGEMENT
USING NEURAL NETWORKS** 92
Prerna Sharma and *Bhim Singh*
INTRODUCTION 92
RELATED WORK 93
ASSUMPTION AND NOTATIONS 94
MATHEMATICAL FORMULATION OF MODEL AND ANALYSIS 96
MULTILAYER-FEED FORWARD NEURAL NETWORKS 99
WORKING ON PROPOSED SYSTEM 102
EXPERIMENTAL RESULTS AND ANALYSIS 102
CONCLUDING REMARKS 102
REFERENCES 102

CHAPTER 7 CYBER SECURITY IN DATA SCIENCE AND ITS APPLICATIONS 105
M. Varalakshmi and *I. P. Thulasi*
INTRODUCTION 105
DATA SCIENCE TODAY 105
MOTIVE AND SIGNIFICANCE OF DATA SCIENCE 106
IMPORTANCE OF DATA 107
IMPORTANCE OF DATA SCIENCE 107
MOTIVATION OF DATA IMPORTANT INDUSTRIES 107
DATA SCIENCE FOR PREFERABLE TRADE 107
DATA ANALYTICS FOR CLIENT ACQUISITION 108
DATA ANALYTICS FOR REVOLUTION 108
DATA SCIENCE FOR ENHANCESURVIVAL 108
PART OF DATA SCIENCE IN CYBER SECURITY 108
CONNECTION ALLYING SUBSTANTIAL DATA AND CYBER SECURITY 109

DATA SCIENCE USED IN CYBER SECURITY 109

Negative Hoping on "Lab-based" Order 110

Utilize Entrance to Sufficient Data 110

Specialize in this Irregularity 110

Utilize Data Science in a Logical Approach 111

UPCOMING CHALLENGES IN CYBER SECURITY DATA SCIENCE 111

OPERATE CLASSIFICATION ISSUES IN CYBERSECURITY DATAFILE 111

RELIABILITY SCHEME RULE 111

AMBIENCE PERCEPTON IN CYBER SECURITY 112

ATTRIBUTE ENGINEERING IN CYBER SECURITY 112

PROMINENT SECURITY ACTIVE CREATION AND ARRAY 112

DISCUSSION 113

CONCLUDING REMARKS 114

REFERENCES 115

CHAPTER 8 ARTIFICIAL NEURAL NETWORKS FOR DATA PROCESSING: A CASE STUDY OF IMAGE CLASSIFICATION 116

Jayaraj Ramasamy, R. N. Ravikumar and S. Shitharth

INTRODUCTION 116

ARCHITECTURE OF ANN 117

Input Layer 118

Hidden Layer 118

Output Layer 118

BENEFITS OF ARTIFICIAL NEURAL NETWORK (ANN) 119

Ability for Processing 119

Network-based Data Storage 119

Capacity to Function Despite a Lack of Knowledge 119

Transmission of Memory 119

Acceptance for Faults 119

DISADVANTAGES 120

Ensure that the Network Structure is Correct 120

Network Activity that has Gone Unnoticed 120

Network's Life Expectancy is Unknown 120

WORKING OF ANN 120

TYPES OF ANN 121

Feedback ANN 121

Feed-Forward 121

SIMPLE NEURAL NETWORK 121

LITERATURE REVIEW 122

PROPOSED SYSTEM 123

RESULTS AND DISCUSSION 124

CONCLUSION 125

REFERENCES 125

CHAPTER 9 CARBON EMISSION ASSESSMENT BY APPLYING CLUSTERING TECHNIQUE TO WORLD'S EMISSION DATASETS 128

Nitin Jaglal Untwal

INTRODUCTION 128

Research Methodology 130

Limitations of the Study 130

Feature Extraction and Engineering 131

Data Extraction 131

Standardizing and Scaling 132
Identification of Clusters by Elbow Method 132
Cluster Formation 134
RESULTS AND ANALYSIS 134
Cluster One – High Rainfall 134
Cluster Two 141
Cluster Three 141
Cluster Four 142
Cluster Five 142
Cluster Six 142
CONCLUSION 143
REFERENCES 143

CHAPTER 10 A MACHINE LEARNING APPLICATION TO PREDICT CUSTOMER CHURN: A CASE IN INDONESIAN TELECOMMUNICATION COMPANY 144
Agus Tri Wibowo, Andi Chaerunisa Utami Putri, Muhammad Reza Tribosnia, Revalda Putawara and *M. Mujiya Ulkhaq*
INTRODUCTION 144
LITERATURE REVIEW AND CONTRIBUTION 146
RESEARCH DESIGN 147
Dataset 147
Data Preparation 148
Exploratory Data Analysis 148
Features Selection 150
MACHINE LEARNING APPLICATION 151
Ridge Classifier 151
Gradient Booster 151
Adaptive Boosting 151
Bagging Classifier 152
k-Nearest Neighbor 152
Decision Tree 153
Logistic Regression 153
Random Forest 153
MODEL PERFORMANCE AND EVALUATION 154
RESULT 155
CONCLUDING REMARKS 159
REFERENCES 160

CHAPTER 11 A STATE-WISE ASSESSMENT OF GREENHOUSE GASES EMISSION IN INDIA BY APPLYING K-MEAN CLUSTERING TECHNIQUE 162
Nitin Jaglal Untwal
INTRODUCTION 163
Introduction to Cluster Analysis 163
Research Methodology 165
Data Source 165
Period of Study 165
Software used for Data Analysis 165
Model Applied 165
Limitations of the Study 165
Future Scope 165
Research is Carried Out in Five Steps 165
Feature Extraction and Engineering 165

Data Extraction 166
Standardizing and Scaling 166
Identification of Clusters by Elbow Method 166
Cluster formation 169
RESULTS AND ANALYSIS 169
Cluster One 171
Cluster Two 173
Cluster Three 174
CONCLUSION 175
REFERENCES 175

CHAPTER 12 DATA MINING TECHNIQUES: NEW AVENUES FOR HEART DISEASE PREDICTION 177
Soma Das
INTRODUCTION 177
ADVERSE IMPACT OF CARDIOVASCULAR DISEASES IN INDIA 179
Smoking 179
Hyperglycaemia 179
Hypertension 179
Obesity 180
Dyslipidaemia 180
Dietary Habits and Exercise 180
Genetic Risk Factors 180
Treatment Gaps 181
The Multilayer Perceptron (MLP) 181
Coactive Neuro-Fuzzy Inference System (CANFIS) 182
Aptamer Biochip-based CDSS –ensemble (Apta CDSS-E) 182
Intelligent Heart Disease Prediction System (IHDPS) 182
Intelligent and Effective Heart Attack Prediction System (IEHPS) 183
Decision Tree Fuzzy System (DTFS) 183
CONCLUDING REMARKS 183
REFERENCES 184

CHAPTER 13 DATA SCIENCE AND HEALTHCARE 186
Armel Djangone
INTRODUCTION 186
So, What is Data Science? 186
Data Science Techniques vs. Data Mining 187
Now, Why is Data Essential? 187
What is an Ideal Data Scientist? 188
Technical and Soft Skills for Healthcare Data Scientists 188
Technical Skills 189
Soft Skills 189
Why is Data Science so Crucial for Organizations? 190
HEALTHCARE DATA: CHALLENGES AND OPPORTUNITIES 191
Opportunities 191
Defining Big Data 193
Challenges 194
Data Science Opportunities for Healthcare 195
HEALTHCARE LEADERSHIP 197
Transactional leader 198
Transformational leadership 198

CONCLUDING REMARKS 200

REFERENCES 200

SUBJECT INDEX 201

FOREWORD

There is a need to provide a new, up-to-date, comprehensive, and innovative review of the developments to show, integrate, synthesize and provide future research directions in the applications of advanced mathematics in data science. Therefore, this book has made a valuable contribution to the literature by providing systematic reviews on the interrelationships between mathematics, statistics, and computer science.

Data Science is one of the most significant advances of this century. It deals with the collection, preparation, analysis, visualization, management, and preservation of this data – both structured and unstructured. Data science incorporates several technologies and academic disciplines to discover, extract, compile, process, analyze, interpret, and visualize data. It includes mathematics, statistics, computer science and programming, statistical modeling, database technologies, signal processing, data modeling, artificial intelligence, machine learning, natural language processing, visualization, and predictive analytics.

Mathematics is very important in the field of data science as concepts within mathematics aid in identifying patterns and assist in creating algorithms. Understanding various statistics and probability theory notions is key to implementing such algorithms in data science.

This book provides a comprehensive account of the areas of the applications of advanced mathematics in data science. It has covered many significant issues, methods, and applications of data science and mathematics in some crucial areas, such as The Role of Mathematics in Data Science, Mathematical Modeling in Data Science, Mathematical Algorithms for Artificial Intelligence and Big Data, Soft Computing in Data Science, Data Analytics: Architecture, Opportunities, And Open Research Challenges, Linear Regression, Logistic Regression, Neural Networks, and a Review on Data Science Technologies.

The book has implications for data science modeling and many real-life applications. Many readers, including undergraduate university students, evening learners, and learners participating in online data science courses, will be benefitted from this book.

I recommend this book to all interested in data science technologies, mathematical modeling, and applications.

S.B. Goyal
Faculty of Information Technology
City University
Petaling Jaya, 46100, Malaysia

PREFACE

The title of our book is Advanced Mathematical Applications in Data Science. The book is dealing specially Data Analysis – Mining and analysis of Big Data, Mathematical modelling in Data science, Mathematical Algorithms for Artificial Intelligence and Big Data, using MATLAB with Big Data from sensors and IOT devices, the relationship between Big data and Mathematical modelling, Big IOT Data analytics, Architecture, opportunities and open research challenges, the role of Mathematics in Data science, linear regression, logistic regression, Neural networks, Decision tree, applications of linear algebra in Data science, Big Data and Big Data analytics, concepts, types and techniques, foundation of Data science, fifty year of Data sciences, Health Bank – a world health for Data science applications in Healthcare, Radio frequency identification, a new opportunity for Data science, towards a system building agenda for data, semantic representation of Data science properly, a review on Data science techniques, Big Data: the next era of Information and Data science in medical imaging, Data science and healthcare, soft computing in Data science, foundation for private, fair and robust Data science, Data science fundamental principles, practical Data sciences for Actuarial task *etc*.

The scope of this book is not only limited to above highlighted areas but much more than that. Today as all of us are aware that most of the decision making and marketing strategies are data driven. So the research in this field is very much important and useful for any kind of day to day decision making and for marketing strategies *etc*. Finally we would thank the Bentham Science publishing house for giving us an opportunity to explore this field.

Biswadip Basu Mallik
Department of Basic Science & Humanities
Institute of Engineering & Management
Kolkata, West Bengal
India

Kirti Verma
Department of Engineering Mathematics
Lakshmi Narain College of Technology
Jabalpur Madhya Pradesh
India

Rahul Kar
Department of Mathematics
Kalyani Mahavidyalaya, Kalyani
West Bengal, India

Ashok Kumar Shaw
Department of Basic Sciences and Humanities
Budge Budge Institute of Technology, Budge Budge
Kolkata, West Bengal
India

&

Sardar M. N. Islam (Naz)
ISILC, Victoria University
Melbourne, Australia

List of Contributors

Armel Djangone	Dakota State University, Business Analytics and Decision Support, Washington Ave N, Madison, United States
Arnob Sarkar	National Atmospheric Research Laboratory, Department of Space, Andhra Pradesh, Government of India
Agus Tri Wibowo	Department of Consumer Service, PT Telekomunikasi Indonesia, Jakarta, Indonesia
Andi Chaerunisa Utami Putri	Department of Consumer Service, PT Telekomunikasi Indonesia, Jakarta, Indonesia
Bhim Singh	Department of Basic Science, Sardar Vallabh Bhai Patel University of Agriculture and Technology, Meerut (U.P.), India
Charanarur Panem	Department of Cyber Security and Digital Forensics, National Forensic Sciences University Tripura Campus, Tripura, India
J. Vijaylaxmi	PVKK Degree & PG College, Anantapur, Andhra Pradesh, India
Jayaraj Ramasamy	Department of IT, Botho University, Gaborone, Botswana
M. Varalakshmi	Marudhar Kesari Jain College for Women, Vaniyambadi, Tirupattur(dt), Tamilnadu, India
Meetu Luthra	Department of Physics, Bhaskaracharya College of Applied Sciences, University of Delhi, Delhi, India
Maheswari	Department of Computer Applications, Fatima College, Madurai, India
Muhammad Reza Tribosnia	Department of Consumer Service, PT Telekomunikasi Indonesia, Jakarta, Indonesia
M. Mujiya Ulkhaq	Department of Industrial Engineering, Diponegoro University, Kota Semarang, Indonesia Department of Economics and Management, University of Brescia, Brescia BS, Italy
Neha Bhardwaj	Department of Mathematics, School of Basic Sciences and Research, Sharda University, Noida, Uttar Pradesh, India
Nitin Jaglal Untwal	Maharashtra Institute of Technology, Aurangabad, India
I. P. Thulasi	Marudhar Kesari Jain College for Women, Vaniyambadi, Tirupattur(dt), Tamilnadu, India
Priya Panneer	Department of Mathematics, Mathematics Marudhar Kesari Jain College for Women, Vaniyambadi, Tirupattur, Tamilnadu, India
Prerna Sharma	Department of Basic Science, Sardar Vallabh Bhai Patel University of Agriculture and Technology, Meerut (U.P.), India
Rashmi Singh	Amity Institute of Applied Sciences, Amity University, Noida, Uttar Pradesh, India
R. N. Ravikumar	Department of Computer Engineering, Marwadi University, Gujarat, India
Revalda Putawara	Department of Consumer Service, PT Telekomunikasi Indonesia, Jakarta, Indonesia

Sardar M. N. Islam (Naz) — ISILC, Victoria University, Melbourne, Australia

Sathiyapriya Murali — Department of Mathematics, Mathematics Marudhar Kesari Jain College for Women, Vaniyambadi, Tirupattur, Tamilnadu, India

Srinivasa Rao Gundu — Department of Digital Forensics, Malla Reddy University, Dhulapally, Hyderabad, Telangana, India

S. Shitharth — Department of Computer Science, Kebri Dehar University, Kebri Dehar, Ethiopia

Soma Das — Life Science, B.Ed. Department, Syamaprasad Institute of Education and Training, Kolkata, India. Honorary Guest Faculty, Sports Science Department, University of Calcutta, Kolkata, India

CHAPTER 1

The Role of Mathematics in Data Science: Methods, Algorithms, and Computer Programs

Rashmi Singh[1,*], Neha Bhardwaj[2] and Sardar M. N. Islam (Naz)[3]

[1] *Amity Institute of Applied Sciences, Amity University, Noida, Uttar Pradesh, India*

[2] *Department of Mathematics, School of Basic Sciences and Research, Sharda University, Noida, Uttar Pradesh, India*

[3] *ISILC, Victoria University, Melbourne, Australia*

Abstract: The field of data science relies heavily on mathematical analysis. A solid foundation in certain branches of mathematics is essential for every data scientist already working in the field or planning to enter it in the future. In whatever area we focus on, data science, machine learning engineering, business intelligence development, data architecture, or another area of expertise, it is important to examine the several kinds of mathematical prerequisites and insights and how they're applied in the field of data science. Machine learning algorithms, data analysis and analyzing require mathematics. Mathematics is not the only qualification for a data science education and profession but is often the most significant. Identifying and translating business difficulties into mathematical ones are a crucial phase in a data scientist's workflow. In this study, we describe the different areas of mathematics utilized in data science to understand mathematics and data science together.

Keywords: Baye's theorem, Classification, Computer programs, Data science, Linear algebra, Machine learning, Matrices, Normal distribution, Optimization, Regression, System of linear equations, Vectors.

INTRODUCTION

To analyze data for the sake of decision making, "Data Science" combines different subfields of work in mathematics/statistics and computation in order to accomplish this. The use of the word "science" suggests that the discipline in question follows methodical procedures to arrive at findings that can be verified.

* **Corresponding author Rashmi Singh:** Amity Institute of Applied Sciences, Amity University, Noida, Uttar Pradesh, India; E-mail: rsingh7@amity.edu

The discipline makes use of ideas that are derived from the fields of mathematics and computer science since the solutions to the following problems can be found in the findings that are achieved *via* kinds of columns given below. such processes: making a Netflix movie suggestion, financial projections for the company, a home's price can be estimated by comparing it to other properties of a similar size and quality in terms of factors like the number of rooms and square footage, a song suggestion for Spotify playlist as discussed [1, 2, 3, 4]. How, therefore, does mathematics come into play here? In this chapter, we give evidence for the claim that mathematics and statistics are crucial because they provide the means to discover patterns in data. Furthermore, newcomers to data science from other fields can benefit greatly from familiarity with mathematics.

DATA SCIENCE

Data science uses the tools and methods already available to discover patterns, generate meaningful information, and make decisions for businesses. Data science builds prediction models with machine learning.

As discussed [5], data can be found in a variety of formats, but it is useful to think of it as the result of an unpredictable experiment whose outcomes are up to interpretation. In many cases, a table or spreadsheet is used to record the results of a random experiment. To facilitate data analysis, variables (also known as features) are typically represented as columns and the items themselves (or units) are represented as rows. To further understand the utility of such a spreadsheet, it is helpful to consider three distinct kinds of columns given below:

● In most tables, the first column serves as an identifier or index, where a specific label or number is assigned to each row.

● Second, the experimental design can be reflected in the columns' (features') content by identifying which experimental group a given unit falls under. It is not uncommon for the data in these columns to be deterministic, meaning they would remain constant even if the experiment was repeated.

● The experiment's observed data is shown in the other columns. Typically, such measurements are not stable; rerunning the experiment would result in different results [6].

Many data sets can be found online and in various software programs.

Data science study may be divided as follows:

1. Acquire, enter, receive, and extract information from signals and data using these key phrases related to data capture. At this juncture, we are collecting both structured and unstructured data in their raw forms.

2. Data Architecture, Data Processing, Data Staging, Data Cleansing, and Data Warehousing all need regular upkeep. At this point, the raw data will be taken and transformed into a format that the next stage can utilize.

3. Data processing consists of data mining, data summarization, clustering and classification, data wrangling, data modeling, *etc.* Once the data has been prepared, data scientists evaluate its potential for predictive analysis by looking for patterns, ranges and biases.

4. Some analytics/analysis methods are exploratory, confirmatory, predictive, text mining, and qualitative. At this point, the data will be analyzed in several ways.

5. Communication is required in a number of different areas, including the reporting of data, the display of data, business intelligence, and decision-making. The final step in the process involves analysts producing the findings in formats that are simple to grasp, such as charts, graphs, and reports.

Applying such algorithms in data science requires familiarity with numerous topics, from mathematics, probability theory, and statistics. However, almost every single topic of today's data science methods, including machine learning, is rooted in rigorous mathematics.

MAIN MATHEMATICAL PRINCIPLES AND METHODS IMPORTANT FOR DATA SCIENCE

Linear Algebra

The fields of data science and machine learning can benefit tremendously from using linear algebra, a branch of mathematics. Learning linear algebra is the most important mathematical ability for anyone interested in machine learning. The vast majority of machine learning models may be written down as matrices. A dataset is frequently represented as a matrix in its own right. Linear algebra is employed in data pre-processing, data transformation, and model evaluation (see [4, 5, 7, 8]).

Matrices

The building elements of data science are matrices. They appear in a variety of linguistic personas, from Python's NumPy arrays to R's data frames to MATLAB's matrices.

In its most basic form, the matrix is a collection of numbers that take the form of a rectangular or array-like array. This can be used to symbolize either an image, a network, or some other type of abstract organization. In practice, the matrices are of assistance in the field of neural networks as well as image processing.

Almost every machine learning algorithm, from the KNN (K-nearest neighbor algorithm) to random forests, relies heavily on matrices to perform its core functionality.

Matrix is a method of grouping related items for easy manipulation and manipulation according to our needs. When training different algorithms, it is frequently utilized in the field of data science as a storage medium for information, such as the weights in an artificial neural network [9, 10, 11].

System of Linear Equation

The relationship between linear dependency and the solution of linear equations is substantial. Since the topic is systems of linear equations, let's begin anew with the equations:

$$D_{1,1}z_1 + D_{1,2}z_2 + ... + D_{1,n}z_n = c_1$$

$$D_{2,1}z_1 + D_{2,2}z_2 + ... + D_{2,n}z_n = c_2$$

$$D_{m,1}z_1 + D_{m,2}z_2 + ... + D_{m,n}z_n = c_m$$

We know D and c as constant terms and need to find z.

The system is equivalent to a matrix equation of the form:

D * z= c

where A is a m x n matrix of coefficients, x and b are column vectors. The equation corresponds to:

$$D = \begin{bmatrix} d_{11} & d_{12} & ... & d_{1n} \\ d_{21} & d_{22} & ... & d_{2n} \\ . & . & ... & . \\ d_{m1} & d_{m2} & ... & d_{mn} \end{bmatrix}, z = \begin{bmatrix} z_1 \\ z_2 \\ . \\ z_n \end{bmatrix}, c = \begin{bmatrix} c_1 \\ c_2 \\ . \\ c_n \end{bmatrix}$$

The Number of Solutions

Three cases can represent the number of solutions of the system of equations Dz = c.

1. No solution

2. Exactly 1 solution

3. An infinite number of solutions

It is because we are dealing with linear systems: two lines can't cross more than once. These three cases are illustrated in Fig (**1**). Here, the first one shows the lines are parallel but distinct (no solution), in the second, lines intersect at one point (one solution) and the third one depicts the lines are identical (infinite number of solution).

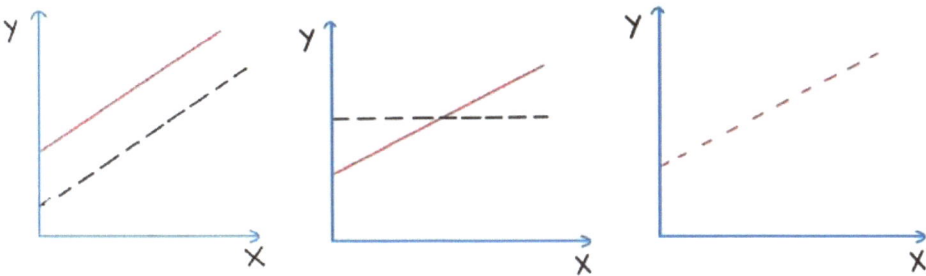

Fig. (1). Number of solutions.

Vectors

In Data Science, vectors are used to mathematically and readily express an object's attributes, which are numerical qualities. Vectors are indispensable in numerous fields of machine learning and pattern recognition.

Vectors are frequently employed in machine learning because they provide a straightforward method of data organization. Vectorizing the data is frequently one of the very first steps in developing a machine learning model.

They are also frequently utilized as the foundation for various machine learning approaches. Support vector machines are one specific illustration. A support vector machine examines vectors in n-dimensional space to determine the optimum hyperplane for a given data set. Fig (**2**) displays the optimal hyperplane with a blue line that separates two classes of instances: squares and circles. The other lines, however, are not proper hyperplanes, as they do not classify the objects properly. The dark-filled instances are called Support Vectors. Essentially, a support vector machine will seek to identify the line with the greatest distance between the data sets of both classes. Due to the higher reinforcement, future data points can be classified with greater certainty.

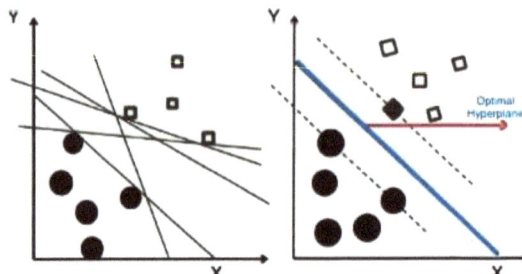

Fig. (2). The optimal hyperplane for a given data set is shown through the blue line.

The following parts will describe the various ways linear algebra can be applied to the field of data science.

Linear algebra is a crucial component of machine learning optimization. Some of the important applications are:

Loss Function

The loss function is utilized to compute how dissimilar our forecast is from the expected output.

The Vector Norm can be used in linear algebra to create a loss function. A vector's Norm can be derived from the magnitude of the vector. Let us examine L1 norm: When the only allowable directions are parallel to the space's axes, the L1 Norm is measured as the distance between the origin and the vector. As demonstrated in Fig. (3), the L1 norm is the distance between the origin (0,0) and the destination (4,5), comparable to how a person travels between city blocks to reach their destination, which comes out to be 9 in this case.

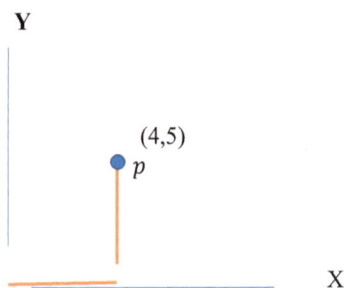

Fig. (3). L1 Norm of a vector p=9.

L1 Norm of vector p = (p1, p2, ..., pn), is given by

$$\| p \| = |p1| + |p2| + \cdots + |pn|.$$

Regularization

In the field of data science, the concept of regularisation is extremely important. It is a strategy that stops models from being overfitted to their data. In point of fact, regularisation is another application of the norm.

Overfitting is a situation in data science, machine learning and statistics when statistical models fit completely against all the training data used in the model. A model like this has poor performance with new data since it has learned everything, even the noise, in the training data. It is not possible for it to generalize the knowledge that it has never come across. Regularization is a technique that penalizes too complex models by including the Norm of the weight vector within the cost function. Given that we want to make the cost function as little as possible, we need to make this Norm as small as possible. This causes components of the weight vector that are not necessary to decrease to zero and prevents an excessively complex prediction function from being generated.

Support Vector Machine Classification

Support Vector Machine (SVM) is an algorithm that is a discriminative classifier as it finds a decision surface and it is a supervised machine learning algorithm.

In SVM, data items are represented as points in n-dimensional space to represent n (number of features). The value of each feature is the value of a certain coordinate. Then, we accomplish classification by locating the hyperplane that distinguishes the two classes the most, *i.e.*, the one with the greatest margin, which in this case is C as shown in Fig. (**4**),

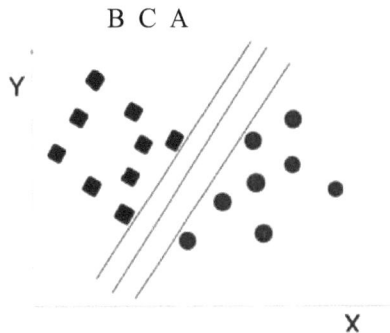

Fig. (4). The margin for the hyperplanes is maximum for C.

When fewer dimension are there then its associated vector space, then the subspace is called a hyperplane. Therefore, a hyperplane is a straight line for a 2D vector space, a 2D plane for a 3D vector space, a 3D plane for a 4D vector space, and so on. Also, using Vector Norm margin is computed.

Statistics

Probability Theory

Probability theory is a subfield of mathematics/statistics that concentrates on investigating random occurrences. Data scientists who work with data that has been influenced by chance need to have this ability [12, 13].

Given that chance occurs in every situation, the application of probability theory is necessary in order to comprehend the workings of chance. The objective is to ascertain how likely it is that a specific event will take place. This is often accomplished by using a numerical scale ranging from 0 to 1, with "0" denoting improbability and "1" denoting absolute certainty.

Normal Distribution

With mean (μ) and standard deviation (σ) as the parameters, a random variable "x" is normally distributed when its probability density function as follows:

$$y = \frac{1}{\sqrt{2\pi}} e^{-\frac{(x-\mu)^2}{2\sigma}}$$

The normal distribution, sometimes known as a bell curve, is shown in Fig. (**5**), with the blue curve. It has symmetry about the middle black line, where the mean, median and mode coincides, and 50% of data values lie on the left side of the black line and 50% on the right side.

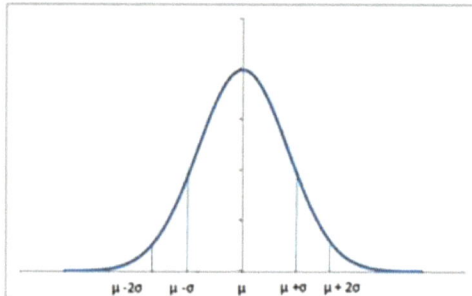

Fig. (5). The standard normal distribution curve.

Since the sum of all possible probabilities is 1, the total area under the curve is 1. So, in both directions, the probabilities around the mean move in a similar manner. That is why the normal distribution of the mean is exactly similar.

Depending on how dispersed the data is, the distribution could vary slightly. If there is a sufficient difference from the mean, there will be a flatter in the normally distributed curve if the range and the standard deviation of the data are very high [6, 14].

Moreover, if there is a larger deviation from the mean, the data's probability decreases, being closer to the mean. Similarly, suppose the standard deviation is low, which indicates that the majority of values are close to the mean. In that case, there is a significant likelihood that the sample means will be close to the mean, and the distribution will be much slimmer, as shown in Fig. (**6**) with black line. Whereas, the pink and red curves are thicker and flatter, this shows a greater standard deviation.

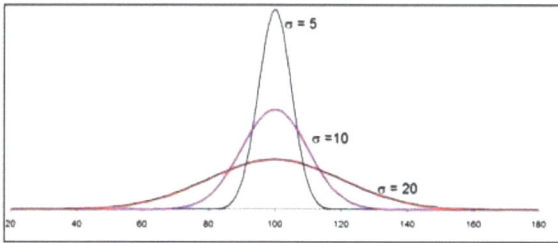

Fig. (6). Variation in standard normal curve with standard deviation.

- The probability of a random variable falling within that interval is given by the area beneath a probability density function.
- Normally distributed sample means represent that the random samples are of equal size from a population's data.

There is a greater likelihood that the sample means will be close to the actual mean of the data than that they would be further away. Normal distributions flatter greater standard deviations than smaller standard deviations.

For model development in data science, data satisfying normal distribution is advantageous. It simplifies mathematics. Depending upon the hypothesis, whether it is the bivariate distribution or normal distribution, models such as LDA, Gaussian Naive Bayes, logistic regression, linear regression, *etc.*, are explicitly developed. Also, Sigmoid functions behave naturally with data when it is normally distributed.

Numerous natural phenomena in the world, such as financial data and forecasting data, exhibit a log-normal distribution. From a study [15], we can convert the data into a normal distribution by employing transformation techniques. In addition, many processes adhere to the principle of normality, including several measurement mistakes in an experiment, the position of a particle experiencing diffusion, *etc.*

Before fitting the model, it is therefore preferable to critically examine the data and the underlying distributions for each variable before fitting the model.

Z Scores

Numerous situations will arise in which we will need to determine the chance that the data will be less than or greater than a specific value. This value will not be equal to 1 or 2 standard deviations of the mean.

The standard score or Z score measures the observed value's distance from the mean in terms of standard deviations. If Z score is greater than zero, it indicates that the recorded value standard deviation is above the mean. If the Z score is negative, then it denotes a value that is below the mean.

Observed value is $\mu+z\sigma$, where μ is the mean and σ is the standard deviation.

Using the Z table, the probability for a specific Z table is determined. There is no need to calculate the area under the normal curve. In the Z table, rows of the Z table have the Z score in tens and columns have the hundredths decimal. The value is equal to the area under the curve shown shaded with green in minus the Z score.

For a given Z score, we can see Z table to find the probability values that will go below that score. It might be negative or positive. For example, if we search for 1.47, we find that 93% of the data falls below that value. Fig. (**7**), depicts in green the area under the bell curve to the left of $z= \mu+2\sigma$.

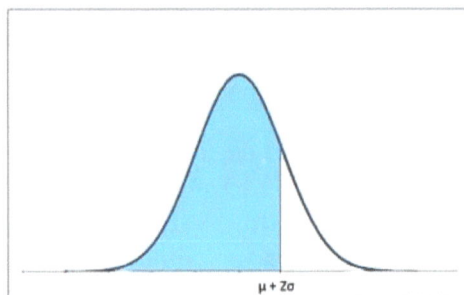

Fig. (7). Area under the normal curve calculated using Z score.

The Central Limit Theorem

When there is a great quantity of data, it might be challenging to comprehend what it all indicates. It is not easy to get a handle on what's going on beneath the surface. In order to figure out how to resolve this issue, we investigate a modest portion of the available data. To ensure the accuracy of the conclusion, we would consider the outcome based on more than one factor. On the other hand, processing this enormous volume of data is a tremendously challenging endeavor. In order to process it, we determine the mean of the data from anywhere between 40 and 50 different people.

Repeatedly selecting a sample of around fifty persons and computing the mean is something that helps us achieve our goal. Doing this fairly regularly also helps. The plotting of the means of these samples can now begin. These sample means represent a highly symmetrical frequency distribution. The frequency of the actual data is the greatest close to the mean and diminishes steadily as we move far from it on either side.

Probabilities can be easily derived from frequencies. We can compute the likelihood for each bin by dividing the frequency of a bin (such as 200 to 300) by the total number of data points in the observation. Consequently, the probability distribution now replicates the shape of the frequency distribution.

The probability distribution gets increasingly symmetrical when the sample size used to determine the means is very large. As the population means centered on the curve, the probability distribution tends to be perfectly symmetrical as the sample size approaches. The resulting curve represents a normal distribution.

Some Other Statistical Methods

Some other statistical methods which are used in data science widely are the following:

Skewness

In real-time case studies, data skewness is one of the significant issues that data scientists frequently confront. In a normal distribution, data are symmetrically dispersed. The symmetrical distribution has zero skewness because all central tendency measures are centered (Mean=Median= Mode).

In positively skewed data, the mean is higher than the median and the findings are skewed to the bottom, as shown in Fig. (**8**). The median is the midpoint value and the mode is always the highest. The mean is greater than the median.

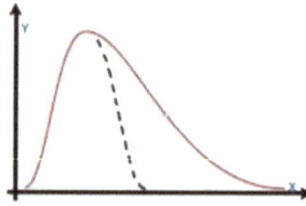

Fig. (8). Positive Skewness: Mean > Median > Mode.

Extremely positive skewness is undesirable for distribution purposes, as it might lead to misleading findings. Data transformation technologies are assisting in normalizing skewed data. The well-known transformation for positively skewed distributions is the log transformation. The log transformation suggests natural logarithm calculations for each value in the dataset.

In negatively skewed data, the mean is smaller than the median, as shown in Fig. (9). Negatively Skewed Distribution is a distribution in which the distribution's mean, median, and mode are negative rather than positive or zero.

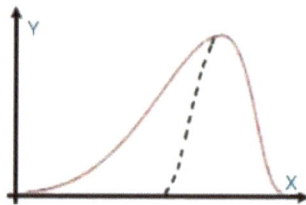

Fig. (9). Negative Skewness: Mode >Median >Mean.

Several transformations can be done to the data in order to preserve its information while simultaneously plotting the data under a symmetrical curve. Despite the fact that this transformation is determined by the features of the data, the following processes are utilized for data transformation:

  I. Re-plotting each data point after taking the square root of each data point.
 II. Taking the cube root of every data point and re-plotting the results.
III. Re-plotting each data point after calculating its logarithm.
IV. Re-plotting each data point after taking its reciprocal.

Kurtosis

The degree of presence of outliers in the distribution is measured by kurtosis.

In statistics and probability theory, excess kurtosis is used to compare the kurtosis coefficient to the normal distribution. Since the kurtosis of normal distributions is

3, extra kurtosis is calculated by subtracting kurtosis from 3. Three possibilities are: excess kurtosis can be negative (Platykurtic), positive (Leptokurtic), or close to zero.

A high kurtosis value typically indicates that the distribution's tails have more extreme values than the tail of the normal distribution. This could result in a length that is six or seven standard deviations from the mean. Similarly, if the kurtosis value is extremely low, the distribution's tail will be shorter than the tail of a normal distribution.

A high value of kurtosis is frequently regarded as riskier since data that are applied to any machine learning algorithm tend to produce outlier values that are further from the mean. Fig. (**10**) indicates the types of kurtosis, leptokurtic has long tails due to the presence of many outliers and platykurtic has short tails due to fewer outliers.

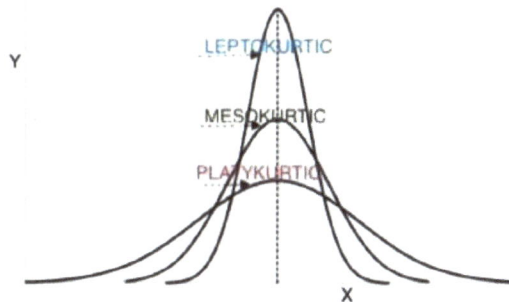

Fig. 10. Types of Kurtosis: Leptokutic, Mesokurtic and Platykurtic.

Applications of Statistics in Data Science through Machine Learning Algorithms

The applications of statistics in data science through Machine Learning Algorithms are discussed in the next few sections below:

Regression

The field of statistics known as regression can be used to make predictions based on an existing dataset. Simple linear regression, multivariate regression, polynomial regression, quantile regression, probit regression, and logistic regression are different forms of regression analytics [10, 11, 16]. We may want to see if teaching a student longer affects their test scores or to know how much money a certain lifestyle costs. Regression can help in answering these questions. Linear regression is a statistical method for forecasting a response by determining the optimal line to represent the connection between a dependent and an independent variable. Let's pretend you have access to a dataset (training set) depicting sales of ice cream y on days with average temperatures of x. Using the training data, a regression model learns weights w that allows for accurate prediction of y.

The objective of learning weights for the regression line is to achieve a level of accuracy that is as close to perfect as possible.

$$S(w) = \sum_{i=1}^{N}(y_i - f(x_i; w))^2$$

In order to calculate the derivative of S(w) and find a solution for zero derivative, the closed form solution can be used to minimize S(w), which is essentially the same thing. As a result, we will be presented with the weights resulting in the shortest distance between the regression line and the training data.

Machine Learning Using Principal Component Analysis to Reduce Dimensionality

Principal Component Analysis (PCA) is a statistical technique for extracting features. PCA is utilized for highly linked and high-dimensional data. As depicted in Fig. (11), the fundamental concept of PCA is to transform the original space of features into the space of primary components [4].

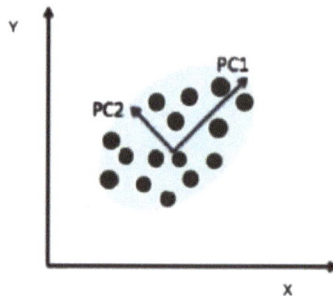

Fig. (11). PCA algorithm showing the transformation from old to new feature space so that the feature correlation is removed.

A PCA transformation accomplishes the subsequent:

a. Decrease the number of features utilized in the final model by concentrating on the components that account for the majority of the variance in the dataset.
b. Eliminates the association between features.

Mathematical Basis of PCA

Consider a strongly correlated features matrix with four characteristics and n observations, as given in Table **1**.

Table 1. Features matrix with 4 variables and n observations.

$\Delta_1^{(1)}$	$\Delta_2^{(1)}$	$\Delta_3^{(1)}$	$\Delta_4^{(1)}$
$\Delta_1^{(2)}$	$\Delta_2^{(2)}$	$\Delta_3^{(2)}$	$\Delta_4^{(2)}$
$\Delta_1^{(3)}$	$\Delta_2^{(3)}$	$\Delta_3^{(3)}$	$\Delta_4^{(3)}$
.	.	.	.
.	.	.	.
.	.	.	.
$\Delta_1^{(n)}$	$\Delta_2^{(n)}$	$\Delta_3^{(n)}$	$\Delta_4^{(n)}$

We may create a scatter plot to visualize the correlations between the features. We may compute the covariance matrix to quantify the degree of connection between attributes using the following equation:

$$\sigma_{jk} = \frac{1}{n} \sum_{i=1}^{n} \left(\frac{\Delta_j^{(i)} - \mu_j}{\sigma_i} \right) \left(\frac{\Delta_k^{(i)} - \mu_k}{\sigma_k} \right)$$

where μ_j and σ_j are the mean and the standard deviation of the feature Δ_4, respectively.

The covariance matrix can be written in matrix form as a 4 x 4 symmetric matrix.

$$\Sigma = \begin{bmatrix} \sigma_1^2 & \sigma_{12} & \sigma_{13} & \sigma_{14} \\ \sigma_{21} & \sigma_{22} & \sigma_{23} & \sigma_{24} \\ \sigma_{31} & \sigma_{32} & \sigma_{33} & \sigma_{34} \\ \sigma_{41} & \sigma_{42} & \sigma_{43} & \sigma_{44} \end{bmatrix}$$

By conducting a unitary transformation (PCA transformation), this matrix can be diagonalized to provide the following:

$$\tilde{\Sigma} - \begin{bmatrix} \lambda_1 & 0 & 0 & 0 \\ 0 & \lambda_2 & 0 & 0 \\ 0 & 0 & \lambda_3 & 0 \\ 0 & 0 & 0 & \lambda_4 \end{bmatrix}$$

Due to the fact that the trace of a matrix remains unchanged when subjected to a unitary transformation, we observe that the sum of the diagonal matrix's eigenvalues equals the total variance of features Δ_1, Δ_2, Δ_3, and Δ_4. Consequently, the following quantities can be defined:

$$\text{Variance Explained Ratio} = \frac{\lambda_j}{\sum_{j=1}^{4} \lambda_j}$$

Notice that when $p = 4$, the cumulative variance becomes equal to 1 as expected.

Classification

Classification is a method used to give categories to a set of data to make accurate predictions and conduct a thorough analysis [17]. When using classification techniques, we are presented with an already existing dataset and are made aware of the classes to which particular instances belong; with this information, a prediction model can subsequently be constructed to address the following problem: Determine, for each new instance that will be added to the dataset, which category does that specific instance fall under.

The Max Entropy algorithm, the K-nearest neighbor algorithm, and the Naive Bayes algorithm are all examples of classification algorithms [18].

In contrast to the idea of regression described earlier, which involves weights being learned to predict continuous values, the Max Entropy method, also known as Logistic Regression, involves weights being learned to forecast categorical values.

K-Nearest Neighbor

The current examples are compared with the data points from the past, and decisions on classification are made based on the extent to which the new cases match the ones that came before them.

Naive Bayes

The Bayes' Theorem is the foundation of the Naive Bayes algorithm, a classification process in which all classified features are independent of one another, regardless of their relationship. Bayes' Theorem provides the basis for the Naive Bayes algorithm.

We can find fantastic examples of the Naive Bayes algorithm in data analysis that make the system work and look so easy.

Some classification applications are: Identifying whether or not an email is considered spam. The process of identifying whether a cat or a dog is depicted in a certain photograph. YouTube video organization by category.

Calculus

For most data scientists, it is just essential to comprehend the principles of calculus and how they may affect various models.

Understanding that the derivative of a function yields its rate of change, for instance, explains why the rate of change approaches zero as the function's graph flattens.

In turn, this will assist a data scientist in comprehending how gradient descent works by locating a function's local minimum. In addition, it will demonstrate that classical gradient descent only works well for functions with a single minimum. If there are several minima (or saddle points), gradient descent may identify a local minimum without locating the global minimum unless many locations are used as a starting point.

When considering ways to address a problem involving data science, there are a great many different subfields of mathematics (other than those discussed above) that may also be helpful.

Graph theory can be used to solve specific types of difficulties. For example, whether attempting to optimize routes for a shipping system or developing a system for detecting fraud, a graph-based approach can occasionally outperform conventional methods.

Because a finite amount of "bits" may be used to represent any given number, the field of discrete mathematics becomes increasingly significant as the use of computers in mathematics grows more widespread. Furthermore, discrete mathematics has a number of fundamental concepts that can be utilized in two ways: first, as limitations, and second, as sources of inspiration for potential solutions to problems.

Optimization or Operational Research Methods

Optimization or Operational Research (O.R.) methods see [19] are used extensively in different areas of data science: data analytics, machine learning, *etc*. It is called The Science of Better. In data science, real-life problems are modeled in mathematical forms. OR/optimization techniques, along with data analytics, computational algorithms, and computer programs, are adopted to solve these problems better.

Optimization methods or mathematical programming aim to find the values of the variables that give the optimum value to the objective function (in the case of non-constrained optimization) through optimization algorithms.

The stages of an optimization modeling work in data science are the following (following [20]):

- define the modeling problem,
- develop the data science model,
- computing the data science model numerically by some suitable algorithms and computer programs,
- analyze or apply the implications of the model results for actions or planning.

Some main techniques are as follows: static optimization, dynamic optimization

and stochastic optimization.

Static models in data science can be linear, non-linear, or integer programming models. Linear programming is a commonly used optimization model or a mathematical programming method with a linear objective function and is subject to linear equality, linear inequality constraints, and non-negativity constraints.

An example of a static optimization model (a linear programming model) is given below:

MIN $C = c_1 X + c_2 Y + c_3 Z$ objective function

(Y, X, Z)

s.t.

$X = bY$ refers to flows and balance constraints,

$Z \geq Z^*$ are the demand constraints,

$X \leq X^*$ are the capacity constraints,

$Z = aX$ are the flows and balance constraints,

$Y \leq Y^*$ resource constraints,

$Y, X, Z \geq 0$ is the non-negativity constraint,

c's = the costs of nodes,

Y, X, Z = the vectors of decision variables.

Dynamic Optimization Model

The following is a dynamic optimization model where a dynamic system is optimized subject to the constraints of the system see [21].

$$\text{MAX } J(u) := \int_0^T e^{-\delta T} \left[px(t) - u(t) \right] dt \text{ subject to}$$

$$x(0) = x_0, x(t) = \rho u(t) \left[1 - x(t) \right] - \beta x(t), 0 \leq u(t) \leq c \left(0 \leq t \leq T \right)$$

$$\lambda(t) - \left(\delta + \beta + \rho u(t) \right) \lambda(t) = p .$$

T = time, x(t) = the state function, u(t) = the control function, t is the planning horizon. The parameters of the model are presented by other symbols.

Stochastic Optimization Methods

In stochastic optimization, random variables are used to formulate the optimization problem and to find the solution.

MIN $C = c_1 Xs + c_2 Ys + c_3 Zs$ objective function

(Ys,Xs,, Zs)

s.t.

Xs = bsYs refers to primary logistics and supply chain flows and balance constraints,

Zs * Zs are the demand constraints,

Xs * Xs are the capacity constraints,

Z = aX are the flows and balance constraints,

Ys * Ys resource constraints,

Ys, Xs, Zs * 0 is the non-negativity constraint.

cs's = the costs of nodes under different scenarios,

Ys, Xs,, Zs = the vectors of decision variables under different scenarios s = 1, 2. ….S.

The applications of Optimization Methods/ OR in data science are discussed in the next few sections below:

In practice, optimization increases the effectiveness of a system. It is adopted in numerous fields, such as data science, computer science, hospital, medicine, supply chain, finance, government, physics, economics, manufacturing, transportation, artificial intelligence, machine learning, *etc.* In an optimization model, the goal can be to minimize the costs of processes, activities, orsystems. In a hospital, the objective may be to reduce the amount of time patients spend in the emergency room before being seen by a doctor. In marketing, the objective may be to maximize profit by targeting the proper customers within the constraints of money and operations. By designing optimal routes, the objective of a humanitarian operation would be to reach as many impacted people as possible to deliver clothing, shelter, food, water, and medical support. In addition, it acts as the foundation for data science algorithms. It is the foundation of the vast majority of machine learning and statistical approaches used in data science [22, 23, 24].

It aids in locating the minimum error or optimal solution to a problem. In regression, for instance, the error is computed as:

$$MSE = \frac{1}{n}\sum\left(y - \hat{y}\right)^2$$

$y - \hat{y}$ is difference between actual and predicted.

Optimization helps to determine the minimum loss function value of machine learning algorithms.

Consider another example:

If we want to fit a function between y and x and we have data on y and x, we can claim that y equals a_1 plus a_2 times x. We have many different samples of x and y, denoted by the notation (x_1, y_1), (x_2, y_2), and so on. This can be generalized as follows: $yn = a_1 + a_2 * x_n$. It is clear that there are n equations but only 2 variables to work with. It is extremely unlikely that all of these equations can be solved. The following is how we define the error function: $e = y_1 - a_1 - a_2 * x_1$

In general, $e_n = y_n - a_1 - a_2 * x_n$

The optimization problem is unconstrained if there are no restrictions on the possible values of the choice variables. This is a common type of linear regression problem. It is often referred to as a functional approximation problem and is regularly utilized in data science.

Some Other Methods

Game theory, set theory, and chaos theory are some common mathematical methods used in data science theory and applications.

Computer Programs

There are many computer programs to numerically implement the mathematical methods discussed above. However, some of the popular computer programs in data science are as follows: PYTHON, JAVA, R, C, GAMBIT, GAMUT, NECTAR, EXCEL, GAMS, MATLAB, MATHEMATICA, MINOS, SAS, STATA.

CONCLUDING REMARKS

The preceding analysis of the functionality and implications of mathematics and statistics led us to the following conclusion that the role of mathematics and statistics is extremely important in the field of data science. This is so because of the ideas that they bring to light and the tools that they make possible.

Specifically for the field of data science, using mathematical techniques, computing algorithms and statistical reasoning will greatly assist in getting results that are scientifically adequate and scientifically adequate results based on appropriate procedures. In the end, the only way to reach at good solutions in data science is to ensure a harmonious interaction between mathematics and statistics.

REFERENCES

[1] G. Peyré, and M. Cuturi, "Computational optimal transport: With applications to data science", *Foundations and Trend. Mach. Learn.,* vol. 11, no. 5-6, pp. 355-607, 2019.
[http://dx.doi.org/10.1561/2200000073]

[2]   M.P. Deisenroth, A.A. Faisal, and C.S. Ong, "Mathematics for Machine Learning". Cambridge University Press, 2020, pp. 1-398.
[http://dx.doi.org/10.1017/9781108679930]

[3]   G. James, D. Witten, T. Hastie, and R. Tibshirani, "An Introduction to Statistical Learning Application in R. 2nd". Springer: New York, NY, 2021, pp. 1-607.
[http://dx.doi.org/10.1007/978-1-0716-1418-1]

[4]   J. R. Hou, S. Nerur, and J. J. Zhang, "Applying data science on structureal equations modelling(SEM): An exploratory study", *Ess. vis. eff. onl. hum. deci.mak. data. sci. appl.,* pp. 114-127, 2019.

[5]   R.L. Graham, D.E. Knuth, O. Patashnik, and S. Liu, "Concrete mathematics: A foundation for computer science", *Comput. Phys.,* vol. 3, no. 5, pp. 106-107, 1989.
[http://dx.doi.org/10.1063/1.4822863]

[6]   T. Hastie, R. Tibshirani, and J. Friedman, "The Elements of Statistical Learning. 2nd". Springer, 2011.

[7]   M.M. Wolf, J.W. Berry, and D.T. Stark, "A task-based linear algebra building blocks approach for scalable graph analytics", *IEEE High Perform. Ext.Comp. Conf. (HPEC),,* 2015pp. 1-6 15-17 September 2015 , Waltham, MA, USA
[http://dx.doi.org/10.1109/HPEC.2015.7322450]

[8]   G. Peyré, and M. Cuturi, "Computational optimal transport: With applications to data science", *Found.Tren.,* p. 272, 2019.
[http://dx.doi.org/10.1561/2200000073]

[9]   M. Udell, and A. Townsend, "Why are big data matrices approximately low rank?", *SIAM J. Math. Data. Sci.,* vol. 1, no. 1, pp. 144-160, 2019.
[http://dx.doi.org/10.1137/18M1183480]

[10] R. Brijder, M. Gyssens, and J. Van den Bussche, "On matrices and K-relations", In: *Int. Symp. Found. Inform. Knowl. Syst.* Springer: Cham, 2020, pp. 42-57.

[11] J. Joshi, and S. Saxena, "Regression analysis in data science", *J. Appl. Anal. Comput,* vol. 14, no. 6, 2020.

[12] R.V. Hogg, E.A. Tanis, and D.L. Zimmerman, "Probability and statistical inference". vol. 993. Macmillan: New York, 1977.

[13] D. Koller, and N. Friedman, "Probabilistic graphical models: Principles and techniques". MIT press: Cambridge, 2009.

[14] A. Field, J. Miles, and Z. Field, "Discovering statistics using r sage publications", 2012.

[15] S.C. Olhede, and P.J. Wolfe, "The future of statistics and data science", *Stat. Probab. Lett.,* vol. 136, pp. 46-50, 2018.
[http://dx.doi.org/10.1016/j.spl.2018.02.042]

[16] R. Koenker, "Quantile regression", *Econom. Soc. Monog.,* vol. 38, p. 26, 2010.

[17] K. Jajuga, A. Sokolowski, and H.H. Bock, "Classification, clustering, and data analysis: Recent advances and applications", In: *Rec. Adv. Appl.* Springer: Berlin, Heidelberg, 2012, pp. 1-508.

[18] S. Boyd, and L. Vandenberghe, "Introduction to applied linear algebra: Vectors, matrices, and least squares". Cambridge university press: Los Angeles, 2018, pp. 1-474.
[http://dx.doi.org/10.1017/9781108583664]

[19] B.D. Craven, and S.M. Islam, "Optimization in economics and finance: some advances in non-linear, dynamic, multi-criteria and stochastic models". vol. 7. Springer Science & Business Media, 2005.

[20] H.A. Taha, "Operations research: an introduction". 8th Edition, Asoke K. Ghosh, Prentice Hall of India, Delhi, 1992.

[21] B.D. Craven, and S.M. Islam, "Operations research methods: related production, distribution and

inventory management applications". ICFAI University Press, 2006.

[22] B.D. Craven, S.M. Islam, and X.X. Huang, "Operations research models for capital budgeting: Some new approaches and models", *Adv. Quanti. Anal. Fin. Accoun.,* no. 12, pp. 215-228, 2014.

[23] F. Rojas, P. Wanke, V. Leiva, M. Huerta, and C. Martin-Barreiro, "Modeling inventory cost savings and supply chain success factors: A hybrid robust compromise multi-criteria approach", *Mathematics,* vol. 10, no. 16, p. 2911, 2022.
[http://dx.doi.org/10.3390/math10162911]

[24] P. Amodio, M. De Giosa, F. Iavernaro, R. La Scala, A. Labianca, M. Lazzo, F. Mazzia, and L. Pisani, "Detection of anomalies in the proximity of a railway line: A case study", *J. of Comput. Math. and Data Sci.,* p. 100052, 2022.

CHAPTER 2

Kalman Filter: Data Modelling and Prediction

Arnob Sarkar[1] and **Meetu Luthra**[2,*]

[1] *National Atmospheric Research Laboratory, Department of Space, Andhra Pradesh, Government of India*

[2] *Department of Physics, Bhaskaracharya College of Applied Sciences, University of Delhi, Delhi, India*

Abstract: We provide here an analysis of Kalman filter, which has wide applications in the experimental and observational fields. Kalman filter is a data fusion algorithm or a mathematical tool which is based on the estimation theory. It basically is a set of mathematical equations which provide a computational mechanism for evaluating the state of discrete processes with noisy data. In fact, observations and data analysis is a very key aspect of all theories. In any set of data, to make it useful, one has to minimize the error/noise by taking into consideration various aspects like the estimated values (the theoretical values), the measurement values, experimental errors and the estimated errors. We have shown here how this can be done using Kalman Filtering technique. Kalman Filter is a tool which can take the observational data and improvise it to identify the best possible value of the parameters involved. Kalman filter and its variants such as the extended Kalman filter have wide applications mainly in the field of communication *e.g.*, in GPS receivers (global positioning system receivers), radio equipment used for filtering and removing noise from the output of laptop trackpads, image processing, face recognition and many more.

Keywords: Acceleration, Big data, Data science, Extended kalman filter, GPS, Kalman filter, Mathematical modelling, Noise, Signals, Speed, Uncertainty.

INTRODUCTION

Why Kalman Filter?

When we have a large set of data, efficient parameter estimation remains one of the most important tasks to perform [1]. There are a number of methods where data estimation or prediction algorithms are implemented to get a proper result. Situations arise when there exists noise in the signal. These noises are the unwanted signals which are responsible for incorrect and undesired output [2].

* **Corresponding author Meetu Luthra:**Department of Physics, Bhaskaracharya College of Applied Sciences, University of Delhi, Delhi, India; E-mail: meetu.luthra@bcas.du.ac.in

Biswadip Basu Mallik, Kirti Verma, Rahul Kar, Ashok Kumar Shaw & Sardar M. N. Islam (Naz) (Eds.)

There are various methods to remove the noise and get appropriate results. These include: Linear curve fitting, Quadratic curve fitting and other degrees of curve fitting.

Linear curve fitting, which solely depends on least square curve fitting, is optimal for small number of data points. But, with continuous noisy data inputs and undefined total number of data points, a suitable algorithm is required where input at every consecutive time interval is taken which includes noise, and a suitable path is estimated or predicted. This task can be accomplished by Optimal Filters.

There are various optimal filters to achieve this and get appropriate predicted results. One such filter is Kalman Filter. Using Kalman Filter, it is possible to counter unwanted signals or data inputs with an unknown total number of data points and make predictions of the desired variables. Kalman Filter is not the only filter to do so. Other filters like *Extended Kalman Filter*, *Unscented Kalman Filter* and *Particle Filters* also perform the same task, but with greater efficiency and are more practical. Although these filters are better, the computation costs are generally higher than the computation costs of Kalman Filter.

Kalman Filter was originally developed by Rudolf E. Kalman in his paper in 1960, where he intended to use the state space approach to an earlier known filter, the Wein's Filter [3].

UNDERSTANDING THE KALMAN FILTER

What is Kalman Filter?

Kalman Filtering is a mechanism by which the true value of the quantity (*e.g.*, velocity, position, *etc.* of an object) can be estimated by using a set of equations and consecutive data values through an *iterative process*. The values being measured contain some or the other kind of errors that are not predictable or are *random* and in addition, there exist inherent uncertainties or variations in the data too.

Kalman Filter is a *two*-step process consisting of a filter and a smoother. It begins with the first step and makes a prediction for the required variables for the next step. *State equations* and *error matrices* are updated. This process is called filtering. After the filtration process, the estimation does not have any information about previously estimated values. Once, a variable of interest has been filtered, it is then smoothed.

State Space Approach

There are systems that depend on time and may change their behaviour over time. Such systems are known as *Dynamic Systems*[1]. One such type of Dynamic System is the Linear Dynamic System where the system varies linearly with time.

It is important to predict how the system behaves after a given time. This is achieved in numerous ways, one of which has been discussed below:

For a Linear Dynamic System[2], a State-Space approach is used. For this State-Space approach, there should be a finite dimensional representation of a particular problem [4].

Let x be a state vector with $N \times 1$ dimension. The variation of this state vector x equals a constant matrix φ multiplied by the state vector (x) itself. The variation can take two forms:

a) **Flow**: System varies continuously with time (t)

$$\frac{dx(t)}{dt} = \phi x(t) \tag{1}$$

b) **Discrete**: The system changes its state at discrete intervals $(..., m - 1, m, m + 1,)$.

$$x_{m+1} = \phi . x_m \tag{2}$$

Here, m is an integer representing the time step t_m.

Mean Squared Error

The following sections build up the basis for the Kalman Filter equation.[3]

A general way of describing a linear dynamic system is:

$$y_k = a_k + n_k \tag{3}$$

y_k is the observed variable which is time-dependent,

a_k is the gain term

x_k is a variable which bears the information

n_k is the additive noise

The main task is to have an estimate of x_k. Defining a new term called the *error*, represented as:

$f(e_k)$, which accounts for the difference between the estimated

value of x_k, *i.e.*, $\mathrm{x}^{\wedge}_k$ and x_k itself.

$$f(e_k) = f(x_k - \hat{x}_k) \tag{4}$$

The shape that $f(e_k)$ largely depends on the particular application. But mostly, this function should be positive and monotonically increasing [5]. Functions exhibiting this behaviour are known as Squared Error Function.

$$f(e_k) = (x_k - \hat{x}_k)^2 \tag{5}$$

Since, we require the extent to which the filter can predict huge data over a period of time, it is important to define the expected value of the error function:

$$LF = E[f(e_k)] \tag{6}$$

where,

LF: Loss function

$E[f(e_k)]$: Expected error

The results in the Mean Squared Error (MSE) function are defined as:

$$\epsilon(t) = E(e_k^2) \tag{7}$$

The estimations of x_k are done in a manner so as to minimise the loss function LF.

KALMAN FILTER EQUATIONS

We first write down the state equations for any process under consideration:

$$_{k+1} = \phi\, x_k + w_k \tag{8}$$

where,

x_k is the state Vector representing the process at time k and has dimensions (nx1).

ϕ: is the state transition matrix of the process from state k to the consecutive state k+1.

This state is assumed to be stationary w.r.t time and has the dimensions (nxm).

w_k: is the white noise associated with the process, with a known value of covariance.

The observations on this variable can be modelled by the equation:

$$z_k = Hx_k + v_k \tag{9}$$

z_k: is the actual measurement of x at time k with dimensions (mx1).

H: is the connection between the state and the measurement vector without noise,

stationary with respect to time and has dimensions (mxn).

v_k: is the measurement error associated with the process and we consider it to be white noise with no cross-correlation with the process noise. And has dimensions (mx1).

The two noise models have covariances assumed stationary with respect to time and are given by:

$$Q = E[w_k w_k^T] \tag{10}$$

$$R = E[v_k v_k^T] \tag{11}$$

The mean squared error (MSE) function is given by:

$$\epsilon(t) = E\ (e_k)^2 \tag{12}$$

This is equivalent to:

$$E\ [e_k\ e_k^T] = P_k \tag{13}$$

P_k : Error covariance matrix[4] at time k.

Expansion of (2.13) gives:

$$P_k = E\left[(x_k - \hat{x}_k)(x_k - \hat{x}_k)^T\right] \tag{14}$$

Let $\hat{x}_k'$ be the priori estimate of $\hat{x}_k$, which can be known by knowing the system considered. We can write an updated equation for the new estimate, combining the old estimate with the measurement data. Therefore,

$$\hat{x}_k = \hat{x}_k' + K_k(z_k - H\hat{x}_k') \tag{15}$$

K_k : is the Kalman Gain.

$z_k - H x^\wedge_k$: is known as innovation or measurement residual.

For the current estimate, we have from equation (15):

$$i_k = z_k - H\hat{x}_k \tag{16}$$

Substituting equation (9) in equation (15), we have:

$$\hat{x}_k' = \hat{x}' + K_k(Hx_k + v_k + H\hat{x}_k') \tag{17}$$

Substituting equation (2.29) in equation (2.14), we get:

$$
\begin{aligned}
P_k &= E\left[(x - \hat{x}_k)(x_k - \hat{x})^T\right] \\
P_k &= E\left[\hat{x}_k + K_k(Hx_k + v_k - H\hat{x}_k') - \hat{x}_k\right]\left[\hat{x}_k' + K_k(Hx_k + v_k \quad H\hat{x}_k') \quad \hat{x}_k'\right]^T \\
P_k &= E\left[K_kHx_k + K_kv_k - K_kH\hat{x}_k'\right]\left[K_kHx_k + K_kv_k - K_kH\hat{x}_k'\right]^T \\
P_k &= E\left[(I - K_kH)(x_k - \hat{x}_k') - K_kv_k\right]\left[(I - K_kH)(x_k - \hat{x}_k') - K_kv_k\right]^T
\end{aligned} \tag{18}
$$

The error in the prior estimate is $(x^\wedge_k - x^\wedge_k')$, which is clearly not correlated with the measurement noise so the expectation may be written as:

$$P_k = (I - K_kH)\, E\left[(x_k - \hat{x}_k')(x_k - \hat{x}_k')^T\right](I - K_kH)^T + K_k E[v_kv_k^T]K_k^T \tag{19}$$

Substituting equation (2.11) and equation (2.14) in equation (2.19):

$$P_k = (I - K_kH)P_k'(1 - K_kH)^T + K_kR\,K_k^T \tag{20}$$

here, P_k' is the prior estimate of P_k.

Equation (2.20) is the *error covariance update* equation. The mean squared error is contained in the diagonal of this covariance, as shown below:

$$P_{kk} = \begin{bmatrix} E[e_{k-1}e_{k-1}^T] & E[e_k e_{k-1}^T] & E[e_{k+1}e_{k-1}^T] \\ E[e_{k-1}e_k^T] & E[e_k e_k^T] & E[e_{k+1}e_k^T] \\ E[e_{k-1}e_{k+1}^T] & E[e_k e_{k+1}^T] & E[e_{k+1}e_{k+1}^T] \end{bmatrix} \tag{21}$$

Trace of a matrix is defined as the sum of its diagonal elements. So, the trace of the above matrix P_{kk} must be *minimized* for the Mean squared error to be minimum.

We first take the derivative of the trace of the matrix P_{kk} with respect to K_k. and then the output is put equal to zero to get the minima. Expanding (2.20) gives:

$$P_k = P_k' - K_k H P_k' - P_k' H^T K_k^T + K_k (H P_k' H^T + R) K_k^T \tag{22}$$

Since the trace of the matrix is equal to the trace of its transpose, thus:

$$T[P_k] = T[P_k'] - 2T[K_k H P_k'] + T[K_k (H P_k' H^T + R) K_k^T] \tag{23}$$

where T[M] represents the trace of the matrix M.

As, $P_k' = (P_k')^T$, being a symmetric matrix, and

$(K_k H P_k')^T = P_k'^T H^T K_k^T = P_k' H^T K_k^T$

Therefore,

$$T[K_k H P_k'] = T[(K_k H P_k)^T] \tag{24}$$

Differentiating with respect to K_k

$$\frac{dT[P_k]}{K_k} = -2(HP_k')^T + 2K_k(HP_k'H^T + R) \tag{25}$$

Being a minimum value, setting it to zero and then rearranging the terms, we have:

$$(HP_k') = K_k(HP_k'H^T + R) \tag{26}$$

Solving for K_k:

$$K_k = P_k'H_T(HP_k'HT + R)^{-1} \tag{27}$$

This is the equation for Kalman Gain.

The measurement prediction covariance associated with it is given by:

$$S_k = HP_k'H^T + R \tag{28}$$

Substituting equation (27) in equation (22), we have:

$$
\begin{aligned}
P_k &= P_k' - P_k'H^T(HP_k'H^T + R)^{-1}HPk \\
&= P_k' - K_kHP'k \\
P_k &= (I - K_kH)P_k'
\end{aligned}
$$

So, we have:

$$P_k = (I - K_k H)P_k' \tag{29}$$

IIcncc, wc obtain the equation for Error Covariance Matrix with optimal gain.

Equation (15), equation (27) and equation (29) develop an estimate of the state variable x_k.

The following equation gives the State projection:

$$\hat{x}_{k+1} = \phi\hat{x}_k' \tag{30}$$

We need an equation which should project the error covariance matrix to the next time interval, k+1 in order to complete the recursion. For this, we first write an expression for the prior estimate,

$$
\begin{aligned}
e'_{k+1} &= x_{k+1} - \hat{x}_{k+1} \\
&= \phi\,(x_k + w_k) - \phi\hat{x}_k \\
&= \phi\,e_k + w_k
\end{aligned}
\tag{31}
$$

Now we extend the equation (2.14) to time $k + 1$:

$$
\begin{aligned}
P'_{k+1} &= E[e'_{k+1}e^T_{k+1}] \\
&= E[(\phi e_k + w_k)(\phi e_k + w_k)^T]
\end{aligned}
\tag{32}
$$

Since the noise w_k exists between k and k+1, e_k and w_k have zero cross-correlation, whereas the error e_k corresponds to the error at time k.

Therefore,

$$
\begin{aligned}
P'_{k+1} &= E\left[e_{k+1}\, e'_{k+1}{}^T\right] \\
&= E\left[\phi\, e_k\, (\phi\, e_k\,)^T\right] + E\left(w_k\, w_k{}^T\right) \\
&= \phi\, P_k\, \phi^T + Q
\end{aligned}
$$

This completes the Recursive Filter.

Summarising the primary equations for the Kalman Filter process

The **State** equations:

$$
X_p = \quad \phi\, X_{k-1} + Bu_k + w_k
\tag{33}
$$

$$
X_{kp} = \quad \phi\, X_{k-1} + Bu_k + w_k
\tag{34}
$$

$$
P_k = \quad \phi\, P_{k-1}\, \phi^T + Q_k
\tag{35}
$$

The Measurement Input equation:

$$
Y_k = CXk_m + Z_k
\tag{36}
$$

The Kalman Gain equation:

$$
K = \frac{P_{kp}H}{HP_{kp}H^T + R}
\tag{37}
$$

The State Matrix Update equation:

$$
X_k = X_{kp} + K\,[Y - HX_{kp}]
\tag{38}
$$

The Process Covariance Matrix Update equation:

$$P_k = (I - KH)\, P_{kp} \qquad\qquad (39)$$

From the above equations, the matrices H and C are used for converting another matrix to a suitable dimension. Matrix, I represent the Identity Matrix.

GENERAL APPLICATIONS OF KALMAN FILTER

There are numerous applications of Kalman Filters. Stating a few of them here:

1. Global Positioning System (G.P.S.) receivers.

2. Tracking a Plane using suitable radars.

3. Weather forecasting over an area.

4. Advanced Driver Assistance Systems (A.D.A.S.).

5. Virtual Reality, for predictive steps.

6. Image processing in a computer.

KALMAN FILTER EQUATIONS IN ONE DIMENSION

To have a clear perspective of Kalman filter, we analysed it in one-dimension. The equations considered previously are generalised for N dimensional case. The special case where the dimension reduces to just one, the equations are tweaked a little.

Abbreviations used in the equations are:

K: Kalman Gain.

EST_k: Current Estimated Value.

EST_{k-1}: Previous Estimated Value.

E_{EST}: Error in the Estimated Value.

MEA: Measurement input value at time k.

E_{MEA}: Error in the Measurement input value at time k.

Using these, the equations for one dimension case are given by:

The *Kalman Gain* equation:

$$K = \frac{E_{EST}}{F_{EST} + E_{MEA}} \tag{40}$$

The *Estimate Update* equation:

$$EST_k = EST_{k-1} + K\,[MEA - EST_{t-1}] \tag{41}$$

The *Error in the Estimate Update* equation:

$$
\begin{aligned}
E_{EST_k} &= \frac{(E_{MEA})(E_{EST_{k-1}})}{E_{MEA} + E_{EST_{k-1}}} \\
&= [1 - K]E_{EST_{k-1}}
\end{aligned}
\tag{42}
$$

The equation **(40)** determines the Kalman Gain (*K*), which depends on E_{EST} and E_{MEA}. The value of *K* is restricted between 0 and 1. This can be proved by considering the following two cases:

1. $E_{EST} \gg E_{MEA}$ then **(40)** approximates to $K \approx 1$.

2. $E_{EST} \ll E_{MEA}$ then **(40)** approximates to $K \approx 0$.

The equation **(41)** updates the Estimated value. The following two cases illustrate the two ideal cases.

1. $E_{EST} \gg E_{MEA}$ and $K \approx 1$, then the new estimated value (EST_k) is changed to a greater extent from the previous value (EST_{k-1}).

2. $E_{EST} \ll E_{MEA}$ and $K \approx 0$, then the new estimated value (EST_k) is not changed that much from the previous value (EST_{k-1}).

The equation **(42)** updates the Error in the Estimated value. The following two cases illustrate the two ideal cases.

1. $E_{EST} \gg E_{MEA}$ and $K \approx 1$, then the error in the estimated value E_{ESTk} remains almost same.

2. $E_{EST} \ll E_{MEA}$ and $K \approx 0$, then the error in the estimated value E_{ESTk} reduces, making estimates more accurate.

The basic algorithm of the Kalman Filtering process is shown in Fig. (**1**).

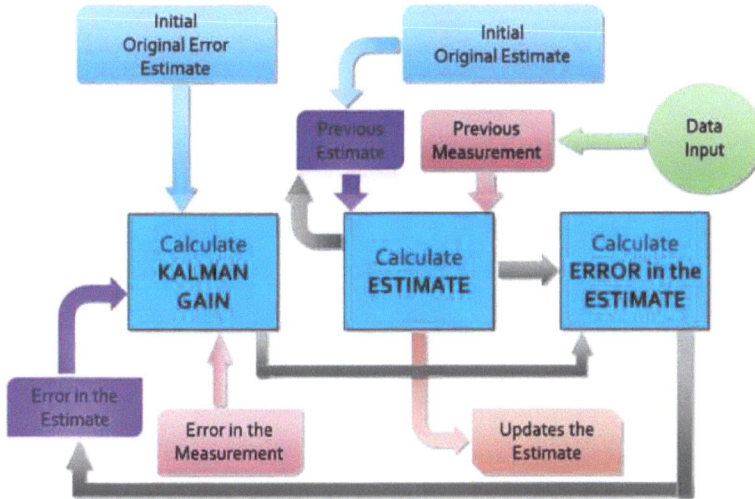

Fig. (1). Algorithm for One Dimension.

We present here some very simple examples to give the reader an insight into the usage of Kalman filter.

EXAMPLE 1: FINDING THE TRUE VALUE OF TEMPERATURE

A room with no drastic change in temperature is considered. The main aim is to find out the actual or *true* value using a temperature sensor, *i.e.*, $72°C$. Every second, the temperature is recorded. This is done till the number of observations reaches a large value.

Let Matrix M represent the Measurement values, where $M =$ [75, 71, 72, 75, 68, 73, 69, ...] in $°C$ *(degree Celsius)* and Error in the Measurement $E_{MEA} = 2°C$. The initial values considered are:

Initial Estimate $EST_o = 68°C$

Initial Error in the Estimate $E_{ESTo} = 2°C$

First Iteration

$$K = \frac{E_{EST}}{E_{EST} + E_{MEA}}$$

$$= \frac{2}{2 + 4}$$

$$= 0.33$$

$$EST_k = EST_{k-1} + K[MEA - EST_{k-1}]$$

$$= 68 + 0.33(75 - 68)$$

$$= 70.33\,°C$$

$$EST_{ESTk} = [1-K]E_{ESTk-1}$$

$$= (1-0.33)2$$

$$E_{ESTk} = [1-K]E_{ESTK-1}$$

$$= (1 - 0.33)2$$

$$= 1.33\,°C$$

Second Iteration

$$K = \frac{E_{EST}}{E_{EST} + E_{MEA}}$$

$$= \frac{1.33}{1.33 + 4}$$

$$EST_k = EST_{k-1} + K[MEA - EST_{k-1}]$$

$$= 70.33 + 0.25(71 - 70.33)$$

$$= 70.50°C$$

$$EST_{ESTk} = [1 - K]E_{ESTk-1}$$

$$= (1-0.25)0.33$$

$$= 1.00°C$$

Further iterations are carried out and eventually, the estimated value (EST_k) reaches the true value. The more data points, the more accurate the final results (final estimates) will be.

EXAMPLE 2: FINDING THE TRUE VALUE OF ACCELERATION DUE TO GRAVITY

Kalman Filtering can be used to find out the true value of a measurable quantity. There are many constants used in physical systems like *acceleration due to gravity*, *Planck's Constant*, *Boltzmann constant*, *etc.* But, to find out their exact value or true value, one should not be restricted to one or two experimental outcomes, as it may not be accurate. To overcome this problem, a large number of observations are taken (preferably using more than one type of apparatus to measure one single parameter). In this example, various observations are recorded for the *time period* of a simple pendulum. These observations are then used to find out the true value of time period of a simple pendulum (of finite length) and thus find out the value of acceleration due to gravity. This true value is found using Kalman Filter technique.

The value of acceleration due to gravity (g) is thus calculated using the formula:

$$g = \frac{4\pi^2 l}{T^2} \tag{43}$$

T: True value of Time Period (in seconds) found out using Kalman Filter.

l: Length of the simple pendulum (in metres).

N: Total number of observations.

The value of parameters used are: l = 1.04m, N= 126

The experimental values of time period are given in Table **1** below:

Table 1. Experimental Values of Time Period in second.

2.021	2.041	2.036	2.024	2.054	2.044	2.051
2.043	2.043	2.047	2.04	2.045	2.053	2.042
2.035	2.025	2.058	2.047	2.046	2.042	2.04
2.057	2.037	2.041	2.033	2.057	2.061	2.065
2.05	2.038	2.042	2.036	2.038	2.04	2.048

(Table 1) cont.....

2.021	2.041	2.036	2.024	2.054	2.044	2.051
2.045	2.036	2.044	2.047	2.042	2.051	2.04
2.047	2.043	2.035	2.058	2.064	2.042	
2.044	2.045	2.052	2.041	2.036	2.023	
2.056	2.064	2.044	2.042	2.043	2.034	
2.042	2.042	2.046	2.053	2.025	2.052	
2.041	2.043	2.03	2.044	2.047	2.04	
2.02	2.054	2.041	2.035	2.041	2.044	
2.044	2.057	2.043	2.036	2.032	2.066	
2.035	2.036	2.025	2.047	2.053	2.038	
2.048	2.045	2.037	2.048	2.044	2.043	
2.037	2.042	2.038	2.061	2.045	2.055	
2.052	2.024	2.036	2.042	2.056	2.037	
2.044	2.04	2.043	2.061	2.037	2.04	
2.046	2.047	2.045	2.042	2.048	2.029	
2.03	2.033	2.042	2.043	2.055	2.04	

The graph in Fig. (**2**) shows the data points found experimentally. The X-axis shows the sample space, and Y-axis indicates the **time period** of a simple pendulum in seconds.

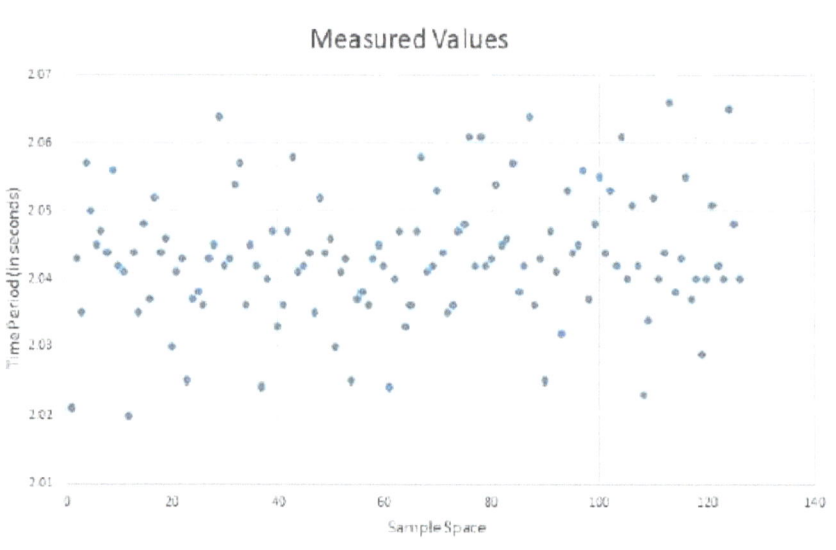

Fig. (**2**). Experimental Observations.

The program below uses basic MATLAB commands.

```
%Length of the Pendulum: 1.04 metre
%To find the True value of Acceleration
gravity
%10 Oscillations each for  126 data sets

clc;
set(0,'defaulttextinterpreter','Latex');

fileID = fopen('TimePeriod_data.txt','r');
formatSpec = '%f';
sizeA = [1 Inf];

A = fscanf(fileID,formatSpec,sizeA);
fclose(fileID);
A = A';
Est = 2.1; %initial estimate
E = zeros(126,1); %Estimated values matrix
EEst = 0.5; %Initial Error in the Measurement
M = A;
EMea = 0.005; %Error in the measurement

for i = 1:126
  E(i) = Est;
  KG = EEst/(EEst + EMea);
  Est = Est + (KG*(M(i) - Est));
  EEst = (1-KG)*EEst;
end
  disp(E);

T = Est;
disp("Estimated Value of Time Period (in seconds):");
disp(Est);

L = 1.04;

g = (4*3.14*3.14*L)/(T*T); disp("The value of acceleration due to gravity is given by
(in m/s^2): ");
disp(g);
```

Fig. (**3**) shows the output screen.

The estimated value of **Time Period** after the Kalman Filter process is equal to 2.0432 *seconds*. Using Equation (3.1), the value of **acceleration due to gravity** for Earth (g) is calculated and is equal to 9.8248 ms^{-2}

Fig. (**4**) shows a graph for the *estimated values* (solid line), which eventually converges to a particular true value. Although, the result may not be accurate because of external factors like air resistance, extensible string, string with mass, *etc.* But these have been neglected. The scattered points show the experimental data values, while the solid line shows the estimated values.

Fig. (3). Output Screen.

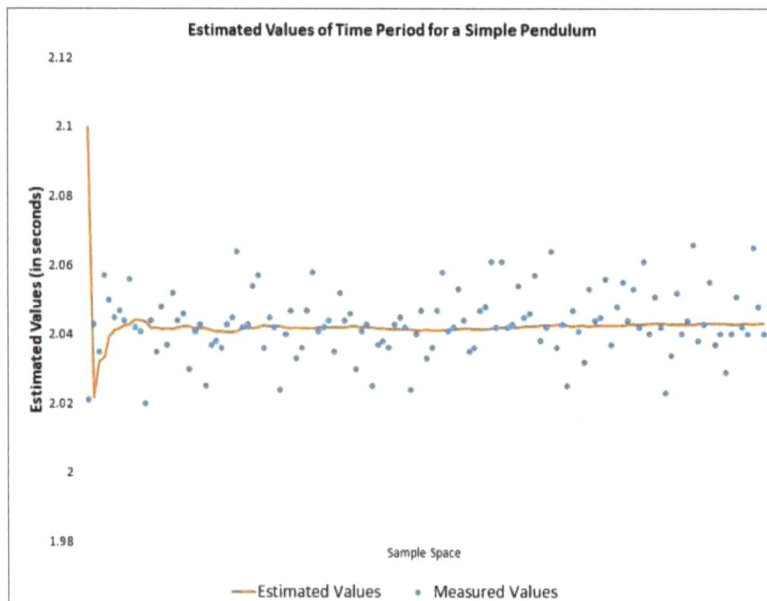

Fig. (4). Experimental Observations with Kalman Filtered Estimated Values.

EXAMPLE 3: VERIFYING HUBBLE'S LAW

Hubble's Law was stated by Hubble in his article (PNAS) in 1929. It is the observed relation between the recession velocity of galaxies and their distance. This law is a landmark in observational cosmology, the study of the big vast universe, which is supposed to be nearly 14-18 billion years [6].

The study of the universe is totally incomplete without the observations which are to be suitably analysed and assessed to make conformity with the theoretical models [7, 8].

Let V_r be the **recessional velocity** in kms^{-1} and D be the **distance** from the observer (Earth in this case) in mega-parsecs Mpc. The Hubble's Law states that:

$$V_r = H_o \times D \tag{44}$$

where, H_o is known as **Hubble's constant**, it represents the constant rate of cosmic expansion caused by the stretching of space-time itself. The Hubble's Law is now well established for the Local Universe ($V_r < 30,000 kms^{-1}$) [9].

Data from **24** different galaxies are obstained[5] and tabulated in Table **2**. The distance D is measured using the Tully-Fisher relation. The recessional velocity V_r is measured using the red-shift method.[6]

Table 2. Galaxies Data.

Galaxy	D(Mpc)	V_r(kmps)	Error in D	Error in V_r
NGC 7814	12	1050	2.881	4
NGC 0157	16.226	1652	5.014	5
NGC 0578	18.282	1628	4.774	3
NGC 0063	18.6	1160	0.164	3
NGC 0289	19.162	1629	3.627	2
NGC 0150	19.291	1584	4.242	4
NGC 0584	20.4	1802	4.463	3
NGC 0596	21.452	1876	4.385	11
NGC 0514	25.669	2472	3.975	1
NGC 0524	26.43	2403	4.171	5
NGC 0448	27.12	1908	7.246	5
NGC 0274	27.525	1750	12.522	10
VV 730	33.3	2700	10.203	2

(Table 2) cont.....

Galaxy	D(Mpc)	V_r(kmps)	Error in D	Error in V_r
NGC 0470	34.726	2374	6.828	3
NGC 0632	38.525	3168	5.843	6
NGC 0048	41.967	1776	17.431	8
MCG -01-02-001	44.5	3709	9.173	4
UGC 12914	50.8	4371	11.02	8
UGC 00139	55.605	3963	7.843	4
NGC 0536	60.69	5189	10.593	5
NGC 0523	62.725	4758	8.049	4
NGC 0452	62.946	4962	4.613	5
UGC 01087	63.275	4485	8.578	1
NGC 0494	65.187	5462	6.595	10

The graph for measured values is shown in Fig. (**5**).

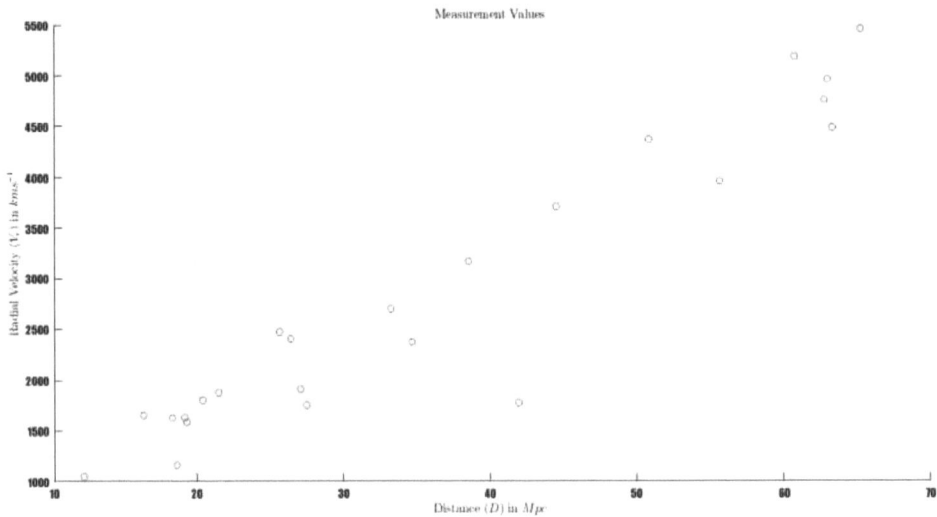

Fig. (5). Measurement Values.

The X-axis represents the Distance (*D*) in *Mpc* and Y-axis represents the Radial Velocity (V_r) in kms^{-1}.

[5]Data collected from: https://ned.ipac.caltech.edu/level5/NED1D/ned1d.html

[6]Refer Appendix for more.

Kalman Filter process is carried out with the following considerations, according to Equations: (34), (35), (36):

1. State matrix is obtained. D defines the distance of the galaxy from the Earth in Mpc and V_r signifies the radial velocity in kms^{-1}.

$$X_k = \begin{bmatrix} V_r \\ D \end{bmatrix}$$

$$(45)$$

$$P_k = \begin{bmatrix} \sigma_{V_r^2} & \sigma_{V_r}\sigma_D \\ \sigma_D\sigma_{V_r} & \sigma_{D^2} \end{bmatrix}$$

$$(46)$$

2. The state equations are obtained. H_o represents the value of Hubble's constant[6] and is equal to $73\ kms^{-1}Mpc^{-1}$.

$$X_{k+1} = \begin{bmatrix} 0 & H_o \\ 0 & 1 \end{bmatrix}\begin{bmatrix} V_r \\ D \end{bmatrix}$$

$$(47)$$

$$P_{k+1} = \begin{bmatrix} 0 & H_o \\ 0 & 1 \end{bmatrix}\begin{bmatrix} \sigma_{V_r^2} & \sigma_{V_r}\sigma_D \\ \sigma_D\sigma_{V_r} & \sigma_{D^2} \end{bmatrix}\begin{bmatrix} 0 & H_o \\ 0 & 1 \end{bmatrix}^T$$

$$(48)$$

[7]Value of Hubble's Constant obtained from https://ned.ipac.caltech.edu/

3. Measurement value is used from the data obtained.

$$Y_m = \begin{bmatrix} 1 & 0 \\ 0 & 1 \end{bmatrix}\begin{bmatrix} V_{rm} \\ D_m \end{bmatrix}$$

$$(49)$$

where, V_{rm} represents the Radial Velocity measurement value and D_m represents Distance measurement value.

Using the Equations **(37)**, **(38)** and **(39)**, Kalman Filtering is done to *estimate* the values of *Distance D* and *Radial Velocity V_r*. The matrices H, C and I are the *Identity Matrix* of order 2x2.

The code snippet attached below uses simple MATLAB commands to calculate the estimated states.

```
clc ;
clear ;
format long ;
set (0, ' defaulttextinterpreter ','Latex ');
S =[ Inf, Inf ];
% Initial Estimated State Matrix
v = 100;
d = 1;
X = [v;d];
disp (X);
Ho = 73;
A = [0 Ho ;0 1];
disp (A);
H = eye (2, 2);
C = eye (2, 2);
I = eye (2, 2);
% Initial Estimated Process Covariance matrix
dv2 = 5;
dd2 = 0.25;
dvd = dv2 *dd2;
ddv = dd2 *dv2;
P = [dv2 dvd ;ddv dd2 ];
% Measurement Values
file_vm = fopen ('velocity . txt ', 'r');
file_dm = fopen ('distance . txt ','r');
file_vm_err = fopen (' velocity_error . txt ', 'r');
file_dm_err = fopen (' distance_error . txt ','r');
format_vm = '%d';
format_dm = '%f';
format_vm_err = '%d';
format_dm_err = '%f';
size_vm = [1, Inf ];
size_dm = [1, Inf ];
size_vm_err = [1, Inf ];
size_dm_err = [1, Inf ];
vm = fscanf (file_vm, format_vm, size_vm);
dm = fscanf (file_dm, format_dm, size_dm);
vm = vm ';
v = 100;
d = 1;
X = [v;d];
disp (X);
Ho = 73;
A = [0 Ho ;0 1];
disp (A);
H = eye (2, 2);
C = eye (2, 2);
I = eye (2, 2);
% Initial Estimated Process Covariance matrix
dv2 = 5;
dd2 = 0.25;
dvd = dv2 *dd2;
ddv = dd2 *dv2;
P = [dv2 dvd ;ddv dd2 ];
% Measurement Values
file_vm = fopen ('velocity . txt ', 'r');
file_dm = fopen ('distance . txt ','r');
file_vm_err = fopen (' velocity_error . txt ', 'r');
file_dm_err = fopen (' distance_error . txt ','r');
format_vm = '%d';
format_dm = '%f';
format_vm_err = '%d';
format_dm_err = '%f';
size_vm = [1, Inf ];
size_dm = [1, Inf ];
size_vm_err = [1, Inf ];
size_dm_err = [1, Inf ];
vm = fscanf (file_vm, format_vm, size_vm);
dm = fscanf (file_dm, format_dm, size_dm);
vm = vm ';
```

Fig. (**6**) shows a plot between the estimated values for Radial Velocity (V_r) in kms^{-1} and Distance (D) in *Mpc* calculated using Kalman Filter.

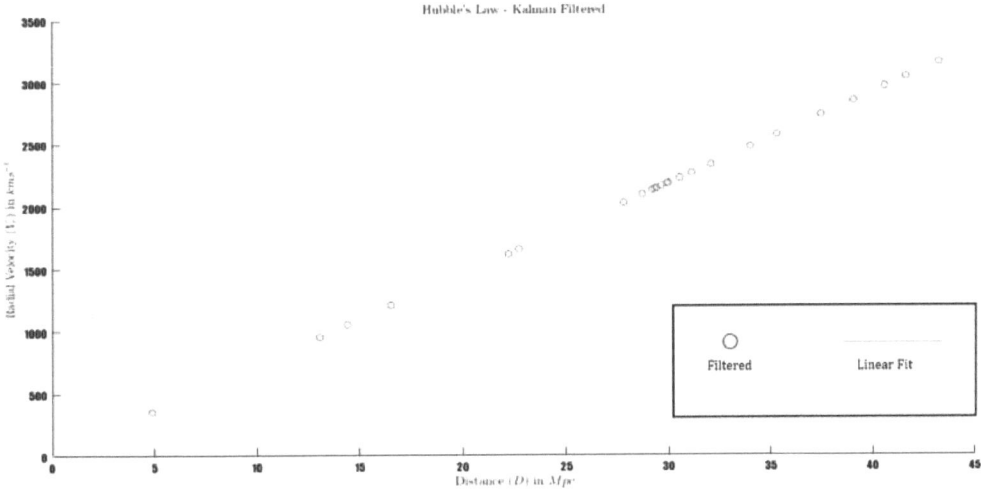

Fig. (6). Kalman Filtered Plot.

The slope obtained from the graph is equal to the **Hubble's Constant**, which is calculated to be: 72.3 $kms^{-1}Mpc^{-1}$.

According to Milne model [10] of the Universe, the *inverse of Hubble's Constant* (H_o^{-1}) gives the *age of the universe* in seconds and is equal to:

$$age = H_o^{-1} = 4.268326 \times 10^{17} \tag{50}$$

which is nearly equal to **13.53 billion Years**.

LIMITATIONS OF KALMAN FILTER

Although being efficient and having a number of advantages, there are a few limitations for Kalman Filter technique:

1. Kalman Filter can only be used for Linear systems. Although it is faster than other Curve Fitting methods, it can still be slower as compared to other Filters.

2. In one-dimensional case, if all the measurements are below or above the True Value, it is never possible to attain the True Value using Kalman Filter technique.

OTHER FILTERS

There are various other filters which are faster and more efficient and are also capable of filtering out **non-linear systems**, but maybe subjected to high computation costs. These are:

1. Extended Kalman Filter

2. Unscented Kalman Filter

3. Particle Filters

FUTURE PROSPECTS

1. The Kalman filter can be used for track reconstruction of atmospheric muon neutrinos.

The Iron Calorimeter at Indian Based Neutrino Observatory (INO) as shown in Fig. (7) is used to study the interactions involving the atmospheric muon neutrinos and anti- neutrinos. The detector measures the momentum and direction to track the muon. The track reconstruction is required for the detector. Using Kalman filter, trajectory estimation is easily done [11].

Fig. (7). INO Iron Calorimeter at VECC.

2. Reconstruction of Electron track in GLAST using Kalman Filter- The Kalman filter can be used to estimate the path of a spacecraft.

3. Modify Kalman Filter according to Non-Linear applications. A large number of practical applications involve nonlinear dynamics. Here, Kalman Filter fails to perform a proper estimation of variables. So, modifications are made to Kalman Filter method to make it useful for non-linear systems also.

CONCLUDING REMARKS- KALMAN FILTER IN A NUTSHELL

We have used Kalman Filters for two situations:

1. Analysing a large number of observations for the time period of a simple pendulum and finding out a true value of its time period and using this result, calculate the actual value of acceleration due to gravity on Earth.

2. Estimation of radial velocity to their corresponding radial distance and verifying Hubble's Law, by considering both the measurement and theoretical values, using a number of observations for the radial velocity and radial distances of various galaxies (Table **2**).

The primary conclusions drawn from the Kalman Filter method are:

- Kalman Filter is independent of the total number of inputs. This means that it is not necessary to mention the total number of inputs. Because of this advantage, dynamic input of variables of interest is possible.
- As the number of data points increases, the estimated value also improves.
- Kalman filter is efficient and much faster, compared to other curve fittings like Linear Fitting.
- The computation costs involved in using this are very low as compared to other filters which might be more useful as far as the efficiency and speed of computation is concerned. But their huge computation costs make them less popular.

APPENDIX – BASIC CONCEPTS

A.1. LINEAR DYNAMIC SYSTEMS

Linear Dynamic Systems are the dynamic systems, having a *linear* evaluation function. From equation (2.1):

$$\frac{dx(t)}{dt} = \phi x(t) \tag{A.1}$$

Let $a(t)$ and $b(t)$ be two different solutions for the above equation. For a Linear Dynamic system, the *linear combination* of these solutions will also be a solution. Let α and β be non-zero constants, then:

$$c(t) = \alpha a(t) + \beta b(t) \tag{A.2}$$

then, $c(t)$ will also be a solution of the Equation (A.1).

A.2. ERROR COVARIANCE MATRIX

Variance and Covariance

Let N be the total number of observations, where N is very large.

Let X_i be the ith measurement.

Let $\bar{X}$ represent the average of measurements.

Deviation from the average value is: $\bar{X} - X_i$. Square of the deviation: $(\bar{X} - X_i)^2$.

The **Variance** is given by:

$$\sigma_x^2 = \frac{\Sigma(\bar{X}-X_i)^2}{N} \tag{A.3}$$

The **Covariance** is given by:

$$\sigma_x\sigma_y = \frac{\Sigma(\bar{X}-X_i)(\bar{Y}-Y_i)}{N} \tag{A.4}$$

The **standard Deviation** is given by:

$$\sigma_x = \sqrt{\sigma_x{}^2} \tag{A.5}$$

$$P = \begin{bmatrix} \sigma_X^2 & \sigma_X\sigma_Y \\ \sigma_Y\sigma_X & \sigma_Y^2 \end{bmatrix} \tag{A.6}$$

These types of matrices are always *Symmetric*.

Variance: Variance is more expanded as compared to Standard Deviation;

$$\sigma_X^2 \text{ and } \sigma_Y^2$$

Covariance: It accounts for the error in measurement/estimate between two variables; $\sigma_X \sigma_Y$ and $\sigma_Y \sigma_X$.

A.3. TULLY FISHER RELATION

Tully and Fisher [12] showed that the width of neutral Hydrogen (HI) width, when expressed in logarithmic scale is linearly correlated with the absolute magnitude, without any additional parameters.

$$M = a.log_{10}W_{HI} + b \tag{A.7}$$

where, M: absolute magnitude a and b are constants. W_{HI} is the 21 cm line width.

According to Virial Theorem, the relation between distance D in *Mpc* can and absolute magnitude M from equation (A.7) be calculated by using the expression:

$$m - M = 5log_{10}D + 25 \tag{A.8}$$

where, m: apparent magnitude.

A.4. RED SHIFTS AND RECESSIONAL VELOCITY

Measured Doppler red shifts give the recession velocity of galaxies. Let z represent the wavelength shift. Therefore:

$$z = \frac{\Delta\lambda}{\lambda} = \sqrt{\frac{1 + \frac{v}{c}}{1 - \frac{v}{c}}} - 1$$

where, v gives the recessional velocity of a galaxy (V_r).

NOTES

[1] Systems whose attributes are changing with time.

[2] Dynamic Systems having linear evaluation functions. Refer Appendix for more.

[3] Referred to www.tina-vision.net; Article: The Likelihood Interpretation of the Kalman Filter.

by N. A Thacker, A.J. Lacey.

[4] Refer Appendix for more details regarding Covariance matrix.

REFERENCES

[1]   D. Koller, and N. Friedmann, "Probabilistic graphical models: Principles and techniques adaptive computation and machine learning",

[2]   B. Carter, and R. Mancini, "Op-amps for everyone". Texas Instruments, 2009, pp. 10-11.

[3]   R.E. Kalman, "A new approach to linear filtering and prediction problems", *J. Basic. Eng.,* vol. 82, no. 1, pp. 35-45, 1960.
[http://dx.doi.org/10.1115/1.3662552]

[4]   M.S. Grewal, and A.P. Andrews, "Kalman filtering theory and practice using matlab". 2nd. Wiley & Sons, 2001.

[5]   R.G. Brown, and P.Y.C. Hwang, "Introduction to random signals and applied kalman filtering". 2nd. Wiley, 1992, pp. 1-400.

[6]   N.A. Bahcall, "Hubble's Law and the expanding universe", *Proc. of. N.A.S,* vol. 112, no. 11, pp. 3173-3175, 2015.

[7]   A.G. Riess, A.V. Filippenko, P. Challis, A. Clocchiatti, A. Diercks, P.M. Garnavich, R. L. Gilliland, C.J. Hogan, S. Jha, and R.P. Kirshner, "Observational evidence from supernovae for an accelerating universe and a cosmological constant", *A.J.,* vol. 116, no. 3, pp. 1009-1038, 1998.
[http://dx.doi.org/10.1086/300499]

[8]   S. Perlmutter, G. Aldering, G. Goldhaber, and R.A. K. P. Nugent, "Supernovae cosmology project.measurements of omega and lambda from 42 high-redshift supernovae", *A.J.,* vol. 517, no. 2, pp. 565-586, 1999.

[9]   G. Paturel, P. Teerikorpi, and Y. Baryshev, "Hubble law: Measure and interpretation", *Found. Phys.,* vol. 47, no. 9, pp. 1208-1228, 2017.
[http://dx.doi.org/10.1007/s10701-017-0093-4]

[10]   E.A. Milne, "Relativity, gravitation and world structure". vol. 135. Oxford University Press, 1935, pp. 635-636.

[11]   T. Ghosh, and S Chattopadhyay, "Track fitting by kalman filter method for a prototype cosmic ray muon detector", *arxiv,* vol. 0908, p. 0851v1, 2009.

[12]   R.B. Tully, and J.R. Fisher, "A new method of determining distances to galaxies", *Astron. Astrophys.,* vol. 54, pp. 661-673, 1977.

CHAPTER 3

The Role of Mathematics and Statistics in the Field of Data Science and its Application

Sathiyapriya Murali[1,*] and **Priya Panneer**[1]

[1] *Department of Mathematics, Mathematics Marudhar Kesari Jain College for Women, Vaniyambadi, Tirupattur, Tamilnadu, India*

Abstract: Mathematics is the rock-solid foundation of everything that happens when science is present, and it is also extremely important in the field of data science since mathematical ideas assist discover models and facilitate the development of algorithms. But, the concepts they present and the tools they enable are the only reasons statistics and arithmetic are so crucial to data science. There is a particular type of mathematical reasoning that is necessary to grasp data, beyond the fundamentals of calculus, discrete mathematics, and linear algebra. For the implementation of such algorithms in data science, a thorough understanding of the various principles of probability and statistics is essential. Machine learning is one of the many modern data science techniques that has a strong mathematical base. The evidence presented in this chapter backs up our earlier claim that math and statistics are the fields that offer the greatest tools and approaches for extracting structure from data. For newcomers coming from other professions to data science, math proficiency is crucial.

Keywords: Applications in medical science, Bayes' theorem, Binomial, Bernoulli, Computer vision, Calculus, Calculus in machine learning, Gaussian normal, Linear algebra, Loss function, Mean squared error, Mean absolute error, Nonparametric statistical methods, Regression.

INTRODUCTION

Data Science

"Data Science" combines many statistical disciplines with computer technology to clarify the significance of data as a factor in decision-making. The term "science" implies that it is a field that relies on systematic process to achieve results that can be tested. Because machine learning is a process that requires arithmetic to complete analyses and during the hunt for data insights, the field of data science requires a working knowledge of mathematics. Math is typically one of the most

* **Corresponding author Sathiyapriya Murali:** Department of Mathematics, Marudhar Kesari Jain College for Women, Vaniyambadi, Tirupattur, Tamilnadu, India; E-mail:sathiyamathvlr@gmail.com

important subjects, even though it may not be the one that is most desired for your academic and professional path in data science. One of the most important paces in a data scientist's communication is to establish and comprehend work daring and condition others toward mathematical ones. Whether a data scientist, engineer who specializes in machine learning, developer who understands business intelligence, data architect, or another industry expert; it's possible that we still don't fully understand how our careers in data science will be organized. Nevertheless, various mathematical techniques and everything that data science uses them for should be considered. We may finally better follow the option of teaching mathematics since we would have a superior understanding of knowledge and attention.

DATA SCIENCE IN MATHEMATICS

Learning the theoretical underpinnings of data science or machine learning can be demoralizing because they include a wide range of mathematical disciplines and extensive web resources. In this essay, the goal is to present resources to raise the mathematical foundation needed for data science practical/research activity.

Data science relies heavily on mathematics since mathematical concepts are essential for understanding design and creating algorithms. Understanding various concepts from probability theory and statistics is essential for using these algorithms in data science. Regression, maximum likelihood estimation, knowledge of distributions (Binomial, Bernoulli, Gaussian (Normal)), and the Bayes' Theorem are all included in this course [1].

MATH AND DATA SCIENCE IN EDUCATION

For data scientists, regardless matter how far in the future their business careers take them, math is a crucial educational strength. It ensures that you can help a firm solve issues and grow more quickly, improve model displays, and successfully integrate complicated data into the management of business risks [2].

It should be ensured to develop the necessary mathematics knowledge and skill sets using a major online workshop provider like Easy to learn. They provide Data Science Certification Courses that guide students through all they need to know in order to pursue a career in data science, including math-related courses and applications.

TYPES OF DATA SCIENCE IN MATH

Linear Algebra

Ability to use linear algebra in data science processes and applications that are different and diverse. We have categorized these applications into several areas where linear algebra will be used to become a strong data scientist. dimension-holding property of basic machine learning. Computer vision, natural language processing, and reduction [2].

First and foremost, the fact is aware of linear algebra and deep learning techniques. Two pertinent data science applications of linear algebra are shown, together with the most valuable product of basic linear algebra's intended use. Simply put, we may refer to linear algebra as the "math of vectors" and "mathematics" of matrices. Principal Component Analysis is one example of how linear algebra is used in data science and machine learning to reduce the amount of data that can be processed. Deep Learning, neural networks, natural language processing, and other applications also use linear algebra.

According to Encyclopedia Britannica, Linear Algebra is a mathematical control that assigns with Vectors and Matrices and more typically Vector Spaces and Linear Transformation. A two-dimensional (or rectangular) array of numbers is one way to define a matrix. Linear algebra would play the role of Robin if Data Science were Batman. It's common to overlook this real sidekick. Nonetheless, it actually drives important areas of data science, such as computer vision and natural language processing.

APPLICATION OF LINEAR ALGEBRA IN DATA SCIENCE

Loss Function

The most effective machine learning algorithm collects data, analyzes it, and then builds a copy using various ways (linear regression, logistic regression, decision tree, random forest, *etc.*). They could then estimate a prospective data enquiry after discovering the solutions [2].

Mean Squared Error

Mean Squared Errors (MSE), which are straightforward to comprehend and typically determined total ably in the majority of regression issues, are almost definitely the most frequently used dropping error speak to. Data research was aided by the Mass Python Athenaeum, Scikit, Tens or Flow each featuring a built-in implementation of the MSE capabilities. Despite this, they all struggle using the same formulae.

$$\text{MSE} - \frac{1}{P} \sum_{i=1}^{P} (y_i - \bar{y_i})^2$$

where P is the numeral of data points in both notice and forecast worth.

MEAN ABSOLUTE ERROR

The Mean Absolute Error (MAE) and Mean Standard Error (MSE) are identical in every way; however, we compute the whole contrast between the safe and unsecure data [2].

$$\text{MSE} = \frac{1}{P} \sum_{i=1}^{P} (| y_i - \overline{y_i} |)^2$$

COMPUTER VISION

The topic of artificial knowledge and skills known as "computer state of seeing" teaches computers how to interpret and comprehend visual information by employing deep learning models, photos, and videos. By doing this, algorithms would be able to precisely establish and characterize an object, or, to put it another way, they would have the ability to visualize data. Linear algebra is utilized in computer vision for tasks like picture identification, some similarities to fact approaches, image complexity, and image depiction as tensors or vectors, as we used to call them [1].

CALCULUS

The components of mathematics covered in calculus, most appropriately known as analysis, include the length, area, and volume of things, as well as the rate at which an amount changes (explained by the slopes of curves). Intermediate data science algorithms require a strong foundation in introductory calculus. That phrase refers to multivariate calculus and differentiation, respectively. Stochastic calculus knowledge will be useful when we get to the more complex algorithms [2].

CALCULUS IN MACHINE LEARNING

The Gradient Drop Algorithm in Linear Regression is the most potent use of Calculus in Machine Learning (and Neural Networks). With linear regression, data are used to identify the line that best fits the data, which is then used to estimate values for one variable based on another. Creating an easy neural network from a score is one of the most crucial ways to study math for data science and machine learning. We would use calculus to assess the network and linear algebra to title it [2].

APPLICATIONS IN MEDICAL SCIENCE

Differential calculus is most commonly employed in medical science. It is employed to compute the bacterial culture's no-approximation growth. Information from a higher level was brought up, and at this point, the application of calculus was crystal clear in the mind [3].

APPLICATION IN ENGINEERING

We employ integration to measure a precise quantity of material when it comes to architecture. Calculus is primarily used in the material of electrical engineering to determine the precise length through integration. A stout wire rope connects the length to the power. Nonetheless, while planning their important and lengthy missions, flight engineers choose calculus [3].

APPLICATIONS IN RESEARCH ANALYSIS

The research analyst carefully examines the application to learn about various types of series. It works well for raising productivity, operating, and other factors. Calculus is also in charge of increasing production and dividend [3].

APPLICATIONS IN PHYSICS

Without integration, physics is just incomplete. It can calculate the center of mass, the center of gravity, and other things, making it eternal in many respects. Calculus is employed in many different areas, such as business planning, credit card payment records, and solving complex geometrical problems [3].

STATISTICS

It is used by data scientists and analysts to examine important global trends. Moreover, statistics has the ability to glean important information from the data. Different functions, principles, and techniques are provided by statistics. It is a theory that puts statistics, data analysis, machine learning, and systems of their kind into practice to comprehend and analyze real-world data [4].

Studying statistics involves gathering data, looking into it, expanding on it, presenting it, and organizing it along a specific path. The theory of measure-theoretical probability, differential equations, stochastic analysis, mathematical analysis, and linear algebra are some examples of mathematical techniques that have already been used for various analytics but are still relatively new. Statistics has something to do with gathering, categorizing, arranging in a methodical way, and displaying numerical data. This enables one to grasp several answers to the problem and anticipate greater suitability of many situations. The conformation of numerical Data is when statistics take over from details, watching, and detail. With the aid of statistics, we were clever enough to identify multiple measures of middle bias and the separation of various values from the center. Statistics acted as a conduit to comprehend the data and action for triumphant solutions. The power of statistics extends beyond just being able to comprehend the data; it also provides ways to assess the success of our intuition, get different approaches for solving the same issue, and arrive at the proper mathematical approximation for a fact.

Types of Statistics in Data Science

Descriptive statistics and inferential statistics are the two types of statistics. In contrast to inferential statistics, which uses the data to explain the descriptive kind, descriptive statistics gives a full account of the data or collection in words in a summarized manner. Both of these are widely employed. In another category of statistics, descriptive data is transformed into inferential data. Most statistics are divided into the twin admirers groups.

Descriptive Statistics

The details are illustrated in the descriptive statistics, which suggests that a representative of the residents completed the outline using utterly unrelated restrictions like average or variation. The simplest method for organizing, arguing for, and making a case for a collection of data is to use descriptive statistics, which makes use of charts, graphs, and description estimates. Often tables or graphs showing specifics like histograms, pie charts, bars, or scatter plots are used to organize and display data. Descriptive statistics were only intended to be illustrative, therefore they did not call for collective action on all of the data's various aspects.

Inferential Statistics

We tend to try to explain the necessity of illustrative Statistics among the inferential statistics. After the data was gathered, examined, and summarized, inferential statistics were used to explain what data's implications were. With the help of inferential statistics, we may determine whether or not the tendencies found in the study sample are typically applicable to the vast population that the representative is drawn from. Inferential statistics are used to draw conclusions and deductions from example in order to get generalized values.

Application of Statistics in the Field of Study

Statisticians are central to machine learning. So without adequate data on applied math fundamentals, we would not be able to use machine learning to tackle real-world problems. Actually, there are a few key facts that make understanding statistics challenging. We're discussing mathematical equations, Greek notation, and other really well-defined concepts, which makes it difficult to arouse a strong interest in the topic. We will name these concerns with simple, understandable explanations, lessons that are appropriately timed, and interactive laboratories to address problems using methods from applied mathematics. Statistics played a fundamental part in identifying problems across all major businesses and the country, from raw information analysis to developing hypothesis testing investigations [3].

Anyone who wants to understand machine learning well should research how applied mathematics forms the basis for regression and classification algorithms. However, statistics also enables the United States to make sense of information and the way it aids in the extraction of meaning from unlabeled data.

VITAL STATISTICS IDEAS OBTAINING STARTED

Rectangular and non-rectangular information formats are understood, as are location calculations, fixed pattern calculations, information distributions, binary and categorical information, correlation, and relationships between various types of data.

DISTRIBUTION OF DATA POINT

The law of very large numbers, the central limit theorem, common mistake, and so forth, Gaussian distribution, t-distribution, Bernoulli distribution, chi-square distribution, F-distribution, Poisson and exponential distributions, as well as sampling bias, choice bias, sampling distribution, bootstrapping, and confidence intervals are just a few examples of the distributions that can be sampled [1].

APPLIED MATH EXPERIMENTS AND SIGNIFICANCE TESTING

A/B testing, organized hypothesis tests (Null/Alternate), resampling, applied arithmetic power, confidence interval, p-value, alpha, t-tests, degree of freedom, and important values for the ANOVA [3].

NONPARAMETRIC STATISTICAL METHODS

Rank data, normality analysis, normalization of data, rank correlation, rank substance analysis, the fact analysis.

APPLICATION OF STATISTICS IN DATA SCIENCE ANALYZING AND CATEGORIZING DATA

As we begin a new data science project, we use data derived from several sources. The information might be derived from earlier operations with the derivation, from a weather sensor, from an influence of photographs or videos, or it could just be some text supplied over voice or message channels. Raw data has the drawbacks of being unstructured and challenging to interpret. Because computers are adept at locating patterns in and working with structured data, we must convert unstructured primary data into structured data in order to conduct various operations on it.

NUMERIC DATA & CATEGORICAL DATA

Numbers can take one of two forms: uninterpreted, like temperature, time, or humidity, or discrete, like the quantity of an event's incidents [3]. Categorical data, simply contain a set of values with no approximation, such as names of the days of the week, countries with particular content, *etc.* Binary data, which can only take the values 0 or 1, yes or no, or true or false, is one of the two types of categorical data. The second type of system for unconditional data is normal data, where the classes are classifications. A numerical classification is an illustration of this (1, 2, 3, 4, or 5).

EXPLORATORY KNOWLEDGE ANALYSIS

In knowledge research, exploratory knowledge analysis (EDA) is a method for organizing the data for production. It primarily involves purging and aiming to recognize the data; doing so, the purpose is to either get the Associate in Nursing's goods that require from it or establish an intuition for deciphering the results for future modeling. EDA is used to gather several types of information about the data, sampling of the data, completing blank values and observe the patterns in the information.

SIGNIFICANCE TESTS

The purpose of significance tests, also known as hypothesis tests, is to determine whether or not the outcomes of an event are random. They are frequently used in historical applied mathematics analysis.

To do a check, we typically gather information on the variables A and B so that any determined difference between A and B should lead to either:

The change in B is arbitrary and independent of A.

A and B are actually dependent on one another.

An irregular experiment is subjected to an applied mathematics hypothesis test to determine whether or not random likelihood might serve as a less expensive means of elucidating the difference between the two variables. The theory of applied mathematics might serve as a safeguard against researchers falling for random likelihood. There are two different types of hypotheses:

Null Hypotheses

The 2 categorical variables square measure freelance (no relation between their values and any correlation is thanks to chance).

Alternative Hypotheses

The two category variables are correlated. There are several other types of significance testing; however, in this article, we will focus on the three that are most often used: the chi-squared test, student's t-test, and analysis of variance test (ANOVA).

CHI-SQUARED CHECK

The chi-squared test determines if two category variables are related or independent by inventing a price "p" that denotes the likelihood that the two variables are independent. This check only applies to categorical information (data that falls into one of several categories), such as gender or color, not to numerical information like height or weight.

STUDENT'S T-TEST

The t-test shows how significant the differences between variables are; in other words, it helps you determine if such differences could be due to chance. The data in each sample must be generally distributed and must have the same variance for the t-test to be valid.

ANALYSIS OF VARIANCE CHECK (ANOVA)

To assess the importance of an experiment's results, an analysis of variance check may be helpful. In other words, they help the United States determine whether to accept the alternative hypothesis or reject the null hypothesis. To see if there is a difference between testing samples, we frequently measure them. There are two types of analysis of variance tests: unidirectional and two-way:

Unidirectional

Unidirectional has one variable quantity, for example, the kind of rice.

Two-ways

Two-way has 2 freelance variables. As an example, the kind of rice and calories.

RESERVATION AND PREDICTION

The ability to reach is the main justification for using statistics in knowledge science. Simple regression, logistical regression, polynomial regression, stepwise regression, ridge regression, lasso regression, and elastic internet regression are only a few of the various types of regression. Yet, we frequently use logistical and linear regressions in knowledge science applications.

Linear Regression

The variable quantity is continuous in simple regression, whereas the variables are frequently distinct or continuous. Using a best work line connecting the various points, simple regression establishes a relationship between a variable quantity and one or more freelancing variables. The term "regression line" usually refers to that work line.

Logistic Regression

To determine the odds of an incident succeeding or failing, logistic regression is used. When a variable needs to be predicted and is binary (0/1, True/False, Yes/No), logistic regression is typically used. In order to perform effectively, logistical regression, which is typically employed for classification problems, occasionally requires an excessive sample size.

CLASSIFICATION OF KNOWLEDGE SCIENCE IN STATISTICS

Knowledge scientists are frequently blunt when dealing with problems that demand a higher level of machine-driven cognition. Consider whether a promotional email is legitimate or spam, or whether a posting is likely to be clicked or not. These problems are referred to as classification challenges. Maybe the most fundamental type of prediction is classification; often, we want to categorize data into binary classes or even a lot of ordinal categorizations. Several categorization methods, including naïve mathematicians, random gradient descent, call trees, random forests, and support vector machines, are frequently utilized in logistical regression. Let's talk about the Naive mathematician and K-nearest neighbor algorithms as examples of categorization algorithms.

Naive Mathematician

Classifiers for naive mathematicians are a subset of the action algorithms based on Bayes' Theorem. It is a collection of algorithms, each of which contributes to a common underlying truth. The fundamental tenet of the mathematical algorithmic program is that each variable has an equal impact on each variable quantity. This algorithmic software is incredibly rapid compared to many subtle strategies and requires a small amount of training knowledge. Nonetheless, it is known that naive mathematicians' estimates are not accurate [3].

K-nearest Neighbors

Although the k-nearest neighbors algorithmic program only saves values of the coaching knowledge and uses these values within the classification approach, it does not intend to build a comprehensive internal model. The great vote of the k nearest adjacent of every created is used to classify from a long forward. This algorithmic program is among the few that may be used, is reliable when it comes to coaching knowledge and is helpful if coaching knowledge is important.

PROBABILITY

For making prediction, applied mathematics is tremendously useful. Predictions and estimates play a significant role in knowledge science. We often create estimates for any analysis with the aid of applied mathematics techniques. As a result, the majority of applied mathematics strategies are dependent on the concept of chance. Chance may be a crucial mathematical concept for knowledge research; it is used, among other things, to decode machine learning outputs and verify hypotheses. In this paragraph, we'll discuss some fundamental notions of chance.

FREQUENCY TABLES

It deals with how to depict a class's count in an extreme distribution. Consider the distribution of the following five colored balls: Red, Red, Green, Blue, and Red in the subsequent (Table **1**). The frequency table is evident from this. The number of balls in Table **1** is indicated as the frequency, along with the color of the balls.

Table 1. Frequency table.

Color	Frequency
Red	3
Green	1
Blue	1

Probability: Allow us to initial have a glance at a number of the terms related to probability:

Experiment: It is an endeavor, having a group of well-defined outputs.

Outcome: It's attainable results of Associate in Nursing experiment.

Events: The set of outcomes from Associate in Nursing experiment.

Probability will be outlined because of the chance of an occasion happening. This chance worth is between zero and one. The chances of all attainable events of Associate in Nursing experiment occurring are adequate. The formula for chance is:

Probability(event) = variety of desired outcomes / variety of total outcomes.

Example:

The results of an experiment where a nice coin was moved are listed below. There will be two possible outcomes: one is that we'll receive heads, and the other is that we'll get tails. The odds of getting heads or tails are equal, or 0.5, because the coin is honest, unlike the one used in Sholay. Let the desired result be a head. Thus, one of the desirable results in this scenario is variety. There are just two possible results: heads or tails; greater victimization than formula.

P(heads) = ½.

The likelihood for event of obtaining tails is calculated in a very similar manner.

HISTOGRAM

Bar graph is employed to explain the distribution of continuous variables. Wikipedia describes a bar graph as Associate in Nursing estimate of the likelihood distribution of endless variable. {we will|we'll|we area unit going to} see what continuous variables and likelihood distributions are later during this article. Below is Associate in Nursing example of a bar graph plot, we're plotting the frequency map of things in a very store. Distribution is employed to make a decision on the quantity of successes in n Bernoulli trials. Let p, be the likelihood for fulfillment and letter be the likelihood for the failure of a Bernoulli trial. Let x be the quantity of successes in a very trial. The entire variety of failures can then be n-x. The likelihood distribution formula is given as:

P(X) = n c(x) * p(x) * (q)n — x currently we all know that likelihood of failure = one likelihood of success. Hence, we will conjointly write the letter as 1-p. P(X) = n C(x) * p(x) * (1 — p) n — x we will plot the values of this distribution as a likelihood mass operate.

CONTINUOUS RANDOM VARIABLES

Continuous random variables are variables that can have any value in a specific range. For instance, the amount of water in a particular jug can have any number between zero and the jug's holding capacity, as well as decimal values. As we've seen before, an infinite probability variable is diagrammatically arranged as a likelihood distribution operation.

SKEWNESS DISTRIBUTION

Data is dispersed in many different ways. As we did below, we will examine the inequality of the distribution victimization histograms or density curves. The distribution's imbalance will be continuously monitored by graphing it.

RIGHT SKEW DISTRIBUTION

A distribution having an extended tail towards the proper aspect of the graph could be a right skew distribution. For a right skew distribution:

Mode < Median < Mean.

LEFT SKEW DISTRIBUTION

A distribution having an extended tail towards the Left aspect of the graph could be a Left skew distribution. For a Left skew distribution Mode > Median > Mean.

NORMAL DISTRIBUTION

A distribution that contains a bilaterally symmetrical structure *i.e.* it doesn't skew either towards right or left, could be a distribution. It's additionally called a bell curve since it's a campana. For a standard distribution, Mode = Median = Mean. Gaussian Distribution (Normal Distribution) is known for its bell-like form, and it's one of the foremost used distributions in Science. Additionally, a number of real-world occurrences, such as individual heights, machine-made object sizes, measurement errors, pressure levels, and marks on a check, show a distribution.

EXPONENTIAL DISTRIBUTION

The Exponential Distribution could be a generalization of the conventional distribution. Therefore, it is additionally called the Generalized distribution. Yet, the Exponential Distribution has a lot of factors such as λ that represents the positive scale parameter (squeezes or stretches a distribution) and κ that represents the positive form parameter (alters the form of the distribution). The Exponential Distribution does not give asymmetrical knowledge, so it's a lot of a skew distribution.

UNIFORM DISTRIBUTION

A uniform distribution, additionally known as an oblong distribution, could be a chance distribution that contains a constant chance, like flipping a coin or rolling a dice. This distribution has 2 sorts. The foremost common sort in elementary statistics is the continuous uniform distribution (which forms the form of a rectangle).

POISSON DISTRIBUTION

Poisson distribution will be found in several phenomena, like inborn disabilities and genetic mutations, automotive accidents, traffic flow, and also the range of writing errors on a page. Also, Poisson distributions area units are utilized by businessmen to form forecasts concerning the quantity of shoppers or sales on bound days or seasons of the year. In business, overstocking can typically mean losses if the merchandise is not oversubscribed. Similarly, understocking would cause the loss of business opportunities as a result of inability to maximize your sales. By mistreatment of this distribution, individuals in business will predict once the demand is high in order to buy a lot of stocks.

IMPORTANT OF INFORMATION SCIENCE

Data is efficacious, and so is the science in decipherment it. Billions of bytes of information area unit are being generated, and currently its worth has surpassed oil yet. The role of an information mortal is and can be of dominant importance for organizations across several verticals.

DATA WHILE NOT KNOWLEDGE SCIENCE

Data must be browsed and analyzed. This calls out for the need of getting top quality information and understanding to browse it and create data-driven discoveries.

DATA CAN PRODUCE HIGHER CLIENT EXPERTISE

For product and merchandise, knowledge science is going to be investing in the facility of machine learning to alter firms to form and turn out merchandise that customers can love. For instance, for an associate degree eCommerce company, a good recommendation system will facilitate them discovering their client personas by examining their purchase history.

DATA USED ACROSS VERTICALS

Data science isn't restricted to solely trade goods or school or tending. There'll be a high demand to optimize business processes mistreatment knowledge science from banking and transport to producing. Thus, anyone United Nations agency desires to be an information mortal can have an entire new world of opportunities open out there. The longer term is knowledge.

POWER OF INFORMATION SCIENCE

Data science is crucial for businesses since it has helped amazing solutions and information choices, travel from one place to another across many business sectors. The revolutionary method of using intelligent machines to gather a lot of information, analyze behavior, and develop is quite astounding. It may be the reason why knowledge in the sciences is growing so rapidly.

FUTURE OF INFORMATION SCIENCE

Currently, businesses have access to enormous databases thanks to the documentation of all client interactions. Information science plays a crucial role in studying and creating machine learning models that are supported by this data. This frequently happens since these databases aim to produce insightful data. It is reasonable to predict that demand for information science will increase as analysis and machine learning capabilities advance. More job opportunities should be available as the field develops since many information scientists are needed for analysis. Information Science has a broad application in all sectors. Computer science is a key component in the future of information science. The most powerful technology that information scientists will likely have to work to defeat in the future is AI, in my opinion. To put it another way, the long haul of knowledge science can align to build it higher through time. Computer science is already helping firms create options and maintain smooth operations. When computer science is applied to real-world problems, it can employ automated methods to sift through vast amounts of data and find patterns that help current firms make better decisions.

DATA SCIENCE IN TRADE

The creation and use of data may be a key economic activity in the world of gifts. Information Science makes it possible because of its capacity to extract data from enormous amounts of knowledge. Data Technology makes our lives easier by gathering and processing large amounts of data rapidly and effectively to deliver results in hours rather than days or weeks [1].

BENEFITS OF KNOWLEDGE SCIENCE

Data Science is widely utilized in the banking and finance sectors for fraud detection and personalized monetary recommendation. Transportation suppliers use information Science to boost the transportation journeys of their customers as example, Transport for London maps client journeys gives personalized transportation details and manages sudden circumstances and exploitation.

STATISTICAL INFORMATION

Data science enables businesses to use social media content to track long-term trends in the consumption of media material. This helps the companies to build target audience-specific content, live content performance, and advocate on-demand content.

DATA SCIENCE IS VERY IMPORTANT IN THE MODERN WORLD

Any business's use of information is crucial. It will increase the value of any wcompany that makes use of its information and help business leaders make decisions based on facts, mathematically applied statistics, patterns, and trends. Information science integrates programming, math, and statistics domain expertise to create insights and knowledge understanding. The discipline of knowledge science has the potential to be extremely lucrative. Numerous businesses are employing information scientists to bolster their analytics teams.

DATA INDIVIDUAL

An individual with data is someone with Massive amounts of data gathered, analyzed, and interpreted by a UN agency to help a business boost sales and enhance operations. Qualified experts in knowledge science create sophisticated analytical methods and mathematical models that are applied to the analysis of knowledge. They then make use of a variety of discoveries and outcomes to look for trends, patterns, and links in knowledge sets. This information will be used to identify operational risks, address the problems faced by small enterprises, assess the repeat purchase rate, and predict client behavior. A person with knowledge of information is typically a storyteller. United Nations agency provides people in a business or organisation with data insights in a simple and efficient way.

DATA SCIENCE WORKS

Data science uses a variety of techniques and technology, ranging from many different fields to enormous amounts of amassed knowledge. These tools generate insights, extract useful information from data collections, and analyze that information for use in making decisions. Information science work draws on a variety of disciplinary areas, including mining, statistics, analysis, machine learning, and even programming. In order to reveal to others patterns that are familiar, data processing adds algorithms to complex knowledge sets, removing relevant and useful knowledge from the sets. Massive volumes of information are processed by machine learning, which is a synthetic knowledge tool since humans lack the capacity to take a sequence of actions over the course of a lifetime. The approximate analysis is impacted by machine learning by complementing the likelihood of what actually occurs at the calculable moment with what might actually take place.

CONCLUDING REMARKS

There were more positions available if a person only had a basic understanding of mathematics, statistics, and certain abstract concepts in the field of contemporary data technology. Data Scientists, Data Analysts, and other professionals perform a variety of tasks on computers. To draw better intuition into an issue and develop a workable solution, one needs to have a one step ahead understanding and aptitude in the field of mathematics.

REFERENCES

[1]　"Role of statistics in data science . online sources available",

[2]　B. O. tayo, "Ph.D KD nuggets essential linear algebra for data science and machine learning", on may 10, 2021.

[3]　G. H. vardhan, "Mathematics as a monarch", 2021.

[4]　M. Logini, "Statistics and probability concepts for data science", 2021.

CHAPTER 4

Bag of Visual Words Model - A Mathematical Approach

Maheswari[1,*]

[1] *Department of Computer Applications, Fatima College, Madurai, India*

Abstract: Information extraction from images is now incredibly valuable for many new inventions. Even though there are several simple methods for extracting information from the images, feasibility and accuracy are critical. One of the simplest and most significant processes is feature extraction from the images. Many scientific approaches are derived by the experts based on the extracted features for a better conclusion of their work. Mathematical procedures, like Scientific methods, play an important role in image analysis. The Bag of Visual Words (BoVW) [1, 2, 3] is one of them, and it is helpful to figure out how similar a group of images is. A set of visual words characterises the images in the Bag of Visual Words model, which are subsequently aggregated in a histogram per image [4]. The histogram difference depicts the similarities among the images. The reweighting methodology known as Term Frequency – Inverse Document Frequency (TF-IDF) [5] refines this procedure. The overall weighting [6] for all words in each histogram is calculated before reweighting. As per the traditional way, the images are transformed into the matrix called as Cost matrix. It is constructed through two mathematical: Euclidean distances and Cosine distances. The main purpose of finding these distances is to detect similarity between the histograms. Further the histograms are normalized and both distances are calculated. The visual representation is also generated. The two mathematical methods are compared to see which one is appropriate for checking resemblance. The strategy identified as the optimum solution based on the findings aids in fraud detection in digital signature, Image Processing, and classification of images.

Keywords: Bag of visual words, Cost matrix, Cosine distance, Euclidean distance.

INTRODUCTION

Recent advances in information retrieval from images, in particular with mathematical methods, are helpful for research [7, 8]. The dissimilarities among a

---
* **Corresponding author Maheswari:** Department of Computer Applications, Fatima College, Madurai, India; E-mail: kpmshri123@gmail.com

Biswadip Basu Mallik, Kirti Verma, Rahul Kar, Ashok Kumar Shaw & Sardar M. N. Islam (Naz) (Eds.)

set of images can be identified by extracting the features from the images. The analysis of images using Bag of Words model is one of the efficient ways.

It describes the images as 'Visual words' rather than pixel values. Visual word is a generalised feature descriptor [9], most frequently, it is a mean value of the cluster of images. The aggregate occurrence of the words is represented as a histogram. It is impossible to distinguish the images from the histogram since it is not very expressive. In anology with this case, the images, mathematical computation and other processes are done through Python Programming.

HISTOGRAM REWEIGHTING – TF – IDF APPROACH

To get the better similarity from the histogram, an approach called reweighting of the histogram can be used. This is implemented through TF – IDF (Term Frequency – Inverse Document Frequency) weighting. The term "frequency" essentially converts histograms into units of length. Inverse Individual dimensions (words) are given weights based on how frequently they appear in all the images. Every bin in a histogram is reweighted, and the "uninformative" terms (*i.e.,* characteristics that appear frequently in images/everywhere) are downweighted and enhance the importance of rare words.

The reweighted words in the histogram are computed using TF-IDF formula:

$$t_i = \frac{n_{id}}{n_d} \log \frac{N}{n_i}$$

where

n_{id} - Occurance of feature i in an image d;

n_d - Total number of features in an image d

n_i - Number of images that contain the feature i

N - Number of images

By substituting the above formula and the overall weighting, t_i is calculated. From the outcome, the similarity is observed by generating the Cost Matrix.

COST MATRIX GENERATION

The cost matrix is the matrix of all possible histogram comparisons (every image is compared with every image). This is one of the effective ways of comparison of images. The entries are the distance between the histograms. The entries in the cost matrix reflect the similarity. The Euclidean distance [10] and Cosine distance (1- cosine smilarity) are derived and higher cost separation between similar and dissimilar images is observed.

EUCLIDEAN DISTANCE AND COSINE DISTANCE

The Euclidean distance is one way to generate cost matrix. The Euclidean metric is given as:

$$\sqrt{\sum (xi - yi)^2} \tag{1}$$

This is a well-known distance measure, which generalizes our notion of physical distance in two- or three-dimensional space to multidimensional space.

Another method is finding the Cosine distance, the cosine distance is calculated as:

$$1 - \frac{x \cdot y}{||x||||y||} \tag{2}$$

Where $\frac{x \cdot y}{||x||||y||}$ is termed as Cosine similarity.

When comparing both, the difference observed is for the unit length vectors, squared euclidean distance differs from cosine similarity up to a constant.

Consider having vector x and y with unit length, then:

$$||x - y||^2 = (x - y)^T (x - y) = x^T x - 2x^T y + y^T y \tag{3}$$

Since $||x|| = ||y|| = 1$ and so,

$$||x - y||^2 = 2 - 2x^T y = 2 - 2\cos\theta \tag{4}$$

The relationship is defined as [5],

$$\text{Euclidean Distance} = \sqrt{2 - 2\cos\_similarity}.$$

The original histograms can be normalized by making all the norms of all vectors equal to 1.

MODEL DESCRIPTION

Step 1: Histogram generation for image

Step 2: Computation of Cost Matrix

Step 3: Reweightng of Histogram using TF – IDF

Step 4: Visualization of original Euclidean, Reweighted Euclidean

Step 5: Normalization of original Histogram

Step 6: Checking for similarity of the normalized histogram

Step 7: Visual comparison of histograms

The following python code is executed to implement each step listed above

Histogram Generation for Image

```python
import numpy as np
N = 4
histograms = np.array([ [1,2,1,0,0],
                        [3,0,1,1,0],
                        [3,1,1,0,2],[5,2,1,0,0]
                      ])
```

Computation of Cost Matrix

```python
import matplotlib.pyplot as plt


def compute_cost_matrices(histograms):

    cost_matrix_eucl  = np.zeros((N,N))
    cost_matrix_cos   = np.zeros((N,N))

    for row, hist_row in enumerate(histograms):
        for col, hist_col in enumerate(histograms):
            eucl_dist = np.linalg.norm(hist_row-hist_col)
            cost_matrix_eucl[row, col] = eucl_dist
```

```
                cos_sim = np.dot(hist_row, hist_col) / (np.linalg.
  norm(hist_row)* np.linalg.norm(hist_col))
                cost_matrix_cos[row, col] = cos_sim
      return cost_matrix_eucl, cost_matrix_cos


def plotCostMatrix(ax, cost matrix, title):
      axh = ax.imshow(cost_matrix, cmap='viridis')
      plt.colorbar(axh, ax = ax)
      ax.set_title(title)


cm_eucl, cm_cos = compute_cost_matrices(histograms)
```

Reweighting of Histogram using TF – IDF

```
def reweight_tf_idf(histograms):
    re_hists  = np.zeros(histograms.shape)
    N = histograms.shape[0]
    n_i = np.sum(histograms > 0, axis=0)
    for hist_id in range(histograms.shape[0]):
        n_d  = np.sum(histograms[hist_id])
        for bin_id in range(len(histograms[hist_id])):
            re_hists[hist_id, bin_id] = histograms[hist_id, bi
n_id]/ n_d * np.log(N/n_i[bin_id])
    return re_hists

re_hists = reweight_tf_idf(histograms)
print(re_hists)
```

The resultant Matrix is

```
[[0.         0.14384104 0.         0.         0.         ]
 [0.         0.         0.         0.27725887 0.         ]
 [0.         0.04109744 0.         0.         0.3960841 ]
 [0.         0.07192052 0.         0.         0.         ]]
```

Visualization of Original Euclidean, Reweighted Euclidean

```
weighted_hist = np.array([ [0,0.14,0,0,0],
  [0,0,0,0.23,0],
  [0,0.04,0,0,0.4],
  [0,0.07,0,0,0]])
cm_eucl, cm_cos = compute_cost_matrices(histograms)
cm_eucl_w, cm_cos_w = compute_cost_matrices(weighted_hist)
print(cm_eucl_w)
fig, ax = plt.subplots(1,3, figsize=(16,4));
plotCostMatrix(ax[0], cm_eucl, "Original Euclidean")
plotCostMatrix(ax[1], cm_eucl_w, "Reweighted Euclidean")
plotCostMatrix(ax[2], 1- cm_cos_w, "Reweighted Cosine Distance
")
```

```
[[0.         0.26925824 0.41231056 0.07       ]
 [0.26925824 0.         0.46314145 0.24041631]
 [0.41231056 0.46314145 0.         0.40112342]
 [0.07       0.24041631 0.40112342 0.         ]]
```

The Visualization of original Euclidean Distance and Reweighted Euclidean Distance for the generated values through histogram are shown in Fig. (**1**) and Fig. (**2**), respectively.

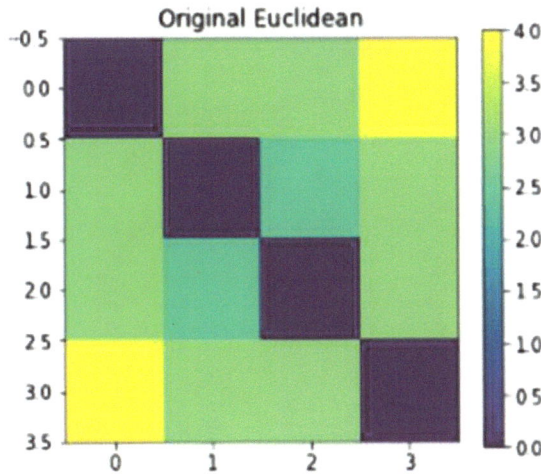

Fig. (1). Original Euclidean Distance.

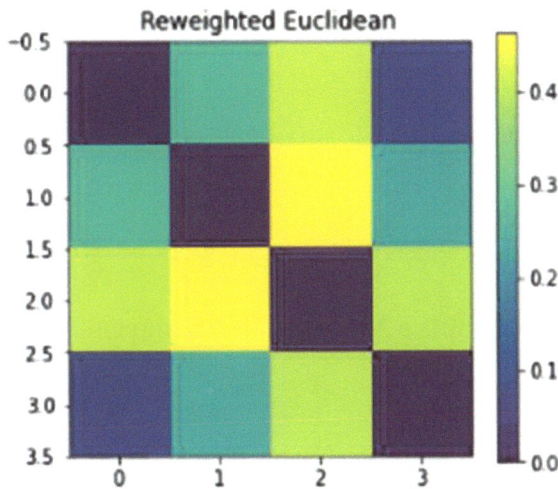

Fig. (2). Reweighted Euclidean Distance.

The reweighted Cosine Distance is calculated and the outcome is visualized as shown in Fig. (**3**).

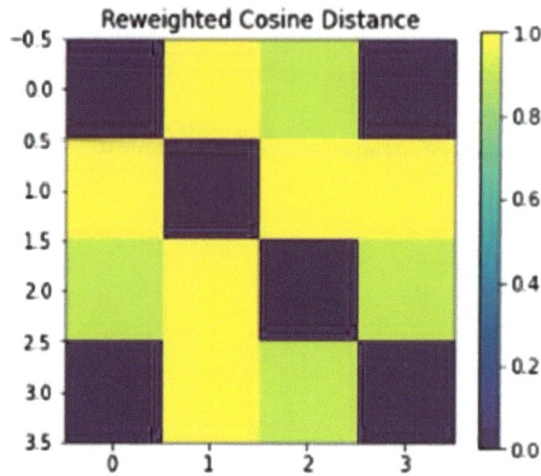

Fig. (3). Reweighted Cosine Distance.

Normalization of Original Histogram

```
def normToUnitLength(v):
    v_length = np.linalg.norm(v, axis=1)
    v_norm = v
    v_norm = v_norm / v_length[:,np.newaxis]
    return v_norm
v = np.array([[3,4], [-1,1], [-1,-2]])
v_circle = normToUnitLength(v)
v = np.array([[6,6], [2,3], [2,0]])
v_circle = normToUnitLength(v)
hist_norm = normToUnitLength(histograms)
print(np.linalg.norm(hist_norm,axis=1))
```

```
[1. 1. 1. 1.]
```

Checking for Similarity of the Normalized Histogram

```
cm_eucl, cm_cos = compute_cost_matrices(histograms)
cm_eucl_norm, cm_cos_norm = compute_cost_matrices(hist_norm)
cm_eucl_w, cm_cos_w = compute_cost_matrices(weighted_hist)
print("squared Euclidean vs adapted cosine difference")
print(np.fabs(cm_eucl_norm**2 - (2 - 2*cm_cos_norm)))
fig, (ax1, ax2) = plt.subplots(1, 2, figsize=(14,6))
plotCostMatrix(ax1, cm_eucl_norm**2, "Squared Euclidean")
plotCostMatrix(ax2, 2 - 2*cm_cos_norm, "Adapted Cosine")
```

```
squared Euclidean vs adapted cosine difference
[[4.44089210e-16 4.44089210e-16 1.11022302e-16 3.33066907e-16]
 [4.44089210e-16 0.00000000e+00 5.55111512e-17 1.38777878e-16]
 [1.11022302e-16 5.55111512e-17 0.00000000e+00 1.11022302e-16]
 [3.33066907e-16 1.38777878e-16 1.11022302e-16 0.00000000e+00]]
```

Using the above Figs. (**4** and **5**), the similarities are observed by comparing the squared Euclidean and Cosine.

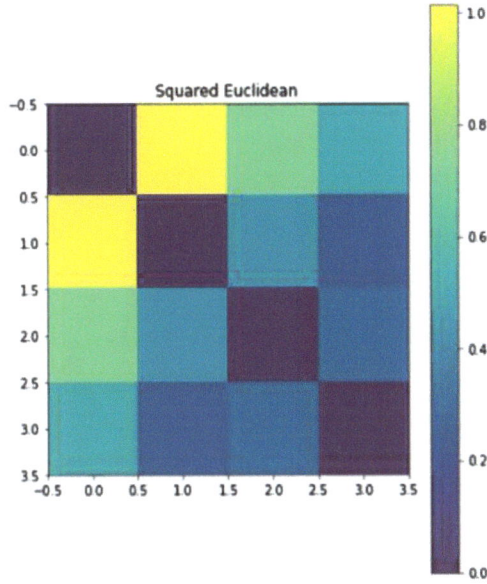

Fig. (4). Squared Euclidean.

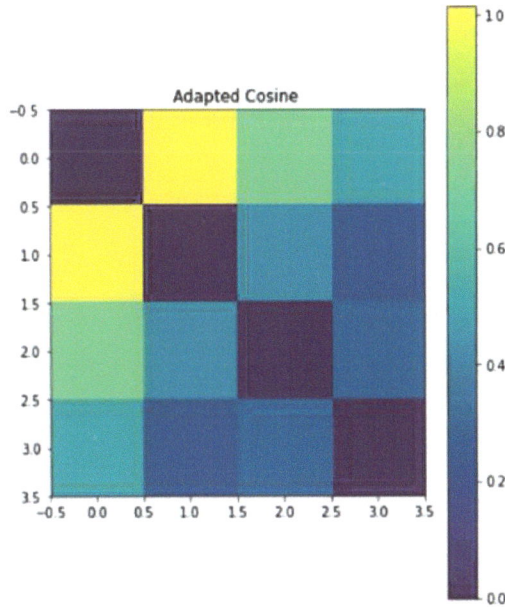

Fig. (5). Adapted Cosine.

Visual Comparison of Histograms

```
hist_weigh_norm = normToUnitLength(weighted_hist)
cm_eucl_w_norm, cm_cos_w_norm = compute_cost_matrices(hist_wei
gh_norm)

fig, axs = plt.subplots(2, 4, figsize=(20,8))

plotCostMatrix(axs[0][0],cm_eucl,"Original Euclidean Distance"
)
plotCostMatrix(axs[1][0], 1 - cm_cos, "Original Cosine Distanc
e")
plotCostMatrix(axs[0][1], cm_eucl_norm, "Normalized Euclidean
Distance")
plotCostMatrix(axs[1][1], 1 - cm cos norm, "Normalized Cosine
Distance")

plotCostMatrix(axs[0][2], cm_eucl_w, "Reweighted Euclidean Dis
tance")
plotCostMatrix(axs[1][2], 1 - cm cos w, "Reweighted Cosine Dis
tance")

plotCostMatrix(axs[0][3], cm_eucl_w_norm, "Reweighted Normaliz
ed Euclidean Distance")
plotCostMatrix(axs[1][3], 1 - cm_cos_w_norm, "Reweighted Norma
lized Cosine Distance")
```

The generated histograms with original Euclidean distance and normalized Euclidean distance, shown in Fig. (**6**), are compared and the similarities and differences are observed.

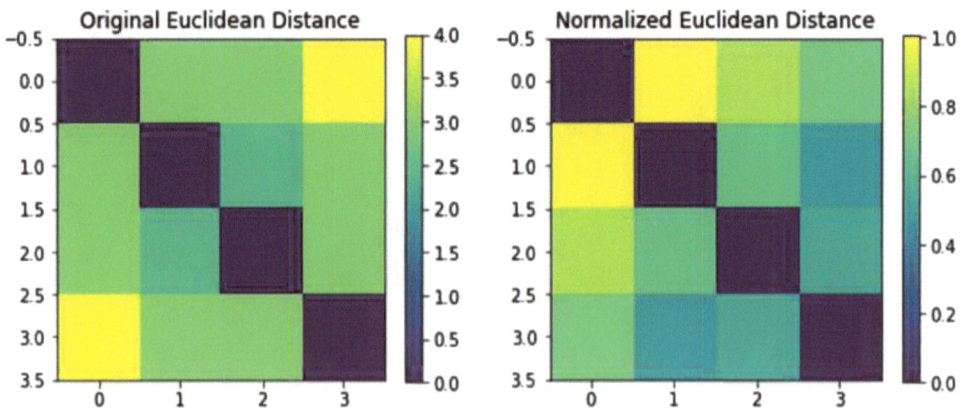

Fig. (6). Comparision of Original & Normalized Euclidean Distance.

The histograms with reweighted Euclidean distance and reweighted normalized Euclidean distance, shown in Fig. (**7**), are compared and the similarities and differences are observed.

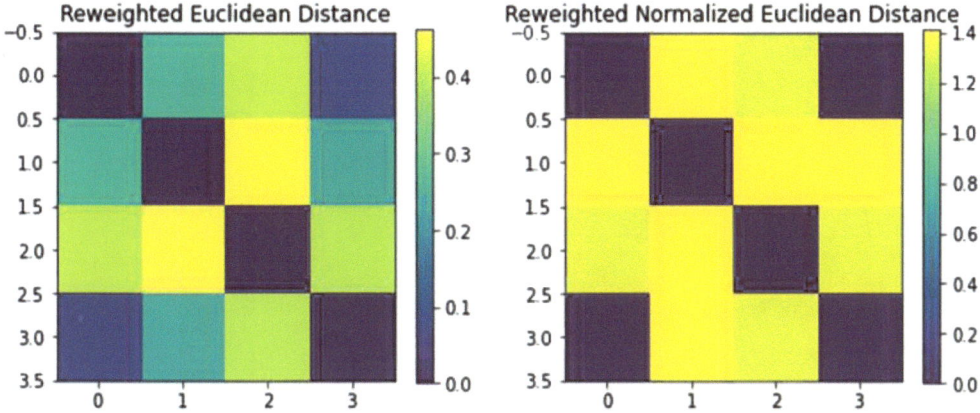

Fig. (7). Comparision of Reweighted Euclidean & Reweighted Normalized Euclidean Distance.

Like Euclidean distance the cosine distance and normalized cosine distance are generated and compared using Fig. (**8**).

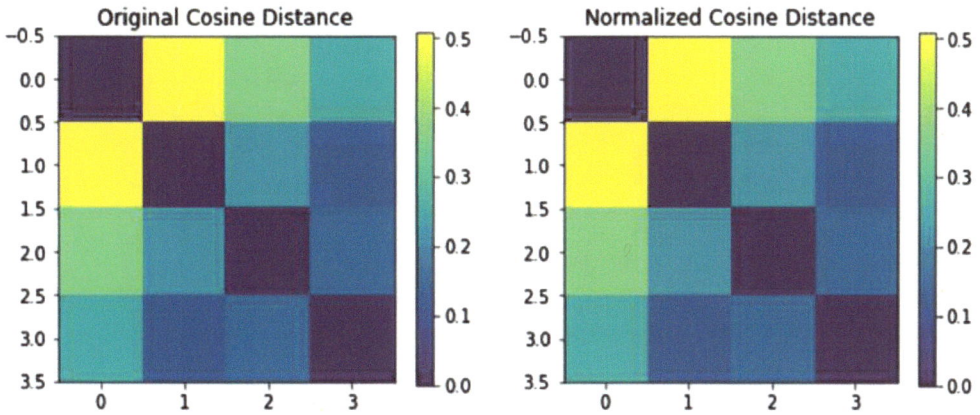

Fig. (8). Comparision of Original & Normalized Cosine Distance.

Fig. (**9**) shows the histogram of reweighted cosine distance and reweighted normalized cosine distance for comparison.

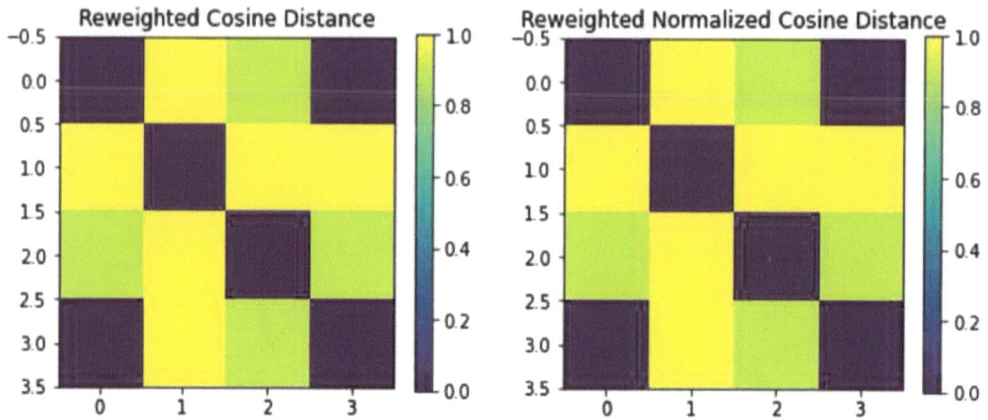

Fig. (9). Comparision of Reweighted Cosine & Reweighted Normalized Cosine Distance.

CONCLUSION

The result of the similarities among the images using the original histograms and normalized is not up to the mark. By applying the TF-IDF and by using Cosine Distance the similarities among the images outside the diagonal are able to observe effectively. The difference is more prominent for cosine distance rather than for Euclidean distance. Further normalization of TF-IDF rewighted histograms, optimized level of result can be obtained for both Eucledian and Cosine distance.

REFERENCES

[1]   D. Aldavert, "A study of Bag-of-Visual-Words representations for handwritten keyword spotting". International Journal on Document Analysis and Recognition (IJDAR) 18.3 223-234, 2015.
      [http://dx.doi.org/10.1007/s10032-015-0245-z]

[2]   R. Shekhar, and C.V. Jawahar, "Word image retrieval using bag of visual words", *10th IAPR Int. Worksh. Docum. Anal. Sys.,* 2012.
      [http://dx.doi.org/10.1109/DAS.2012.96]

[3]   N.D. Cagatay, and M. Datcu, "Bag-of-visual-words model for classification of interferometric SAR images", *Proc. Eur. Conf. Synth. Aperture Radar, EUSAR.,* pp. 243-246, 2016.

[4]   Z. Mehmood, S.M. Anwar, N. Ali, H.A. Habib, and M. Rashid, "A novel image retrieval based on a combination of local and global histograms of visual words", *Math. Probl. Eng.,* vol. 2016, pp. 1-12, 2016.
      [http://dx.doi.org/10.1155/2016/8217250]

[5]   J. Yang, Y.G. Jiang, A.G. Hauptmann, and C.W. Ngo, "Evaluating bag-of-visual-words representations in scene classification", *Proc. int. worksh. multime. inform. retri.,* pp. 197-207, 2007.
      [http://dx.doi.org/10.1145/1290082.1290111]

[6]   Y.G. Jiang, C.W. Ngo, and J. Yang, "Towards optimal bag-of-features for object categorization and semantic video retrieval", *Proc. CIVR,* pp. 494-501, 2007.
      [http://dx.doi.org/10.1145/1282280.1282352]

[7]   X. Chen, X. Hu, and X. Shen, "Spatial weighting for bag-of-visual-words and its application in

content-based image retrieval", In: *Proc. Pacif.Asia. Conf. Knowl. Disc. Data. Min.* vol. 5476. Springer: Berlin, Heidelberg, 2009, pp. 867-874.
[http://dx.doi.org/10.1007/978-3-642-01307-2_90]

[8]   P. Tirilly, V. Claveau, and P. Gros, "A review of weighting schemes for bag of visual words image retrieval", IRISA: Rennes, France, 2009.

[9]   K. Mikolajczyk, and C. Schmid, "A performance evaluation of local descriptors", *IEEE Trans. Pattern Anal. Mach. Intell.,* vol. 27, no. 10, pp. 1615-1630, 2005.
[http://dx.doi.org/10.1109/TPAMI.2005.188] [PMID: 16237996]

[10]   A.A.A. Karim, and R.A. Sameer, "Image classification using bag of visual words (BoVW)", *Al-Nahrain J. Sci.,* vol. 21, no. 4, pp. 76-82, 2018.
[http://dx.doi.org/10.22401/ANJS.21.4.11]

CHAPTER 5

A Glance Review on Data Science and its Teaching: Challenges and Solutions

Srinivasa Rao Gundu[1], **Charanarur Panem**[2,*] and **J. Vijaylaxmi**[3]

[1] Department of Digital Forensics, Malla Reddy University, Dhulapally, Hyderabad, Telangana, India

[2] Department of Cyber Security and Digital Forensics, National Forensic Sciences University Tripura Campus, Tripura, India

[3] PVKK Degree & PG College, Anantapur, Andhra Pradesh, India

Abstract: The word "data science" has become more popular in recent years, with a growing number of people embracing it. Only a small minority of people, on the other hand, are able to offer a clear explanation of what the term refers to when it is used in context. With no defined term to communicate and understand one another, it is difficult for organizations that are devoted to the collaboration, utilization, and application Data Science to communicate and understand one another.

As a result of technological advancements, it has become increasingly difficult to define and execute Data Science in a way that is compatible with how it was previously considered and understood in the past.

Specifically, we could now set out to develop definitions of Data Science that are representatives of current academic and industrial interpretations and perceptions, map these perspectives to newer domains of Data Science, and then determine whether or not this mapping translates into an effective practical curriculum for academics. Aspects of data science that differentiate it include how it is now used and how it is projected to be used in the future. Data science is also characterized by its ability to forecast the future.

Keywords: Curriculum, Data science, Quality, Practices, Problem solving.

INTRODUCTION

Despite the increasing relevance of data science, there is still no commonly accepted method of teaching it in both academia and industry.

** **Corresponding author Charanarur Panem:** Department of Cyber Security and Digital Forensics, National Forensic Sciences University Tripura Campus, Tripura, India; E-mail:panem.charan@gmail.com*

Students in data science courses at universities and colleges around the nation are growing more diverse in terms of their backgrounds, including practitioners, academic scholars, and data scientists. Interviews with twenty data scientists who teach in a variety of settings ranging from small-group workshops to massive online courses were conducted in order to gain a better understanding of how these practitioner-instructors transfer their expertise and how this differs from teaching conventional forms of programming, such as Python. To be effective, teachers must be sensitive to a diverse range of student backgrounds and expectations, teach technical workflows that integrate authentic practices around code, data analysis, and communication, and overcome challenges such as choosing authenticity over abstraction in software setup, finding and curating relevant datasets, and preparing students to live with uncertainty in data analysis, among other things. It is feasible that as a consequence of this research, more effective ways of teaching data science will be created, as well as an increase in the number of persons who are data-savvy [1].

"Data Science" (DS) has been a well-known word for quite some time now, and with good reason. It is difficult to define the background, skills, and collection of talents required by a Data Scientist, and it is much more difficult to find a definition that accurately describes these characteristics. This has resulted in the absence of any academic topic or programme that would allow certified Data Scientists to be trained at any academic institution or university. While some individuals believe that DS is a legitimate academic topic, others believe that it is more correctly defined as a mixture of traits and knowledge that would be impossible to uncover in a single person rather than an academic subject. According to the results of this study, data science is characterized in a number of ways by professionals from both the commercial and academic sectors [2]. The study has culminated in the proposal that a Master's Degree in Data Science is developed at the university level as a consequence of the findings.

As described by Wing (2019), the phrase data science is defined as the study of extracting value from data and the extraction of knowledge from data to meet business difficulties. Alternatively, "data science theory, method, and technology" or "data science technique and technology" or "data science technique and technology" have all been used to refer to this concept. In accordance with Irizarry, it is thought that the acronym DS stands for "data extraction", which refers to "the entire complex and multi-step procedures required extracting value from data". One of the fundamental premises of data science is the notion that "all procedures required" should be used in order to extract the most amount of value possible from massive, filthy, and unorganized datasets. Nonetheless, it is possible to construct an overarching definition from this broad notion that spans a wide variety of diverse sub-disciplines while keeping the overall concept in mind [3].

Upon closer inspection, we will be able to see that the definitions of what it takes to be a Data Scientist are much too broad and unclear in their application. To be able to provide degree programmes in developmental disabilities and define curricular requirements in this field, it is essential to have a clear definition of what constitutes a developmental disability.

According to certain circumstances, the needs of businesses and the leadership of academic institutions may be critical in determining what constitutes fundamental knowledge in data science and, as a result, the curriculum that will prepare data scientists to make contributions to businesses and society as they progress through their careers. Collaboration between industry and academia would be beneficial for designing a DS curriculum since it would enable the curriculum to be implemented immediately after development.

Data science is developing at a fast speed, and this will continue to be the case in the foreseeable future. It is vital to acknowledge that data scientists must be adaptive and versatile in order to be successful in their industry [4]. When learning new skills and abilities understanding the vocabulary and knowledge necessary to browse accessible resources, search for critical information, and judge the quality of a given resource is an important part of the process of learning new skills and abilities. Understanding the vocabulary and knowledge necessary to browse accessible resources, search for critical information, and judge the quality of a given resource is an important part of the process of learning new skills and abilities. It is necessary for students to get instruction and examples of appropriate behaviour from their instructors in order to comprehend how to make use of what is currently available and develop general approaches for gaining the next talent, which is not always obvious. It is preferable for teachers to utilize conventional tools in order to educate their students rather than outdated, proprietary, or specialized technology. As a direct consequence of these concerns, we strongly recommend all new course authors to take into consideration tools while developing their courses.

The possession of a technical background alone may not be enough to ensure long-term success in a data science position, particularly in the early stages of one's professional career. A lot of data science careers have been automated, resulting in a decrease in the total number of data science experts. Among the suggestions is the notion that data scientists should focus on building talents that are more difficult to automate [5]. Examples include business insight; explanation; and storytelling, to name a few examples. Specifically, we recommend that, in addition to analytical abilities and subject understanding, data science talents who are both imaginative and resistant to automation be recognized.

A rising number of students are becoming more interested in learning about and practicing data science, which is leading to a rise in the number of qualified data scientists available on the job market. As a result of the present increase in demand, a much greater number of individuals than in the past have shown an interest in learning more about data science and analytical techniques. The urge to teach students from historically underrepresented groups in technical areas such as computer science and engineering may result in students from historically underrepresented groups benefiting from data science training [6].

In order to meet the great demand for this education from both students and industry, we must guarantee that it is available to all students who are interested in pursuing a degree in this subject, regardless of their financial circumstances. Data science education must be accessible to anybody who is interested in earning a degree in the area.

THE IMPACT OF DATA SCIENCE ON THE SOCIETY

There is a slew of consequences that are becoming more apparent as data science and its uses improve. It was anticipated by Nolan and Temple Lang in the first place that data analysts would need to be statistically sound, computationally competent and data literate, and they were accurate. There are multiple ways in which analysing data has had a tremendous influence on society and our everyday lives, as well as countless applications of data science, that should be included in data science education. Students who have received excellent statistical and computational training are likely to have a larger impact on the world in the future than they have had in the past. For data scientists, relevant, real-world information must be a major emphasis of their courses throughout their educational path [7].

EDUCATIONAL GOALS OF DATA SCIENCE

It has been argued by Nolan and Temple Lang (2010) that the present focus on problem solving flexibility and practical applications in data science extends beyond the emphasis on problem solving flexibility and practical applications to address social ramifications and data ethics. Data science is comprised of many components, the most important of which are statistical analysis, machine learning, and programming. The integration of these components is also critical. However, this new discipline must be taught as a multidisciplinary endeavor, with the curriculum that reflects the wide range of challenges, concerns, and realities that arise when dealing with massive amounts of data.

In addition, it should be aimed to make data science education more accessible to anybody who is interested in pursuing a career in the area of information technology. Understanding and analysing data are becoming an increasingly vital ability in a society that is becoming more and more dependent on technology and data collection and analysis. If an individual already has a solid foundation in mathematics and computers, they may not need further training in data literacy abilities. People who are interested in and need the development of critical and practical abilities in applied mathematics, machine learning, and statistical analysis may enroll in courses that will help them develop these talents in these subjects. A student's first course in data science should explain how and why data practice is necessary, as well as emphasize the context, ramifications, and practicality of data practice, before moving on to more complex subjects. This may cause students who were previously apprehensive about pursuing technical programmes and applications to reconsider their decision as a consequence of their experiences [8].

DATA SCIENCE IN PRACTICE AS A PROBLEM SOLVING

For problem-solving, it is the abilities that can't be automated that are needed most. Additionally, they have the ability to formulate questions, invent methods to answer them, analyze findings, and use visualization and storytelling to draw data-driven conclusions, among other skills. Creative problem solving is a more robust talent that is less likely to become obsolete as a consequence of technology improvements, despite the fact that students study particular projects, implementations, tools, and analyses as part of their courses. In order to fulfill the core goals of data science, which are to answer questions and solve problems through the use of data and everything that comes with it, data scientists must also have strong technical and analytical abilities including software. Furthermore, these abilities make up a significant portion of the course material. The problem-solving nature of our data science courses is reflected in our group projects, which need both creativity and tenacity to move from an open-ended project description to conceptualizing and resolving a data-driven challenge.

From our perspective, students should be exposed to the tools and talents needed to succeed as a professional data scientist, as well as the creative aspects of data science, throughout their education in data science. Statistical teamwork is challenging for statisticians because they lack computational thinking skills, according to the argument of Nolan and Temple Lang. Computational skills are becoming more important in today's data-driven and technology workplaces, particularly in computer science, and this trend will only continue in the future. This means that courses must employ industry-standard technology and demonstrate best practices in their particular fields in order to be considered effective. It is essential that students who take a practical data science course demonstrate expertise in one of the most regularly used tools, as well as the capacity to acquire a new tool, and demonstrate meaningful work that shows their strengths to future employers [9].

Rather than functioning as a replacement for statistics or programming classes, data science courses should be structured around the underlying concept of data analysis. Instead of substituting for statistics or programming classes, a student's ability to connect with messy datasets might be hindered in statistics classes due to time constraints, and these courses may solely use idealized datasets for their teaching and demonstration goals instead. It is difficult to devote enough time to data manipulation and manipulation in beginner programming courses, because understanding grammar and programming ideas takes up a large chunk of the curriculum. Prior to enrolling in Data Science in Practice, most students have already completed an entry-level programming course usually in Python and a basic statistics course. This preparation will help students in a data science course, where examples and analysis are based on real-world data. Having a deep grasp of the restrictions and potential of data-driven work, as well as technical skill that is applicable to dealing with real data, it may be appropriate to focus the instructional emphasis on this understanding [10].

Throughout our course, we need to demonstrate a consistent usage of diverse, heterogeneous datasets, which is an important component of data practice. There is more time for pupils to explore the data's context when a full computational and statistical framework is in place. This will help students study more effectively. With the extra time, they'll be able to move data from its raw form to the format needed for analysis, which is a must for every data scientist.

LITERATURE REVIEW

For example, according to Donoghue, 2020, Anderson *et al.* 2014; Yan *et al.* 2019, Brunner *et al.* 2016, Devaux's research on undergraduate courses and programme building has primarily concentrated on the content of introductory or overview courses, as well as the development of new undergraduate courses. Research on undergraduate courses and programme development has mostly concentrated on the content of introductory or overview courses, as well as the design of undergraduate courses under Devaux's research programme.

The use of previously given courses to establish a whole degree programme in data science is unprecedented, and there has been little precedence for doing so in the past. Using such a method is both time-consuming and ineffective; thus, it should be avoided at all costs. For a high-quality curriculum to be implemented, it is necessary to conduct a review of present courses as well as the introduction of new ones, taking into consideration any credit restrictions that may be in place at the time of implementation. Another alternative being considered by several colleges is to simply rename their courses in order to more accurately reflect the increased importance placed on disability studies by the University of California. In order to be effective, we must take an objective approach while also doing a comprehensive examination of the program's overarching aim and objectives. To be more specific, Tang's query was, "What are the fundamental and philosophical foundations of DS as an academic discipline?"

For successful data management and visualization, several studies have shown that they should all be taught as part of a standard course curriculum. Statistical modeling should also be taught as part of a typical course curriculum (Hicks and Irizarry, 2018; Zeng, 2017; Yavuz and Ward, 2018). Numerous proponents have advocated for some years now for the incorporation of computer programming, statistics, and information technology into the DS curriculum (Hardin, *et al.,* 2015).

As a result of the failure to reach a consensus on the components of a professional Master's-level DS programme that would include the expectations of what graduates should know and be able to execute when they graduate, this is a major setback. Given the enormous number of DS Master's degree programmes that are available, it seems that standardized admissions standards are in urgent need of being established (Wing *et al.,* 2018).

However, despite the fact that there are many different DS sub-disciplines and that there is no universal agreement on curriculum standards, there appears to be some commonality among topics such as data visualization, data wrangling and statistical modeling in many programmes. Other topics such as programming, reproducible research, and statistics also appear to be common among programmes (Schwab-McCoy, *et al.,* 2020).

DEMANDS OF THE DATA SCIENCE INDUSTRY AND THE DATA SCIENCE CURRICULUM

DS is the topic of a large number of inquiries from the sector. DS themes, for example, may not be anticipated to be universal throughout all academic programmes, which may conflict with the expectations of employers of graduates from academic programmes. Is it possible to conclude that colleges and universities have educated students for the challenges of business while also preparing them to lead, explore, and develop in this extremely diversified and rapidly evolving DS subject?

According to a study conducted by 365 Data Science in 2020, machine learning, statistics, and Python programming talents are the most in-demand qualities for Data Scientists in the field of data science (Krastev, 2020). Another skill that was often mentioned was computer programming. Other skills that were mentioned were data visualization, statistical modeling, and predictive modeling. In the presentation, there was no discussion of data cleaning or wrangling, which was disappointing [11].

According to the data, deep learning, clustering, and natural language processing were among the skills that were most frequently identified in the survey findings under the umbrella phrase "machine learning methodologies". Deep learning, clustering, and natural language processing were among the skills that were most frequently identified in the survey findings under the umbrella phrase "machine learning methodologies" such as NLP. Statistical prediction and Python libraries with machine learning capabilities are the second and third most popular programming languages, respectively, according to the list of the most popular programming languages. Having a practical understanding of computer programming is essential for Data Scientists in order to complement and grow their Machine Learning skills [12].

When resolving problems using Machine Learning, statistical analysis, and programming, according to the results of 365 Data Science study conducted in 2015, data science seems to be at the centre of the problem-solving process. In order to be successful in the area of Machine Learning, it is required to gain highly specialized abilities. In light of the findings of this research, it should come as no surprise that the Data Scientist's major emphasis should be on applications rather than theory and concepts, rather than theory and conceptions.

In order to develop Machine Learning models, the most often used programming languages are R and Python. This is due to the reason such as because of its ability to swiftly analyze and visualize data and because of its modules such as Tensor Flow and Keras. R is the most extensively used programming language in the world. Employees and managers are aware of the value of R and Python in the modern workplace, and they have adopted these technologies. According to the results of the 365 DS survey, fluency in Python was revealed to be the most sought-after computer aptitude, followed by R and SQL. In addition, the most often cited database and cloud storage systems, such as Spark, AWS, and Hadoop, were included in this list, as were the most frequently mentioned web services. Data visualizations were created using both Tableau and Microsoft Power BI tools, depending on the requirements of the project. Tableau was used in the majority of cases.

INHERENT PROBLEMS IN DATA SCIENCE CURRICULA DEVELOPMENT

There are several obstacles to overcome in order to create a graduate-level programme in DS. The most challenging part of developing a data science programme, particularly at the master's degree level, is combining the huge topic areas into a time frame that potential students can reasonably finish. A demanding curriculum that covers all of the different DS sub-disciplines may be supported by professors, but administrators may want to restrict the amount of credits students can receive or employ already existing courses that may not be as relevant as professors want.

There is a lot of discussion about how difficult it is for instructors to accommodate the various cultural backgrounds and expectations of their pupils. Because of this, DS attracts students from many walks of life. Instead of having hard-core requirements, students who have strong backgrounds in a certain subject may opt out of certain courses or take alternative ones if they don't need them, while students who have less experience can take foundation courses to help them catch up.

Data scientists are in high demand, both now and in the future. Data Science degree programmes at colleges and universities may see a surge in applications even if the sector has a shortage of workers. Graduate students, rather than undergraduates, are considered by many educators to be a better fit for Data Science (DS). While many college freshmen and seniors are aware of DS, few high school seniors are. In the workplace, those with some experience will realize the value of using data, and will seek more education in order to take advantage of it. Because of this, students who have worked in the business before enrolling in an educational programme are more likely to profit from it, since their past expertise with data gives them an advantage.

There seems to be some correlation between the skills and competencies sought by industry and the curriculum offered by academics. When it comes to the DS area, what academics consider to be essential curriculum components frequently doesn't match up with what businesses need.

An instructor's unique perspective on the world and understanding of the most pressing topics to be addressed are evident in how each DS course is put up. There may be a gap between the course structure and the scheduled course in the curriculum as a consequence of this strategy. There are times when a sense of detachment might be beneficial. Technology and algorithm advancements will necessitate changes in what is now available, as well as improvements and augmentations that may be expected in the future. On the other side, adherence to a curriculum's blueprint or structure serves as a basis around which courses are often developed.

TEACHING DATA SCIENCE

Universities, schools, and research labs throughout the country are launching new data science programmes, and online courses like MOOCs and boot camps are among the most popular offerings in both academia and business. Despite the growing popularity of data science, there is no agreement on what should be included in a curriculum for data science education.

On the subject of data science education in the actual world, to our knowledge, there has been no comprehensive examination. Course design guidelines and case studies of how instructors have taught certain courses in their various professions are the only publications now available on this subject, both of which may be found online. All faculty members in the department of computer science (CS) as well as faculty members from other departments, are represented in this collection. In general, there are two types of articles. Academics in the field of computer science have written on their experiences, for example, teaching data science to students who are not computer science majors and improving courses for students who are not computer science majors. Students in topics such as bioinformatics, business administration, and statistics may use data science field guides written by academics from a variety of academic disciplines. When it comes to data science as a component of statistics courses, the focus is more on computational processes and tools than on the theoretical aspects of the mathematics that underpins them. Educators often write on a wide range of topics when they describe their experiences teaching outside of the traditional educational framework. University researchers may benefit from seminars organized by Software and Data.

In order to educate researchers from academic institutions the best practices in data science, many professional organizations organize hackathons, hack weeks, and apprenticeships. Attendees from academic institutions get vital data science expertise at these events.

A comprehensive picture of how contemporary data science is taught by practitioner-instructors in both industry and academia has been painted for the first time, according to the authors, by combining findings from multiple academic research studies in this way that goes beyond anecdotal experiences within individual courses.

According to data science practitioners who also educate undergraduate and graduate students in the discipline, the majority of those in attendance were data science practitioners and teachers. Professionals who are at the forefront of their disciplines and are more intimately connected to the professional network that students desire to have access to when they learn from practitioners. This is an enormous competitive advantage for students. Wilson refers to "end-user teachers" as those who educate without formal pedagogical training, as defined by Wilson as an analogue to "end-user programmers". A lack of research on practitioners-instructors in computer science courses like data science or statistics is to our knowledge the situation at this moment.

Everyone should have a basic understanding of computers. Human-computer interaction (HCI) and computer education research have exploded in recent years on the issue of teaching programming to a wider spectrum of students. This study builds on previous attempts to make programming more comprehensible for those who aren't programmers. However, an increasing number of studies are focusing on students who desire to pursue professions in domains other than computer science or programming; hence, computing education research is becoming more diverse. As an example, Ni and colleagues looked at the problems that high school teachers experience while learning to programme in preparation for a career in computer science teaching. According to research by Dorn *et al.,* many online and graphic designers thought they were artists as well after the outcomes of the investigation.

CONCLUDING REMARKS

There is an increasing need for data scientists across a broad variety of industries. To enable data science education, researchers must develop new types of tools and processes. To effectively teach data science, it is necessary to not only build new technology systems but also to produce instructional materials. Discussions on justice, ethics, and algorithmic bias are critical to the way data science is taught.

REFERENCES

[1]   J.S. Saltz, and N.W. Grady, "The ambiguity of data science team roles and the need for a data science workforce framework", *IEEE Int. Conf. Big. Data. (Big Data),* pp. 2335-2361, 2017.
[http://dx.doi.org/10.1109/BigData.2017.8258190]

[2]   J. Liu, "From statistics to data mining: A brief review", *2020 Int. Conf. Comp. Data. Sci. (CDS),* pp. 343-346, 2020.
[http://dx.doi.org/10.1109/CDS49703.2020.00073]

[3]   K. Moolthaisong, and W. Songpan, "Emotion analysis and classification of movie reviews using data mining", *2020 Int. Conf. Data. Sci. Artif. Intel. and Busin. Anal.(DATABIA).,* pp. 89-92, 2020.
[http://dx.doi.org/10.1109/DATABIA50434.2020.9190363]

[4]   S. Yang, F. Wang, Z. Lin, D. Jiang, and T. Zhou, "Publication volume of major databases related to ideological and political education: Using big data and internet technologies", *2nd Int. Conf. Big. Data. Inform. Educ. (ICBDIE).,* pp. 465-469, 2021.

[http://dx.doi.org/10.1109/ICBDIE52740.2021.00112]

[5]   D. Lande, V. Andrushchenko, and I. Balagura, "Data science in open-access research on-line resources", *2018 IEEE Sec. Int. Conf. Data. Stre. Min. Proces. (DSMP),* pp. 17-20, 2018.
[http://dx.doi.org/10.1109/DSMP.2018.8478565]

[6]   B.A.M. Duhart, and N. Hernández-Gress, "Review of the principal indicators and data science techniques used for the detection of financial fraud and money laundering", *2016 Int. Conf. Compu. Sci. and Computa. Intell.(CSCI).,* pp. 1397-1398, 2016.
[http://dx.doi.org/10.1109/CSCI.2016.0267]

[7]   F. Amin, W-K. Lee, A. Mateen, and S.O. Hwang, "Integration of network science approaches and data science tools in the internet of things based technologies", *2021 IEEE Reg. 10 Symp. (TENSYMP),* pp. 1-6, 2021.
[http://dx.doi.org/10.1109/TENSYMP52854.2021.9550992]

[8]   A. Alazeb, M. Alshehri, and S. Almakdi, "Review on data science and prediction", *2021 2nd Int. Conf. Comp. Data. Sci. (CDS),* pp. 548-555, 2021.
[http://dx.doi.org/10.1109/CDS52072.2021.00100]

[9]   S. Labou, H.J. Yoo, D. Minor, and I. Altintas, "Sharing and archiving data science course projects to support pedagogy for future cohorts", *2019 15th Int. Conf. eSci. (eScience),* pp. 644-645, 2019.
[http://dx.doi.org/10.1109/eScience.2019.00099]

[10]   Q. Zhong, and Y. Wang, "Analysis of factors affecting the sales of popular science books based on big data", *2020 Int. Conf. Big. Data. Econ. Inform. Manag. (BDEIM),* pp. 66-69, 2020.
[http://dx.doi.org/10.1109/BDEIM52318.2020.00024]

[11]   C. V. Krishna, and H. R. Rohit, "A review of artificial intelligence methods for data science and data analytics: Applications and research challenges", *2nd Int. Conf. I-SMAC (IoT in Social, Mobile, Analytics and Cloud) (I-SMAC)I-SMAC (IoT in Social, Mobile, Analytics and Cloud) (I-SMAC),* pp. 591-594, 2018.
[http://dx.doi.org/10.1109/I-SMAC.2018.8653670]

[12]   I. K. Nti, J. A. Quarcoo, J. Aning, and G. K. Fosu, "A mini-review of machine learning in big data analytics: Applications, challenges, and prospects", *Big. Data. Min. Anal.,* vol. 5, no. 2, pp. 81-97, 2022.
[http://dx.doi.org/10.26599/BDMA.2021.9020028]

CHAPTER 6

Optimization of Various Costs in Inventory Management using Neural Networks

Prerna Sharma[1,*] and **Bhim Singh**[1]

[1] *Department of Basic Science, Sardar Vallabh Bhai Patel University of Agriculture and Technology, Meerut (U.P.), India*

Abstract: The process of maintaining the right quantity of inventory to meet demand, minimising logistics costs, and avoiding frequent inventory problems, including reserve outs, overstocking, and backorders is known as inventory optimisation. One has a finite capacity and is referred to as an owned warehouse (OW), which is located near the market, while the other has an endless capacity and is referred to as a rented warehouse (RW), which is located away from the market. Here, lowering the overall cost is the goal. Neural networks are employed in these works to either maximise or minimise cost. The findings produced from the neural networks are compared with a mathematical model and neural networks. Findings indicate that neural networks outperformed both conventional mathematical models and neural networks in terms of optimising the outcomes. The best way to understand supervised machine learning algorithms like neural networks is in the context of function approximation. The benefits and drawbacks of the two-warehouse approach compared to the single warehouse plan will also be covered. We investigate cost optimisation using neural networks in this chapter, and the outcomes will also be compared using the same.

Keywords: Business environment, Inventory, Neural networks, Warehouse.

INTRODUCTION

Every businessman needs a warehouse as it is an important location in the trading. Due to the current state of the market and its globalisation, the business community is extremely competitive, and everyone works hard to satisfy their consumers' needs. As a result, wholesalers and merchants always retain a stock of the products in their stores. Suppliers provide certain discounts on full sale purchases throughout the holiday season as well as various trade credit financing plans to attract the attention of their merchants in this unforgiving business environment.

---

* **Corresponding author Prerna Sharma:** Department of Basic Science, Sardar Vallabh Bhai Patel University of Agriculture and Technology, Meerut (U.P.) India; E-mail: prernam2002@gmail.com

Biswadip Basu Mallik, Kirti Verma, Rahul Kar, Ashok Kumar Shaw & Sardar M. N. Islam (Naz) (Eds.)

Retailers need extra space to store the products they buy in bulk during the accessible period in order to take advantage of these supplier programmes, but due to limited space in busy markets, retailers struggle to find storage space at their own single warehouse and must therefore rent another storage room to house their excess product purchases. To get out of this predicament, they lease another storage unit for a short time. This rental warehouse is utilised as an additional storage facility offered by public, private, or governmental organisations, and these facilities are used as the storage space that results from their use. In order to gain space on a hiring basis for storage needs, the idea of two warehouses was introduced in the inventory modelling. When modelling an inventory. Hartley introduced the idea of a two-warehouse system for the first time, and many authors have since used it, referring to one as a "Own warehouse" with a restricted capacity and the other as a "Rented warehouse" with an unlimited capacity. In this idea, it is frequently stated that because the owner of an additional warehouse provides better protection and preservation facilities, the carrying cost of items in rented warehouses is higher than those in owned warehouses. As a result, it is wise to store the items in rented warehouses first in order to reduce the holding costs incurred in rented warehouses.

Neural networks were inspired by the type of computation done by an individual intellect because they are simple and straightforward representations of the organic nervous system. Broadly speaking, a neural network is a highly unified network of several neurones, which are processing components in planning inspired by the brain. A neural network is believed to reveal parallel distributed distribution since it can be highly parallel.

Neural networks exhibit characteristics such as pattern relationships or mapping properties, generalisation, sturdiness, fault tolerance, and quick and simultaneous information processing.

RELATED WORK

In the year 2010, the authors [1] studied about multi-product inventory optimization using uniform crossover genetic algorithm. In other studies [2] and [3], authors have studied inventory optimization supply chain management and efficient supply chain management using genetic algorithms. Authors have studied about inventory analysis using genetic algorithm in supply chain management [4, 5, 6]. Kannan *et al.* discussed a genetic algorithm approach for a model for closed loop supply chain [7]. Jawahar and Balaji [8] studied for the two-stage supply chain distribution problems with a fixed charge using a genetic alogorithm. Authors rase the problem of modified Pareto genetic algorithm and multi-criterion optimization genetic algorithm [9]. Yimer and Demirli [10] presented same approach of dynamic supply chain scheduling. Similar types of studies were performed by various authors such as Wang *et. al.*. [11], Ram Kumar *et. al.* [12], Sherman *et. al.* [13]. Some authors have presented inventory model for breakable items [14]. A study [15] solved constrained knapsack problem in fuzzy environment for improved genetic algorithm. Two storage inventory problems involing dynamic demand and interval valued lead-time over finite time horizon were propoed by Dey *et al.* [16] Jawahar and Balaji [17] proposed "A genetic algorithm-based heuristic to the multi-period fixed charge distribution problem". Yadav *et al.* [18-22] studied various aspects on warehouse inventory model having deteriorating items with time-dependent demand, shortages and also with variable holding cost. Auto-warehouse model for deteriorating items were studied [23, 24] and after that authors have proposed it holding cost under particle swarm optimization. A focus on optimal ordering policy for non-instantaneous deteriorating articles with tentatively permissible delay in payment under two storage management was shown by Sharma *et al.* [25].

Table **1** represents the comparison between optimized results with neural network and the proposed sytem.

ASSUMPTION AND NOTATIONS

B_I: Maximum amount of inventory backlogged.

C_A: Ordering cost.

k: A Definite time interval to which holding cost remains constant.

h_w: It is holding cost per unit time in Ownware-house.

H_C: holding inventory cost.

h_r: The holding cost in rented ware house.

$I^r(x)$:Inventory level in rented warehouse.

$I^i(x)$:Inventory level in own ware-house.

$I^s(x)$:When the product has shortages, it denotes the inventory level.

L_c: The opportunity cost.

L_C: lost sale cost.

P_1: Purchase cost.

P_2: Cost of purchase.

S_C: shortages cost.

Q_1: Capacity of own warehouse.

Q_2: Capacity of rented warehouse.

X: The length of replenishment cycle.

$X^C(x_1, X)$: For inventory system, total relevant inventory cost per unit time.

x_1: In rented warehouse, time up to which inventory becomes zero.

x_2: The time at which shortages begin and inventory level vanishes in own warehouse.

Z_{max}: Highest Inventory level per cycle for placing order.

μ: Deterioration cost for rented warehouse.

θ: Deterioration cost for own warehouse.

• The lead time approaches to zero and the replenishment rate is infinite.

• For the inventory system, the time horizon is infinite.

• Goods of own warehouse are frenzied only after the using up the goods kept in rented warehouse because of the greater holding cost in rented warehouse than in own ware-house.

• The OW has some degree of the capacity of storage and rented warehouse has infinite capacity.

• Demand changes with time and is considered as linear function of time and

given by $D(x) = \begin{cases} \alpha & \text{if} \quad x = 0 \\ \alpha + bx & \text{if} \quad x > 0 \end{cases}$; where $\alpha > 0$ and $b > 0$.

• For deteriorating aritcles, a fraction of on hand inventory deteriorates per unit time in both the warehouse with distinct rate of deterioration.

• Shortages are permitted and demand is impartially backlogged at the starting of the next replenishment.

• The unit inventory cost or holding cost in the rented warehouse is greater than that of the own warehouse.

• Assuming that the holding cost is fixed till a certain time in rented warehouse and increases according to a part of the ordering cycle length. For that holding cost (h_r), we have k time moment prior to which holding cost is constanth_r=h_rx if x>k

MATHEMATICAL FORMULATION OF MODEL AND ANALYSIS

$$\frac{dI^r(x)}{dx} = -(\alpha + bt) - (\mu I^r(t)); \ 0 \le x \le x_1 \tag{1}$$

$$\frac{dI^{1w}(x)}{dx} = -\theta I^{1w}(x); \qquad\qquad 0 \le x \le x_1 \tag{2}$$

$$\frac{dI^{2w}(x)}{dx} = -(\alpha + bx) - (\theta I^r(x)) \qquad x_1 \le x \le x_2 \tag{3}$$

$$\frac{dI^s(x)}{dx} = -f(\alpha + bx) ; \qquad\qquad x_3 \le x \le X. \tag{4}$$

Now, inventory level at distinct time intervals is shown by solving the differential equations from (1) to (4) having the following boundary conditions:

$$I^r(x_1) = 0, \quad I^{1w}(0) = Q_1; \qquad I^{2w}(x_2) = 0; I^s(x_2) = 0.$$

Therefore differential equation (1) gives:

$$I^r(x) = \{\frac{\alpha}{\mu} + \frac{b}{\mu^2}\{(\mu x_1 - 1)\} e^{\mu(x_1 - x)} - \{\frac{\alpha}{\mu} + \frac{b}{\mu^2}(\mu x - 1)\}; \tag{5}$$

$$I^{1w}(x) e^{-\theta x_1}; \tag{6}$$

$$I^{2w}(x) = \{\frac{\alpha}{\theta} + \frac{b}{\theta^2}\{(\theta x_2 - 1)\} e^{\theta(x_2 - x)} - \{\frac{b}{\theta} + \frac{b}{\theta^2}(\theta x - 1)\} \tag{7}$$

$$I^s(x) = f\{b(x_2 - x) + b/2(x_2^2 - x^2)\}. \tag{8}$$

Now at t=0, $I_r(0)$=Q2

Therefore equation (5) yields:

$$Q_2 = \left\{ \left(\frac{b}{\mu^2} - \frac{\alpha}{\mu} \right) + \left(\frac{\alpha}{\mu} + \frac{b}{\mu^2} \right) (\mu x_1 - 1) e^{-\mu x_1} \right\}. \tag{9}$$

Greatest amount of inventory backlogged at the time of shortages (at $x=X$) is as below:

$$B_1 = -I^s(X) = f\{ \alpha(X - x) + \frac{b}{2}(X^2 - x^2). \tag{10}$$

Inventory lost amount, during the shortages period:

$$L_1 = (1 - B_I) = (1 - f\{ \alpha(X - x) + \frac{b}{2}(X^2 - x^2): \tag{11}$$

The greatest inventory to which has to be ordered is given as:

$$\begin{aligned} Z_{max} &= Q_1 + I^r(0) + B_I \\ &= Q_1 + \left\{ \left(\frac{b}{\mu^2} - \frac{\alpha}{\mu} \right) + \left(\frac{\alpha}{\mu} + \frac{b}{\mu^2} \right) (\mu x_1 - 1) e^{-\mu x_1} \right\} + f\{ \alpha(X - t_2) + \frac{b}{2}(X - x^2) \end{aligned} \tag{12}$$

Now continuity at $\chi = \chi_1$ shows that $I^{1w}(\chi_1) = I^{2w}(\chi_1)$.

Therefore from eq. (6) and (7) we have:

$$b\theta^2 x_2^2 - \alpha\theta^2 x_2 - (\theta^2(Q_1 + Z) + b - \alpha\theta) = 0 \tag{13}$$

$$\text{where, } Z = \{ \frac{\alpha}{\theta} + \frac{b}{\theta^2}(\theta x_1 - 1)\} e^{-\theta x_1} \tag{14}$$

$$t_2 = \varphi(x_1)$$

$$\text{where} \varphi(x_1) = \frac{-\alpha^2 \theta^4 \pm \sqrt{D}}{2cb} \text{ and}$$

$$D = \alpha^2 \theta^4 + 4b\theta^2 (b - \alpha\theta + \theta^2 (W_1 + \left\{ \frac{\alpha}{\theta} + \frac{b}{\theta^2}(\theta x_1 - 1) \right\} e^{-\theta x_1})$$

The present worth holding cost=H$_c$

$$H_c = \int_0^k h_r \, I^r(t)dt + \int_k^{x_1} h_r x \, I^r(x)dt + \int_0^{x_1} h_w \, I^{1w}(x)dt + \int_{x_1}^{x_2} h_w \, I^{2w}(x)dt$$

$$H_c = h_r(\alpha x_1 k + b x_1^2 k - \frac{bk^2}{2\mu} - \frac{bx_1^2}{3\mu} + \alpha x_1^3 + b x_1^4 - \frac{\alpha k}{\gamma} - b x_1 k^2 - \alpha x_1 k^2$$

$$+ \frac{b x_1 k^2}{\gamma}$$

$$+ \frac{\alpha k^2}{\mu} + \frac{bk^3}{3\mu}) + h_w(Q_1 x_1 + \frac{b x_2^2}{\theta} - \frac{b x_1 x_2}{\theta} + \frac{b x_1^2}{2\theta} - \frac{b x_2^2}{2\theta}) \tag{15}$$

Shortages cost

$$S_C = S_c f(\frac{\alpha T^2}{2} - \frac{\alpha x_2^2}{2} + \frac{bT^3}{6} - \frac{b x_2^3}{6} - \alpha x_1 T + \alpha x_2^2 - \frac{b x_2^2 T}{2} + \frac{b x_2^3}{2}) \tag{16}$$

Opportunity cost/Lost sale cost

$$L_c = L_c(1 - (\frac{\alpha X^2}{2} - \frac{\alpha x_2^2}{2} + \frac{bX^3}{6} - \frac{b x_2^3}{6} - \alpha x_1 X + \alpha x_2^2 - \frac{b x_2^2 X}{2} + \frac{b x_2^3}{2}) \tag{17}$$

Purchase cost

$$P_2 = P_c\left(Q_1 + \{(\frac{b}{\mu^2} - \frac{\alpha}{\mu}) + \{\frac{\alpha}{\mu} + \frac{b}{\mu^2}(\alpha x_1 - 1)e^{-\mu x_1}\} + f\{\alpha(X - x_2) + \frac{b}{2}(X^2 - x_2^2)\}\right). \tag{18}$$

Hence, the total applicable inventory cost per unit per unit of time is denoted and defined as follows:

$$X^C(x_1, X) = \frac{1}{X}[C_A + P_2 + S_C + L_C + H_c] =$$
$$= \frac{1}{x}[C_A + P_c\left(Q_1 + \{\frac{b}{\mu^2} - \frac{\alpha}{\mu}\} + \{\frac{\alpha}{\mu} + \frac{b}{\mu^2}(\alpha X_1 - 1)e^{-\mu x_1}\} + f\{\alpha(X - x_2) +$$
$$\frac{b}{2}(X^2 - x_2^2)\}\right) + S_c f(\frac{\alpha X^2}{2} - \frac{\alpha x_2^2}{2} + \frac{bX^3}{6} - \frac{b x_2^3}{6} - \alpha x_1 X + \alpha x_2^2 - \frac{b x_2^2 X}{2} + \frac{b x_2^3}{2}) + L_C\left(1 -$$
$$(\frac{\alpha X^2}{2} - \frac{\alpha x_2^2}{2} + \frac{bX^3}{6} - \frac{b x_2^3}{6} - \alpha x_1 X + \alpha x_2^2 - \frac{b x_2^2 X}{2} + \frac{b x_2^3}{2})) + h_r(\alpha x_1 k + b x_1^2 k - \frac{bk^2}{2\mu} -$$
$$\frac{b x_1^2}{3\mu} + \alpha x_1^3 + b x_1^4 - \frac{\alpha k}{\gamma} - b x_1 k^2 - \alpha x_1 k^2 - b x_1^2 k^2 + \frac{b \, x_1 k^2}{\mu} + \frac{\alpha k^2}{\mu} +$$
$$\frac{b \, k^3}{3\mu}) + h_w(Q_1 x_1 + \frac{cb}{\theta} - \frac{b x_1 x_2}{\theta} + \frac{b x_1^2}{2\theta} - \frac{b x_2^2}{2\theta})] \tag{19}$$

The total applicable inventory cost is lowest if

$$\frac{\partial X^C}{\partial x_1} = 0 \text{ and } \frac{\partial X^C}{\partial X} = 0 \tag{20}$$

Subject to following conditions

$$\left(\frac{\partial^2 X^C}{\partial x_1^2}\right)\left(\frac{\partial^2 X^C}{\partial X^2}\right) - \frac{\partial^2 X^C}{\partial x_1\,\partial X} > 0 \tag{21}$$

MULTILAYER-FEED FORWARD NEURAL NETWORKS

The working of the multilayer-feed forward neural network is described from the following equation. The output of the ith neuron in the first concealed layer is given below:

$$net_i^1 = \sum_{j=0}^{m} P_{ij}^0 Q_j^0$$
$$Y_i^1 = f(net_i^1)$$

The output of ith neuron in the first concealed layer is used as the input to the neurons in the next concealed layer. In the same way, we can find the output of ith neuron in any layer l:

$$net_i^l = \sum_{j=0}^{H^l} P_{ij}^{l-1} Q_j^{l-1}$$
$$Y_i^l = f(net_i^l)$$

The output of the ith neuron in that layer Yi-1.

$$net_i^{l-1} = \sum_{j=0} H^{l-2} P_{ij}^{l-2} Q_j^{l-2}$$
$$Y_i^l = f(net_i^{l-1})$$

The error signal at the output of the lth neuron is described as:

$$e_j^{l-1} = t_j - Y_j^{l-1}$$

To diminish the error in the network, some degree of the error is optimized with respect to the weight vector. We consider the square of the error as a measure. The objective function or cost function, denoted as J is given by:

$$J = \frac{1}{2}\sum_{i-1}^{0}\left(e_i^{l-1}\right)^2.$$

Differentiating partially, the objective function (*J*), with respect to W_{jk}^{l-3}. Mathematically, it can be given as:

$$\frac{\partial J}{\partial P_{ij}^{l-2}} = \frac{1}{2}\sum_{i-1}^{0}\frac{\partial\left(e_i^{l-1}\right)^2}{\partial P_{ij}^{l-2}}.$$

Now considering the following expression:

$$\frac{\partial\left(e_i^{l-1}\right)^2}{\partial P_{ij}^{l-2}} = 2 \times e_i^{l-1}\frac{\partial e_i^{l-1}}{\partial P_{ij}^{l-2}}$$

$$\frac{\partial\left(e_i^{l-1}\right)^2}{\partial P_{ij}^{l-2}} = 2 \times e_i^{l-1}\frac{\partial\left(t-Y_j^{l-1}\right)}{\partial P_{ij}^{l-2}}$$

$$\frac{\partial\left(e_i^{l-1}\right)^2}{\partial P_{ij}^{l-2}} = 2 \times e_i^{l-1}\frac{\partial\left(Y_j^{l-1}\right)}{\partial P_{ij}^{l-2}}$$

$$\frac{\partial\left(e_i^{l-1}\right)^2}{\partial P_{ij}^{l-2}} = 2 \times e_i^{l-1}f'\left(net_i^{l-1}\right)\frac{\partial\left(net_i^{l-1}\right)}{\partial P_{ij}^{l-2}}$$

$$\frac{\partial\left(e_i^{l-1}\right)^2}{\partial P_{ij}^{l-2}} = 2 \times e_i^{l-1}f'\left(net_i^{l-1}\right)Q_j^{l-2}.$$

Therefore, the partial derivative of the objective function with respect to the weight connection between the output layer and the previous layer is as follows:

$$\frac{\partial J}{\partial P_{ij}^{l-2}} = \frac{1}{2} \times 2 \times e_i^{l-1} f'\left(net_i^{l-1}\right) Q_j^{l-2}$$

$$\frac{\partial J}{\partial P_{ij}^{l-2}} = \delta_i^{l-1} Q_j^{l-2}, \quad where \delta_i^{l-1} = e_i^{l-1} f'\left(net_i^{l-1}\right).$$

As applied in the generalized perception algorithm, the change in weight is the negative gradient $(-\Delta)$ of the objective function.

$$\Delta P_{ij}^{l-1} = -\eta \frac{\partial J}{\partial P_{ij}^{l-1}}$$

$$\Delta P_{ij}^{l-1} = -\eta \delta_i^{l-1} Q_j^{l-2} \ .$$

Accordingly, the partial derivative for W_{jk}^{l-3} can be calculated:

$$\frac{\partial J}{\partial P_{jk}^{l-3}} = \delta_i^{l-2} Q_k^{l-3}$$

$$\Delta P_{jk}^{l-3} = -\eta \delta_i^{l-2} Q_k^{l-3}$$

In general, the variation in weight of any layer l, $0 \le l < L-1$ is described by:

$$\Delta P_{jk}^{l} = -\eta \delta_i^{l+1} Q_k^{l}$$

$$\delta_j^{l+1} = e_i^{l-1} f'\left(net_j^{l+1}\right)$$

$$e_j^{l+1} = \sum_{i=1}^{H^{l+2}} \delta_i^{l+2} P_{ij}^{l+2}$$

WORKING ON PROPOSED SYSTEM

The following data which is randomly chosen in proper units has been applied to find the optimal solution and authenticate the model of the three players producer, distributor and retailer. The data is shown as γ=200, C=500, Q=300, c=0.70, h_w=30, h_r=55, P_C=500, μ=0.043, θ=0.054, S_C=450, k=2.34, f=0.09 and Lc=200. Q_1=100, C_A= 650. The standards of decision variables are calculated for the model for two cases separately.

Generations as 900, Population as 190, Cooperative factor as 14, Cognitive learning factor as 14, Social learning factor as 10.10, Inertial constant as 10.10 and number of neighbours as 110.

EXPERIMENTAL RESULTS AND ANALYSIS

In this chapter, optimized costs are evaluated. In addition, optimized results are compared with neural network on the same mathematical model as the previous researcher had used. The proposed algorithm is also applied to the same mathematical model.

Table 1. Results of mathematical model, neural networks and proposed system.

Costfunction	X^c (χ^*_1, X)	Best	Max.	Avg.	Std.
χ^*_1	34.474	-	-	-	-
χ	41.70	-	-	-	-
X*	52.24	-	-	-	-
Total relevant Cost	112.491	112.491	-	-	-
Neural networks	9.541	9.541	9.541	9.510	9.020

CONCLUDING REMARKS

In this chapter, a new neural network has been projected for the optimization of two warehouse inventory model with the aim of minimizing the entire relevant cost. Two distinct cases have been discussed to optimize the relevant cost. Furthermore, the projected neural networks are very useful to optimize the cost. The algorithm is implemented in MATLAB. The algorithm is applied to mathematical-model to optimize the cost. Therefore, it can be accomplished that this neural network is a well-designed and capable method for optimization.

REFERENCES

[1]   S. Narmadha, V. Selladurai, and G. Sathish, "Multi-product inventory optimization using uniform crossover genetic algorithm", *Int. J. Comput. Sci. Inf. Secur.,* vol. 7, no. 1, pp. 170-178, 2010.

[2]   P. Radhakrishnan, V.M. Prasad, and M.R. Gopalan, "Inventory optimization in supply chain management using genetica algorithm", *Int. J. of Comp. Sci. and Netw. Sec.*, vol. 9, no. 1, pp. 33-40, 2009.

[3]   S.R. Singh, and T. Kumar, "Inventory optimization in efficient supply chain management", *Int. J. of Computer Appl. In Engi. Sci.*, vol. 1, no. 4, pp. 428-434, 2011.

[4]   Y. Jiang, M. Chen, and D. Zhou, "Joint optimization of preventive maintenance and inventory policies for multi-unit systems subject to deteriorating spare part inventory", *J. Manuf. Syst.*, vol. 35, pp. 191-205, 2015.
[http://dx.doi.org/10.1016/j.jmsy.2015.01.002]

[5]   L. Thakur, and A.A. Desai, "Inventory analysis using genetic algorithm in supply chain management", *Int. J. of Engg. Res. and Tech.*, vol. 2, no. 7, pp. 1281-1285, 2013.

[6]   H. Zhang, Y. Deng, F.T.S. Chan, and X. Zhang, "A modified multi-criterion optimization genetic algorithm for order distribution in collaborative supply chain", *Appl. Math. Model.*, vol. 37, no. 14-15, pp. 7855-7864, 2013.
[http://dx.doi.org/10.1016/j.apm.2013.05.021]

[7]   G. Kannan, P. Sasikumar, and K. Devika, "A genetic algorithm approach for solving a closed loop supply chain model: A case of battery recycling", *Appl. Math. Model.*, vol. 34, no. 3, pp. 655-670, 2010.
[http://dx.doi.org/10.1016/j.apm.2009.06.021]

[8]   N. Jawahar, and N. Balaji, "A genetic algorithm based heuristic to the multi-period fixed charge distribution problem", *Appl. Soft. Comput.*, vol. 12, no. 2, pp. 682-699, 2012.
[http://dx.doi.org/10.1016/j.asoc.2011.09.019]

[9]   Z.H. Che, and C.J. Chiang, "A modified pareto geneticalgorithm for multi objective build-to-order supply chain planning with product assembly ", *Adv. in Eng.Softw.*, vol. 41, no. 7–8, pp. 1011-1022, 2010.

[10]   A.D. Yimer, and K. Demirli, "A genetic approach to two-phase optimization of dynamic supply chain scheduling", *Comput. Ind. Eng.*, vol. 58, no. 3, pp. 411-422, 2010.
[http://dx.doi.org/10.1016/j.cie.2009.01.010]

[11]   K.J. Wang, B. Makond, and S-Y. Liu, "Location and allocation decisions in a two-echelon supply chain with stochastic demand : A genetic-algorithm based solution", *Expert. Syst. Appl.*, vol. 38, no. 5, pp. 6125-6131, 2011.
[http://dx.doi.org/10.1016/j.eswa.2010.11.008]

[12]   N. Ramkumar, P. Subramanian, T.T. Narendran, and K. Ganesh, "Erratum to A geneticalgorithm approach for solving a closed loop supplychain model: A case of battery recycling", *Appl. Math. Model.*, vol. 35, no. 12, pp. 5921-5932, 2011.
[http://dx.doi.org/10.1016/j.apm.2011.05.026]

[13]   S.H.A. Li, H.P. Tserng, S.Y.L. Yin, and C.W. Hsu, "A production modeling with genetic algorithms for a stationary pre-cast supply chain", *Expert. Syst. Appl.*, vol. 37, no. 12, pp. 8406-8416, 2010.
[http://dx.doi.org/10.1016/j.eswa.2010.05.040]

[14]   P. Guchhait, M.K. Maiti, and M. Maiti, "Multi-item inventory model of breakable items with stock-dependent demand under stock and time dependent breakability rate", *Comput. Ind. Eng.*, vol. 59, no. 4, pp. 911-920, 2010.
[http://dx.doi.org/10.1016/j.cie.2010.09.001]

[15]   C. Changdar, G.S. Mahapatra, and R.K. Pal, "An improved genetic algorithm based approach to solve constrained knapsack problem in fuzzy environment", *Expert. Syst. Appl.*, vol. 42, no. 4, pp. 2276-2286, 2015.
[http://dx.doi.org/10.1016/j.eswa.2014.09.006]

[16]   J.K. Dey, S.K. Mondal, and M. Maiti, "Two storage inventory problem with dynamic demand and

interval valued lead-time over finite time horizon under inflation and time-value of money", *Eur. J. Oper. Res.,* vol. 185, no. 1, pp. 170-194, 2008.
[http://dx.doi.org/10.1016/j.ejor.2006.12.037]

[17]   N. Jawahar, and A.N. Balaji, "A geneticalgorithm for the two-stage supplychain distribution problem associated with a fixed charge", *Euro. J. of Oper. Res.,* vol. 194, no. 2, pp. 496-537, 2009.

[18]   A.S. Yadav, P. Maheshwari, A. Garg, and A. Swami, "Analysis of genetic algorithm and particle swarm optimization for warehouse with supply chain management in inventory control", *Int. J. Comput. Appl.,* vol. 154, no. 5, pp. 10-17, 2016.

[19]   A.S. Yadav, P. Maheshwari, A. Garg, A. Swami, and G. Kher, "Modelling and analysis of supplychain management for deteriorating items with geneticalgorithm and PSO", *Int. Of Appl. or Innov. In Engg. And Mgmt.,* vol. 6, no. 6, pp. 86-107, 2017.

[20]   A.S. Yadav, P. Maheshwari, A. Swami, and A. Garg, "Analysis of six stages supplychain management in inventory optimization for warehouse with artificial bee colony algorithm using genetic algorithm", *Selforganizology,* vol. 4, no. 3, pp. 41-51, 2017.

[21]   P. Yadav, "Soft Computing optimization of two warehouse inventory model", *Asian J. Mathe. Comp. res.,* vol. 19, no. 4, pp. 214-223, 2017.

[22]   A.S. Yadav, P. Maheshwari, A. Swami, and G. Pandey, "A supply chain management for chemical industry for deteriorating items with warehouses using genetic algorithm", *Selforganizology,* vol. 5, no. 1-2, pp. 1-9, 2018.

[23]   R.K. Singh, A.S. Yadav, and A. Swami, "A two-warehouse model for deteriorating items with holding cost under particle swarm optimization", *Int. J. Adv. Eng.Manage. Sci.,* vol. 2, no. 2, pp. 858-864, 2016.

[24]   R.K. Singh, A.S. Yadav, and A. Swami, "A two-warehouse model for deteriorating items with holding costunder inflation and soft computing techniques", *Int. J. Adv.Eng.Manage. Sci.,* vol. 2, no. 6, pp. 869-876, 2016.

[25]   S. Sharma, A. Singh, and A. Swami, "An optimal ordering policy for non instantaneous deteriorating items with conditionally permissible delay in payment under two storage management", *Int. J. Comput. Appl.,* vol. 147, no. 1, pp. 16-25, 2016.
[http://dx.doi.org/10.5120/ijca2016910967]

CHAPTER 7

Cyber Security in Data Science and its Applications

M. Varalakshmi[1,*] and **I. P. Thulasi**[1]

[1] *Marudhar Kesari Jain College for Women, Vaniyambadi, Tirupattur(dt), Tamilnadu, India*

Abstract: The implementation of data science in cyber security to help preserve against attacks and improve approach to better conflict cyber warning has many welfares. Honestly, data science has changed cyber security and the reaction has been profound and transformed. Cyber security uses data science to keep digital devices, services, systems, and software Safe from cyberattacks. Here, we talk about cyber security data science, present day uses for the cyber security field and data guide quickwitted managerial systems that can safeguard our system from cyber-attacks.

Keywords: Cyber security, Data science, Hack, Mathematics, Research, Statistics, Warning.

INTRODUCTION

Data science is a multifaceted field which works with the study methodology, algorithms, action, and method to understand commotion, correct and incorrect data, and apply the data across a wide-ranging application sector.

Combining statistics, data analysis, informatics, and their pertinent processes to identify and evaluate real words is a good concept. It differs from engineering and is used to approach and for ideas derived from diverse domains of mathematics, statistics, data science, and domain knowledge.

DATA SCIENCE TODAY

In the last 3 decades, data science has conservatively developed to carry establishment and management worldwide. It's currently employed by administration, biogenetics, and conjointly even cosmologists. According to the analysis, data science using vast amounts of data wasn't only about gathering data; it also included updating existing systems for managing data and the methods used to gather and analyze it.

* **Corresponding author M. Varalakshmi:** Marudhar Kesari Jain College for Women, Vaniyambadi, Tirupattur(dt), Tamilnadu, India; E-mail: varalakshmijanaki93@gmail.com

Biswadip Basu Mallik, Kirti Verma, Rahul Kar, Ashok Kumar Shaw & Sardar M. N. Islam (Naz) (Eds.)

Data science has developed into a vital component of commercial and academic analyses. Artificial intelligence, machine learning, voice recognition, the digital economy, and search engines are all components of technology. The organic sciences, health care, medical information studies, compassion, and public sciences have all become part of data science's analytical domain. Business science, government, business, and finance are presently influenced by data science.

One peculiar—and maybe harmful—result of the information science uprising has been a gradual shift towards writing more robust programmes. The data scientists have decided to extend unnecessary complex algorithms by investing an excessive quantity of flow and energy, when simpler special jobs may be done just as effectively. As a consequence, "novel" modifications that are noticeable happen less often.

Many data scientists today think that extensively revising is just too hazardous, therefore they instead try to shatter ideas into a tiny portion. Each component is tested before being properly phased into the information flow. Although more conservative programming is faster and more cost-effective, it also discourages exploration and prevents creative, "out-of-the-box" thinking and discoveries.

By using these safe-playing strategies, one may save time and money, avoid making costly errors, reduce the chance of running into serious obstacles, and get around real progress. Google stated: "One topic we tend to spend a lot of time discussing is how we prevent incrementalism when more significant changes are needed. It's difficult since these testing tools will greatly inspire the engineering staff, but they might also end up providing them with a strong incentive to comprehend just minor improvements. We definitely want those little improvements, but we also tend to want to think beyond the box.

MOTIVE AND SIGNIFICANCE OF DATA SCIENCE

Information is mostly used to look for patterns in statistical data. It uses several statistical techniques to explore and get knowledge from the specifics. The data should be completely surveyed by a data researcher from the data production, conflict, and preparation. They then have the responsibility of creating forecasts using the data. Data science is designed to draw conclusions from the data. With these outcomes, he will always be qualified to help businesses make well-dressed business decisions.

IMPORTANCE OF DATA

Data are crucial for model evaluation, characterisation, verification, activity, calibration, validation, and prognostication of the long-term structural robustness and presentation of materials in harsh environments. A lot of models would be useless if there were no reliable data to estimate and test them.

IMPORTANCE OF DATA SCIENCE

Data can work wonders. Industries want data to help them make informed decisions. Data science transformed recent data into comprehensive comprehension. Ultimately, information science is desired by enterprises. A data scientist is a magician who understands how to create magic with data. Every data a good data scientist comes across will be able to be mined for meaningful information. It benefits the business in the right manner. He is a guru and the organisation needs a stable data steering solution. The foundational fields of statistics and computer science are all strong points of data science. The ability to solve problems logically in business.

Use up the responsibility of data science focuses on the examination and direction of details; it depends on the industry's expertise in each sector, so data scientists must have lofty knowledge of the field.

MOTIVATION OF DATA IMPORTANT INDUSTRIES

Businesses need data. They need it in order to represent recommendations based on his or her data and provide a better customer experience. Now, allow me to walk you through the specific area where these businesses want to develop well-dressed data handling determination [1].

DATA SCIENCE FOR PREFERABLE TRADE

By offering a useful understanding of client preferences and behaviours, data science in trading may be utilised for channel optimisation, client segmentation, lead targeting and professional lead grading, real-time interactions, and other purposes. Never before has information been more readily available or necessary for managing a firm.

Industries need data to research their marketing strategy and create effective advertisements. Businesses often spend an enormous amount on the retailing of their goods. This sometimes may not provide the expected results. Hence, researching and looking at the client report industries will result in fantastic adverts.

DATA ANALYTICS FOR CLIENT ACQUISITION

The best way to attract new consumers or clients to your company is *via* client purchases. Expert clients use specific strategies to persuade actionable clients to take action. This procedure aims to provide a methodical, realistic viewpoint to attract new customers and boost revenue for the company.

By looking at customers' preferences, the industry may gather more clients. This enables the sectors to adjust outcomes to best meet the needs of their potential customers. Statistics hold the key to helping businesses embrace their consumers. Because of this, a statistics researcher's goal is to help businesses better understand their customers and communicate their needs to them.

DATA ANALYTICS FOR REVOLUTION

Out of an abundance of data, industries build the finest revolution. By comprehending and identifying perception in the conventional models, the data researcher contributes to the revolution in the results. They acknowledge customer feedback and aid the sectors' search for content that adheres admirably to the feedback and reviews. Industries make decisions and implement them correctly by using information from customer feedback [1].

DATA SCIENCE FOR ENHANCESURVIVAL

Information from customers is helpful in forming the best organisation. Healthcare sectors use the information at their disposal to assist their clients in their daily activities. The purpose of data research in these techniques of production was to comprehend the ideal information, conduct case studies, and create goods that remove challenges that customers confront.

Each of the data-centric industries in the aforementioned example utilises the data differently. Data are used in many ways depending on the needs of the sector. So, the goals of data scientists depend on how much business enjoys themselves. These are the main characteristics of data science and its context.

PART OF DATA SCIENCE IN CYBER SECURITY

Experts in cyber security develop reliable and efficient security solutions to preserve the integrity and security of corporate data, networks, systems, and everything else. Experts in data science mine useful information from enormous volumes of raw data to create models and provide actionable insight.

CONNECTION ALLYING SUBSTANTIAL DATA AND CYBER SECURITY

With the assistance of applications for analysing massive amounts of data as well as numerous tools for searching and discovering, a company may manage the analysis of group information. Expert container survey provides almost accurate forecasts as well as reveals future trends, techniques, and useful judgment.

Let's take one force as an example and have them locate the most of the virtual fractures in their organisation at night when no one is at work. Either way, one may consider how little the chance is that they will kill someone on their network. Anybody may utilise the revealed information to claim that latent charges will be removed from their current place in the near future.

DATA SCIENCE USED IN CYBER SECURITY

In terms of cyber security, our goals are to recognise warning signs, prevent incursions, and pounce, correctly connect spam with hacking, and prevent fraud. Data science and machinery studies are often used to help people more effectively notice these warnings [2].

In order to distinguish between spam and hack, for instance, data from a wide range of representative sources is often utilised for broad teaching purposes.

Here, faultless examination and notification of hack and spam discoveries are the holy grails. Reduce improper productivity, which wastes unneeded energy and flow. The same procedure applies for determining direction and storm. When malware wants to attack a system, there will often be a little incursion at the start to figure out how the network functions.

Ransomware, as is often the case, has increased by a share of 37 in the recent year. It is common practice to accurately assess deviation and malformation in user behaviour that is also the result of a looter. To stop the invader from getting any further assistance, the traditional obstructive estimate may then take hold. Below will usually be a link to several ongoing events that will determine if the invasion is finished.

Data analytics may be used to connect the dots between these "small" malformations and aid in the colouring of an expansive notion of what could be occurring. The approach is similar to prevent duplication. You were able to detect fraud in the Mastercard transaction using samples from your data collection, demonstrating the value of knowledge in spotting dishonest behaviour.

Negative Hoping on "Lab-based" Order

The benefits of using data science for cyber security purposes include the significant illustration of information that is familiar with effective examine warning. One example of a common issue with cyber-security plans is that they are developed using a predetermined sequence of incidence.

Despite the "Rules" being often dismantled by technocrats. It is crucial to consider all of the original information you have obtained from the original reader when formulating a strategy to recognise the warning so that true normal and abnormal behaviour can be distinguished.

Utilize Entrance to Sufficient Data

Malware and spam are easier to recognise than visible differences. Also, a large sample of data is accessible to identify hacker activity for training purposes. While it includes visible deviation, the opposing pointer confuses many other minute variances. Instead than anticipating predetermined rules, it is imperative that we assess all the original evidence that we possibly can in order to understand what is typical and what isn't.

If any anomalies are investigated, data science is known to analyse every new user behaviour with a relationship to the location. A person may compare real-time search of that information with utilising large "data lakes" to help identify warning. That provocation would be applied to all data, which comes from different networks and types of wood.

Specialize in this Irregularity

It is necessary to comprehend how behaviour could have happened in order to prevent false positives. So, any relatively commonplace activity will be suitable for cyber security purposes.

There are always going to be deviations from what are supposed to be routine operations. For instance, many of us rush to a unique nation and register there, use a different device to start up, or immediately pivot to make a purchase commitment that deviates from the prior score record.

A trade depends on many aspects, yet the same kinds of behaviours might signify different commodities depending on what's occurring in the big picture example. There will be a great lot of new, unrelated conflicts, which will lead to numerous erroneous assumptions.

Utilize Data Science in a Logical Approach

Data science studies extensive network data to take action at the business level. On the other hand, networks where massive amounts of data are sent are secured by data reliability software, such as virtual private network services. Data analytics and data dependability are mutually related. In order to anticipate impending threats, data analytics will be used to analyse the trend and movement of hacks over longer periods of time.

Another use of data analytics may be creating a dawn for each customer and differentiating it with real-time information. Another suggestion is that groups should become used to putting together collections of performances and activities that may be considered unconventional. Data sciences are often used to reduce false positives and to satisfy the cautious procedure, so in such situation, being watchful is not a difficult task. The burden on reliability teams may be decreased if the response to awareness is adequately self-operating and participates in the present moment.

UPCOMING CHALLENGES IN CYBER SECURITY DATA SCIENCE

In order to separate insights from relevant information about data-driven acute determining for cyber security outcomes, there are many study items and provocations in cyber security data analytics.

OPERATE CLASSIFICATION ISSUES IN CYBERSECURITY DATAFILE

The cyber data file may offer instability examples linked to a chosen invincible action or it may be clattering, incorrect, insignificant, out of context, or improper. These issues in a data set have a greater impact on the grade of the knowledge process and lower the performance of the models that use machine learning and knowledge. Such informational problems must be effectively addressed before building the cyber models in order to develop a data-driven strategy for firewall conclusion. Thus, understand these problems in cyber data and effectively modify them utilising an already-existing design or a recently-offered design for a specific problem domain, such as hack research. It is necessary to prevent and note intrusions, which may be done using data analytics for cyber security.

RELIABILITY SCHEME RULE

Reliability scheme regulations provide a safe perimeter and allows a buyer to approve, monitor, and clear traffic jams on a network that is backed by a user group. During the explore, the scheme rules with general and excellent unique rules are put aside, and the law that is similar to the jam is appealed. The majority of cyber security systems use static, brought out by human skill or attitude-based scheme rules.

AMBIENCE PERCEPTON IN CYBER SECURITY

First, you must survive cyber security in order to escape the relevant cyber data carrying numerous inferior characteristics. Even though databases are used for data clarification and instrument research methods, a pertinent pattern is often examined to ensure appropriate reporting. To determine if a questionable work is present or not, more general contingent factors like profane, structural, correlation among instants or linkages, and colony will be useful. Hence, various analytical gaps in cyber security might be reasons for alerts, flexible cyber security, conclusion.

ATTRIBUTE ENGINEERING IN CYBER SECURITY

Due to the greater capacity of the network data with the high number of jam qualities, the regulation and effectiveness of an instrument learning based security technique has always faced an excessive amount of competition [1].

Several concepts, like PCA, SVD, and others, have been used to detect the enormous amplitude of the information. In addition, the dependent relationship between uncertain actions and the low-level trademark inside the data file may be appropriate.

Such preliminary information will be included in anatomy for further refinement. As a result, a further analysis problem inside the cyber security data analytics may be how to choose the outstanding trademark or snippet the countless additional taking into account both the poor levelling quality nevertheless as the variables characteristic.

- PCA- principal component analysis
- SVD- Singular value decomposition

PROMINENT SECURITY ACTIVE CREATION AND ARRAY

The cyber security system was poorly specified in many locations, which should have led to a large number of false alarms that are unexpected in an intelligence system. For instance, an IDS in a highly real-world network generates around 9 million spirited alarms per 24 hours. A networks-based obtrusion noting approach typically scans the incoming traffic for related samples that are comparable to the threat to identify vulnerabilities and raise security warnings. To respond to each such alert, however, may not be necessary [2].

While it requires a significant amount of your time and effort, it may pave the way for self-imposed DoS. To combat these problems, a crucial step is required: before presenting them to users—which may raise further analytical concerns in cyber security data analytics—tally the providers, be aware of the contemporary element, analyse it, and rate it.

DISCUSSION

A literature review to grasp the facts on cyber security, changes in policy that entail obtrusion noting concepts, and numerous machine swotting concepts in the task of cyber security. In connection with our analysis of live tasks, analysis problems based on confidence datasets, data feature problems, strategy rule spawning, literacy techniques, data security quality engineering, safeguarding alert generation, current analysis, and more.

Everyone is noted as needing more analytical knowledge within the realm of cyber security data analytics. The scope of data analytics for cyber security is broad. Such user-driven responsibilities include detecting and preventing intrusions, managing approach power, creating security policies, and identifying anomalies like spam.

The focus of cyber security information analytics will be hacker detection, blocking, various hacks spotting and protecting techniques. Such supported the formation could be kind for safety, professionals comprise the research and supports that who are wish within the dominion specific side of security system.

The output of information science in the field of cyber security is widely used in areas of administration, including network security, network security, and cloud security, mobile and online applications, as well as other relevant cyberspaces. Moreover, because data breaches often occur in the banking, healthcare, and governmental sectors, better cyber security solutions are crucial.

On the other hand, the information-driven security compound may also be heavily reliant on blockchain technology, where all efforts are made to use machine learning techniques on a larger volume of security event data in order to extract useful insights, and distributed ledger is hoped to serve as a platform to store such data.

Although the focus of this article is on preserving cyber security data science training in order to examine incomplete security data and write for an intelligent security solution based on data-driven higher perception, it could also be related to massive data analysis in terms of details clarifying and decisiveness. Massive data is concerned with large or compound data sets that include characteristics of increased data volume, velocity, and diversity.

Huge data analysis primarily consists of two components: data management, which includes a data depot, and analysis, which often includes a report and a method of looking for patterns in large datasets. relationships, rules, and other valuable information that is not publicly known. Hence, several current data analysis techniques like artificial intelligence (AI), data processing, and machine learning might play a key role in processing enormous amounts of data by reducing complex issues to simpler ones.

Potential approaches for achieving this include paragon, divide-and-conquer, incremental learning, sampling, granular computing, feature, and instance selection. These approaches may be favoured for improving agreement, lowering costs, or for more efficient processing. In these situations, the idea of data science for cyber security, especially machine learning based modelling, may help the process of automating and making decisions for intelligent security solutions.

Research might take into account improved algorithms or samples for handling enormous amounts of data on parallel computing platforms like Hadoop, Storm, and others. Constructing a data-driven security model for a few chosen safety concerns and important observed developments to estimate the model's potency and efficacy and to assess the usability inside the real-world application domain may be a job for the foreseeable future.

CONCLUDING REMARKS

In this article, I must describe how cybersecurity systems use data-drawn intelligence decision-making in intelligent cybersecurity systems and services. This study is inspired by the complete importance of firewall and data analytics, and methodologies. We have also spoken about how it affects safety information, namely how to remove the impression of security actions and datasets alone.

By reporting the state of the art with respect to security incident data and correlating with protocol services, we have made it our mission to calculate cyber security data analytics. We have also discussed how AI may affect the field of cybersecurity in general and this cybersecurity provocative act in particular.

We have discussed relevant security analysis. Among the team of persistent analysis, the conventional security solution has received more attention than is necessary, accompanied by the least amount of AI work. The purpose of this paper's objectives is to illustrate how perceptions, assumptions, models, and considerations related to cyber security data analytics are divided.

Also, we have discussed a number of important issues in order to evaluate the case for the direction of future research in the field of data analytics for cyber security. In order to solidify the skills, we have also assumed a comprehensive multilayered structure of cyber security info analytics template support the machine learning method, whereas the information science is actually gathered from various sources, and the data science is accompanied by the most recent data driven ways for assuming intelligence security service.

This structure includes certain significant elements, such as the creation of security data, AI-based security modelling, augmentation learning-based security modelling, and increment learning and energy for intelligent cybersecurity system and repair. We paid particular attention to the notion of a data-driven intelligence security solution while designing the search and focusing in particular on the insight from security data.

This paper's summary avoided discussing the relevance of data-driven intelligent higher cognitive tasks in cyber security systems and assistance from a machine literacy standpoint. Both security researchers and advocates may find the whole study and conservation to be very intimating.

In light of the study, we have concentrated on other issues and provided guidance for more analyses. Other areas for investigation include factual correction of the data-driven sample's allusion, which serves as a basis for an intelligent cybersecurity model.

I looked for a paper on data science and cyber security to find a potential direction that I can use as a suggestion for academics and producers of new cybersecurity applications.

REFERENCES

[1]   U.J. Gelinas jr, S. G. Sutton, and J. Fedorowicz, "Business processes and information technology.cincinnati: southwestern/thomason learning", 2004.

[2]   G. Liu, K. Y. Lee, and H. F. Jordan, "TDM & TWDM de Bruijn network and shuffle nets for optional communication & quot", *IEEE Trans. Comput.,* vol. 46, pp. 695-701, 1997. [http://dx.doi.org/10.1109/12.600827]

CHAPTER 8

Artificial Neural Networks for Data Processing: A Case Study of Image Classification

Jayaraj Ramasamy[1,*], R. N. Ravikumar[2] and S. Shitharth[3]

[1] *Department of IT, Botho University, Gaborone, Botswana*

[2] *Department of Computer Engineering, Marwadi University, Gujarat, India*

[3] *Department of Computer Science, Kebri Dehar University, Kebri Dehar, Ethiopia*

Abstract: An Artificial Neural Network (ANN) is a data processing paradigm inspired by the way organic nervous systems, such as the brain, process data. The innovative structure of the information processing system is a crucial component of this paradigm. It is made up of a huge number of highly linked processing components (neurons) that work together to solve issues. Neural networks handle data in the same manner that the human brain does. The network is made up of several densely linked processing units (neurons) that operate in parallel to solve a given problem. They are unable to be programmed to execute a specific activity. ANN, like humans, learns by example. Through a learning process, an ANN is trained for a specific application, such as pattern recognition or data categorization. In biological systems, learning includes changes to the synaptic connections that occur between neurons. This is also true for ANNs. Artificial Neural Networks are used for classification, regression, and grouping. Stages of image processing are classified as preprocessing, feature extraction, and classification. It can be utilized later in the process. ANN should be provided with features and output should be classified. This paper provides an overview of Artificial Neural Networks (ANN), their operation, and training. It also explains the application and its benefits. Artificial Neural Network has been used to classify the MNIST dataset.

Keywords: Artificial neural network, Biological neural network, Neurons, Classification.

INTRODUCTION

Artificial neural network relates to a biological subfield of artificial intelligence that looks similar to a human brain model. The structure and composition of a

---

* **Corresponding author Jayaraj Ramasamy:** Department of IT, Botho University, Gaborone, Botswana; E-mail: jayaraj.ramasamy@bothouniversity.ac.bw

Biswadip Basu Mallik, Kirti Verma, Rahul Kar, Ashok Kumar Shaw & Sardar M. N. Islam (Naz) (Eds.)

biological neural network are used to design ANN architecture. Artificial neural networks [1], like the brain [2], are made up of neurons that are linked together at different network levels. These neurons are referred to as nodes. In Artificial Neural Networks, inputs are represented by dendrites from Biological Neural Networks, nodes are represented by cell nuclei, weights are represented by synapse, and output is represented by axon. An Artificial Neural Network is a sort of neural network that attempts to mimic the structure of neurons that make up the human brain in order for computers to interpret things and make decisions in a biological manner. Machines are designed to act simply as connected cells in the brain in a way to build an artificial neural network. There are around 100bn neurons in the human brain [3 - 6]. So every neuron has a connection between 1,000 to 100,000 points. The brain stores information in a way that it might be dispersed and can be recovered more than one piece of this knowledge from memory at the same moment if necessary. The brain may be thought of as a collection of incredibly strong multicore processors, as shown in Fig. (**1**) and Fig. (**2**) showing a typical BNN and an ANN diagram, respectively.

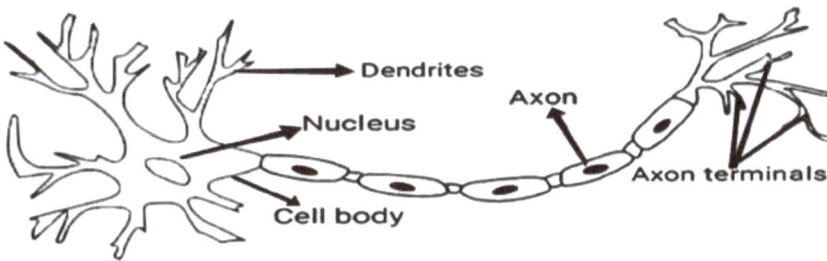

Fig. (1). Biological Neural Network (BNN).

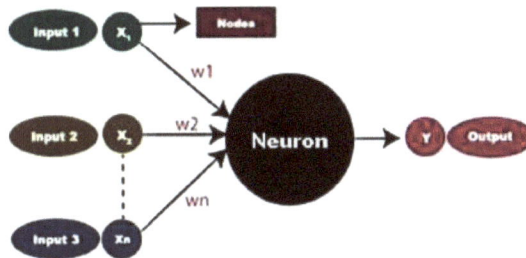

Fig. (2). Artificial Neural Network (ANN).

ARCHITECTURE OF ANN

We must first describe a neural network in order to appreciate the design about an artificial neural network. A neural network is defined by the placement of a great number of artificial neurons, referred as units, together in sequence of layers as shown in Fig. (**3**).

Let's take a glance at the many levels that a neural network might have.

• In the input layer, there are three input nodes.

• In the hidden layer, there are five hidden nodes.

• In the output layer, there are two output nodes.

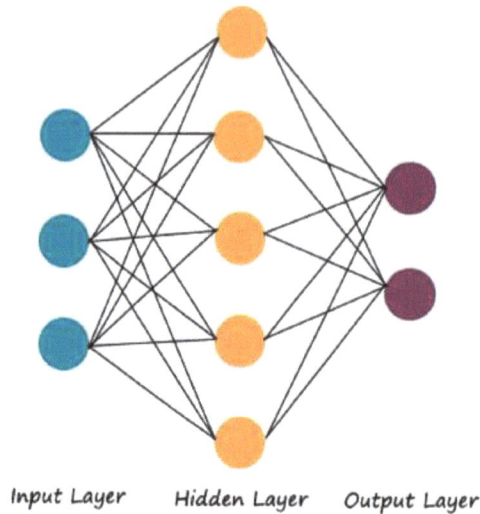

Fig. (3). Architecture of Artificial Neural Network.

Input Layer

It takes input in a variety of formats provided by the programmer, as the name indicates. Input nodes are indeed the outside-world inputs/information that the system use in addition to learning and making inferences. The information is sent from the input nodes to the next layer.

Hidden Layer

We have hidden layer located in between the visible and outgoing layer. It does all of the calculations required to identify hidden traits and patterns. The hidden layer is a cluster of neurons which do all of the operations on the information. There can be any number of hidden layers in a neural network. A single hidden layer is present in its most basic network.

Output Layer

The hidden layer transforms the input, leading in output that is sent over the same layer. When an input is received, the weighted total of the values, as well as a bias, are computed by the artificial neural network (ANN). A transfer function is used to express this calculation. It creates a balanced total, which is then fed to activation function to get the desired result. Functions determine how well a node fire or not. Those who are fired are the only ones who make it all to the outgoing layer. The model's output/conclusions are stored in the output layer, which keeps track of all calculations' outcomes. A single or more nodes might be found in the outgoing layer. The output nod e=1 in a binary classification problem, but the output node in a multi-class classification problem is more than one.

BENEFITS OF ARTIFICIAL NEURAL NETWORK (ANN)

Ability for Processing

Artificial neural networks (ANN) do have quantitative score that allows them to do several tasks at the same time.

Network-based Data Storage

Instead of being kept in a database, data for conventional computing is stored on the system as a whole. The network does not stop working because a few pieces of data are missing in one location.

Capacity to Function Despite a Lack of Knowledge

Even if there is inadequate data after ANN training, this information may deliver data. The relevance of incomplete information determines the loss of performance in this scenario.

Transmission of Memory

Instances should be picked and the system encouraged based on the predicted outcome by delivering such instances to the system in order for an ANN to adjust. The number of instances chosen determines a network's succession, and if the occurrence is not present in all of its features, the structure may generate inaccurate results.

Acceptance for Faults

Damage with one or many ANN cells has no effect on the network's ability to produce output, giving it fault-tolerant.

DISADVANTAGES

Ensure that the Network Structure is Correct

There are no formal rules for constructing artificial neural networks. The ideal network structure is determined by knowledge, effort, and mistake.

Network Activity that has Gone Unnoticed

This is the most serious issue with regard to ANN. When ANN develops a testing solution, it gives no explanation as to why or how it was made. It jeopardizes the integrity of the system.

Network's Life Expectancy is Unknown

The connection is restricted to a certain amount of errors, which will not provide us with optimal outcomes.

WORKING OF ANN

The Neural Network is best described as a balanced directed graph, with neurons serving as nodes. The link between neuron outputs and their inputs may be shown using directed edges with weights. An external source provides an incoming signal in the form of a pattern and an image in the shape of a vector to the Artificial Neural Network. The Artificial Neural Network receives an input signal in terms of a pattern and a visual in the form of a vector from an independent factor. The notations x(n) of every subsequent input will then be used to allocate these inputs numerically [7]. After that, every input is scaled by the relative weights to it. These weights, in general, reflect the power of the associated neurons within the neural network [8 - 12]. If the precise calculation equals zero, distortion is applied to make the outcome non-zero, or another mechanism to build up the system in responding has been used. The biased and weight inputs are identical, therefore weight = 1. In this case, the weighted inputs might range from 0 to positive infinity. The sum of connection weights is guided through the activation function to maintain the response in acceptable parameters, and a defined highest value is compared.

The activation function is a collection of signals that are utilized to produce the desired outcome. Activation functions occur in a number of forms and sizes, but they are generally setting of functions that are either linear or non-linear. The Binary, Tan hyperbolic sigmoidal, linear activation functions are some of the most often utilized sets of activation functions [13].

TYPES OF ANN

Artificial Neural Networks are divided into different types depending on the actions of the neuron and network in the brain. An artificial neural network works in the same way as a neuron and its network operates in the human brain. Artificial neural networks, which have a lot in common with their more complicated biological counterparts, will succeed at their duties.

Feedback ANN

This ANN's output is sent to a network to attain the finest internal outcomes. According to University of Massachusetts research, because they reflect information back into themselves, feedback networks are well-suited to tackling optimization concerns. Feedback ANNs are used to correct internal system errors.

Feed-Forward

In this network, a neural network has at least one neuron layer, a and visible (input) and output layer. The network's intensity may be assessed by studying its input and assessing its output, which is dependent on collective behavior of the linked neurons. This network's key advantage would be that it learns to analyze and recognize input patterns.

SIMPLE NEURAL NETWORK

The best forecasts are likewise made by a basic Neural Network. These are the types of educational computational model using a network of operations to comprehend and transform data input in one type into an expected outcome, sometimes in a different format. Neural Network is a type of method that uses a method inspired and linked to the brain to uncover patterns, relationships, and information in data as shown in Fig. (**4**).

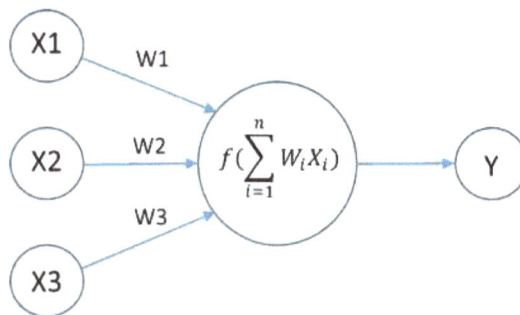

Fig. (4). Simple Neural Network.

1. Input units are passed in the first stage. Specifically, data is sent to the hidden

layer with weights attached. We can have as many hidden layers as we choose.

The picture inputs x1, x2, x3…. xn are passed in the preceding image.

2. Each hidden layer is made up of neurons. Each neuron receives all of its inputs.

3. After passing on the information, the hidden layer does all calculations.

LITERATURE REVIEW

Lan Wu *et al.* [1] proposed an enhanced deep convolutional neural network. In comparison to the conventional network LetNet-5, the upgraded network may assign alternative convolution kernels to conduct convolution based on the quantity of information in the image region, allowing for greater extraction of the image's effective information. The deep convolutional neural network has improved with n=2 has a recognition accuracy of 92.43 percent and a loss rate of 0.098; the n =3 deep convolution neural network has a recognition accuracy of 94.01 percent and a loss rate of 0.087, and the classical Letnet-5 network has a recognition rate of 86.62 percent and a loss rate of 0.127.

Lead Ming Seng *et al.* [2] in this study, they used fast.ai to search the MNIST database and trained the CNN ResNet-18 model to detect handwritten digits. The architecture was then updated using several pre-trained models. They have used five PyTorch pre-trained models for this project: GoogLeNet, ResNet-50, ResNeXt-50, MobileNet v2 and Wide ResNet-50.

Tohidul Islam *et al.* [3] In this article MNIST database provides 28,000-digit images for training and 14,000-digit test images. Multi-layer artificial neural network has a test performance accuracy of 99.60 percent. In the future, they intend to work on new datasets and to further optimize the ANN parameters in order to achieve greater accuracies with a shorter implementation time.

Prajwal Kumar *et al.* [4] described and analyzed the use of GANs in the production of handwritten digits. The MNIST database is used in this article, which contains includes 60,000 images for training and 10,000 images for testing. So, based on the findings, it is concluded that DCGAN incorporates convolutional neural networks into the GAN architecture, employs better parameters and convolutional layers to increase GAN performance, and can create realistic images in less training time.

Wan Zhu [5] proposed a neural network model which works well, with an accuracy rate of 97.65%. The updated model using Autoencoder performs poorly because its accuracy rate is just 74.38 percent, however, the modified model using CNN obtains 98.84 percent, which is somewhat better than our initial neural network.

PROPOSED SYSTEM

In this study, we have worked with MNIST handwritten digits, which are shown in Fig. (5). Artificial Neural Network has been used to perform classification on the dataset [14 - 16].

Fig. (5). MNIST Handwritten Digits.

NumPy is used to analyze matrix values, Matplotlib is used for data visualization, and Keras is used to create the NN model. Once the dataset is loaded, we will use four variables: X_train, y_ train, X_test, and y_test, X is a feature and y are the label. The data sets in total are 70000 of which 60000 have been used for training and the rest 10000 for testing, all of which have the same size (28 by 28 pixels) [17]. The first 28 pixels of each row represent the image's height in pixels, while the latter 28 represent the image's width. Since all labels are represented as a single number, the values of the target label are kept in array of one dimensional. However, this is not the type of label representation that a Neural Network expects, therefore we must convert it to a one-hot representation before training the model. It is simple to do by using the Keras module's categorical () method.

One hot encoding of class with label 5, for a total of 10 classes; the result is a simple collection within all values except the one at index 5. One-hot encoding is the name given to this sort of representation. In our case, we'd want to encode all of the targeted labels y_train and y_test in a single pass. The initial step is to develop a sequential model. After that, we can start adding layers to it. Because we need to convert the 28 by 28-pixel (2-dimensional) picture into 784 data and utilize a Neural Network model with a flattened layer (1-dimension). Then, with the use of a sigmoid activation function, we assign these 784 values to 5 neurons. In reality, we may select any number of neurons for this layer. However, in this situation, we have taken 5 neurons. The next step is to create another thick layer (activation function softmax is used) that will serve as our output layer [18]. Because there are ten different classes in the Classification issue, we need to employ ten neurons in the final layer. We picked categorized cross entropy for the error function parameter after creating the Neural Network classifier model [19] since it is the optimal one to employ in multi - classification tasks. Then we utilize the Adam optimizer, which is likewise the best in most circumstances [20]. Finally, accuracy must be added to the metrics input to evaluate the effectiveness of the classifier. We must utilize the fit () method on our model to train the Neural Network.

We can see that the accuracy is increasing in our 5-iteration training approach (both towards training and test data). This result is rather amazing because we can get almost 75% accuracy with a pretty simple Neural Network model, though it can still be improved. Then we must predict things on a set of images in our X test variable. The output image shows the first ten test images, as well as the estimates in those digit images. As we've seen, the vast majority of that hand-written digits are categorized properly. Just the ninth (left) image is a misclassified test since it ought to be a 4 since it has been projected as a 5 shown in Fig. (**6**).

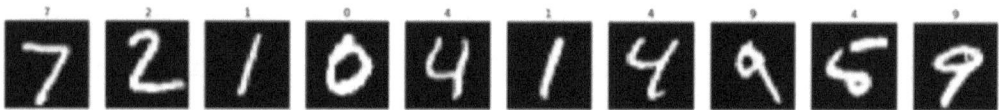

Fig. (6). Image Predictions.

RESULTS AND DISCUSSION

We carried out the project with the assistance of the MNIST database, and we utilized the handwritten digit-based database to examine the architecture of generated output, considering the use of numbers ranging from 0 to 9. To get realistic images, we train the ANN with regard to the appropriate number of epochs and batch normalization; the model accuracy is shown below in Fig. (**7**).

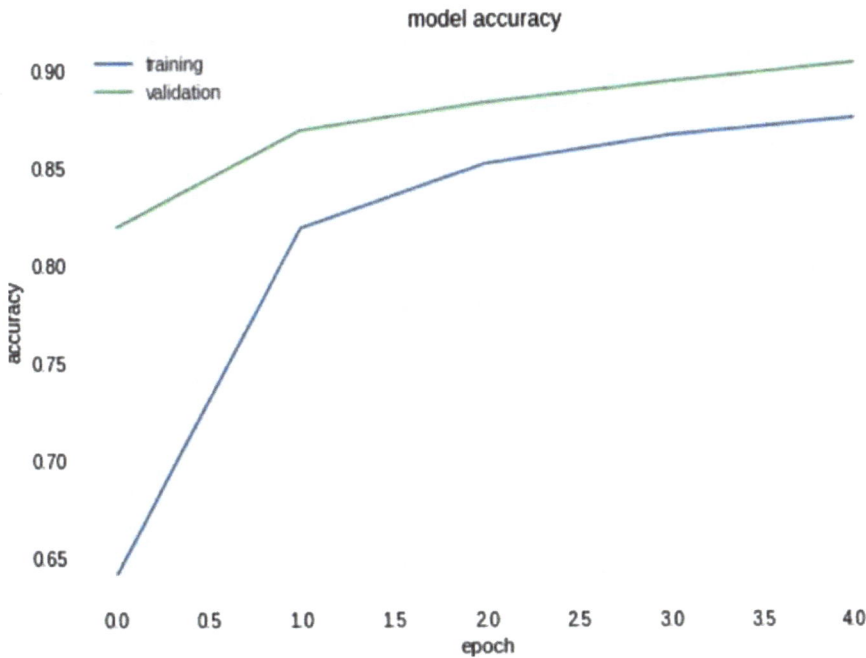

Fig. (7). Model Accuracy.

CONCLUSION

The major goal of this research is to develop an efficient artificial neural network for MNIST Handwritten digits with high accuracy, speed, and simplicity. In this work, we used digit image pixels as feature vectors and ANN as classifiers to recognize handwritten digits. For assessing our tests, we used the freely available MNIST database. According to the data, our experiment attained a recognition accuracy of 75%. In the future, we intend to work on new datasets and to further optimize the ANN parameters in order to achieve greater accuracies with a shorter implementation time. Finally, we are interested in combining a hybrid feature extraction approach with an ensemble classifier.

REFERENCES

[1] L. Wu, X. Jia, and C. Zhu, "Research on application of an improved deep convolutional neural network in handwritten character recognition", *J. Phys. Conf. Ser.,* vol. 1629, no. 1, p. 012002, 2020.
[http://dx.doi.org/10.1088/1742-6596/1629/1/012002]

[2] L.M. Seng, B.B.C. Chiang, Z.A.A. Salam, G.Y. Tan, and H.T. Chai, "MNIST handwritten digit recognition with different CNN architectures", *J. App. Tech. Innov.,* vol. 5, no. 1, p. 7, 2021.

[3] K.T. Islam, G. Mujtaba, R.G. Raj, and H.F. Nweke, "Handwritten digits recognition with artificial neural network", *Int. Conf. Eng. Tech. Technopre. (ICE2T).,* pp. 1-4, 2017.
[http://dx.doi.org/10.1109/ICE2T.2017.8215993]

[4] P. P. Kumar, P. S. Harinadh, M. D. Prasad, and K. G. Naik, "Handwritten digits generation using dcgan",

[5]   W. Zhu, "Classification of MNIST handwritten digit database using neural network", *Proc. res. sch. comp. sci.,* 2018.

[6]   B. Gope, S. Pande, N. Karale, S. Dharmale, and P. Umekar, "Handwritten digits identification using MNIST database via machine learning models", *IOP Conf. Series Mater. Sci. Eng.,* vol. 1022, no. 1, p. 012108, 2021.
       [http://dx.doi.org/10.1088/1757-899X/1022/1/012108]

[7]   K. Kaur, R. Dhir, and K. Kumar, "Transfer learning approach for analysis of epochs on handwritten digit classification", *2nd Int. Conf. Sec. Cyb. Comp. Commun. (ICSCCC).,* pp. 456-458, 2021.
       [http://dx.doi.org/10.1109/ICSCCC51823.2021.9478102]

[8]   Z. Kayumov, D. Tumakov, and S. Mosin, "Recognition of Handwritten Digits Based on Images Spectrum Decomposition", *23rd Int Conf. Dig. Sig. Proces. Appl. (DSPA).,* pp. 1-5, 2021.
       [http://dx.doi.org/10.1109/DSPA51283.2021.9535947]

[9]   W. W. AlQassas, and M. S. El-Bashir, "Recognition impact on rescaled handwritten digit images using support vector machine classification", *World of Comp. Sci. Inform. Tech. J.,* vol. 11, no. 1, 2021.

[10]   R. Wang, Y. Chen, and Z. Zou, "Handwritten digit generation based on generative adversarial networks", *Int. Conf. Electr. Inform. Eng. Big. Data. Comp. Tech. (EIBDCT 2022),* vol. 12256, pp. 407-412, 2022.
       [http://dx.doi.org/10.1117/12.2635378]

[11]   O. Ozcan, Y. Oniz, and M. Ayyildiz, "Handwritten digit recognition using spiking neural networks", *2022 Int. Cong. Human-Comp. Interac.Optim. Rob. Appl. (HORA),* pp. 1-7, 2022.
       [http://dx.doi.org/10.1109/HORA55278.2022.9799818]

[12]   T.N. Truong, C.T. Nguyen, and M. Nakagawa, "Syntactic data generation for handwritten mathematical expression recognition", *Pattern. Recognit. Lett.,* vol. 153, pp. 83-91, 2022.
       [http://dx.doi.org/10.1016/j.patrec.2021.12.002]

[13]   M. Madaan, A. Kumar, S. Kumar, A. Saha, and K. Gupta, "Handwriting generation and synthesis: A review", *Second Int. Conf. Power. Cont. Comp. Tech. (ICPC2T).,* pp. 1-6, 2022.
       [http://dx.doi.org/10.1109/ICPC2T53885.2022.9776932]

[14]   R. Nannapaneni, A. Chakravarti, S. Sangappa, P. Bora, and R.V. Kulkarni, "Augmentation of handwritten devanagari character dataset using DCGAN", In: *Mach. Intell. Smart Sys.* Springer: Singapore, 2022, pp. 31-44.
       [http://dx.doi.org/10.1007/978-981-16-9650-3_3]

[15]   A. Sharma, H. Bhardwaj, A. Bhardwaj, A. Sakalle, D. Acharya, and W. Ibrahim, "A machine learning and deep learning approach for recognizing handwritten digits", *Comput. Intell. Neurosci.,* vol. 2022, pp. 1-7, 2022.
       [http://dx.doi.org/10.1155/2022/9869948] [PMID: 35875749]

[16]   M.A.B. Siddique, M.M.R. Khan, R.B. Arif, and Z. Ashrafi, "Study and observation of the variations of accuracies for handwritten digits recognition with various hidden layers and epochs using neural network algorithm", *4th Int. Conf. Electr. Eng. Inform. Commun. Techn. (iCEEiCT).,* pp. 118-123, 2018.
       [http://dx.doi.org/10.1109/CEEICT.2018.8628144]

[17]   P. Ghosh, A.A. Anjum, A. Karim, M.S. Junayed, M.Z. Hasan, M.Z. Hasib, and A.N. Bin Emran, "A comparative study of different deep learning model for recognition of handwriting digits", *Int. conf. iot. based. cont. netwo. intell. sys. (ICICNIS 2020),* pp. 857-866, 2021.

[18]   A. Karim, P. Ghosh, A. A. Anjum, M. S. Junayed, Z. H. Md, K. M. Hasib, and A. N. Bin Emran, "A comparative study of different deep learning model for recognition of handwriting digits", *ICICNIS,* p. 10, 2020.

[19]   D. Beohar, and A. Rasool, "Handwritten digit recognition of MNIST dataset using deep learning state-

of-the-art artificial neural network (ANN) and Convolutional Neural Network (CNN)", *2021 Int. Conf. Emerg. Smart. Comp. Inform. (ESCI),* pp. 542-548, 2021.
[http://dx.doi.org/10.1109/ESCI50559.2021.9396870]

[20]   H. V. Thang, "Design of artificial neural network architecture for handwritten digit recognition on FPGA", *J. Sci. Tech.Uni. Danang.,* 2016.

CHAPTER 9

Carbon Emission Assessment by Applying Clustering Technique to World's Emission Datasets

Nitin Jaglal Untwal[1,*]

[1] *Maharashtra Institute of Technology, Aurangabad, India*

Abstract: The greenhouse gas emissions mostly include carbon-dioxide as the major component. The CO_2 level is increasing day-by-day which is a great cause of worry for the future world's environment. The reason why greenhouse gases' level increases in the environment is to be assessed and controlled. The greenhouse gases have heat-trapping capacity. A rise in numerous activities, including transportation, power production, agriculture, business, and residential, which are the main drivers of the increase in GHG levels in the atmosphere, is to blame for the rise in GHG emissions. Nitrous oxide, Methane, and Carbon Dioxide are all part of the GHG portfolio. Deforestation, traffic, and soil degradation all contribute to an increase in CO_2. As a result of burning biomass and urban trash, methane levels are also rising. The chlorofloro carbons are also rising due to refrigeration and industrial operations; so keeping the above concern in mind, the researcher had decided to conduct the study title. Carbon Emission Assessment by Applying Clustering Technique to World Emission Datasets using Python Programming. The study considers a period of 169 years (1750-2019). The study is carried out in five steps data fetching in python programming, feature engineering, standardization, clustering. The study generates 6 clusters. Cluster one contains 220 countries, cluster two includes Russia, France, Germany, China, Europe (others). America (others), Asia Pacific. Cluster three includes the United Kingdom. Cluster four includes the United States. Cluster five includes EU-28. Cluster six includes Malawi.

Keywords: Carbon emission, Data extraction, Engineering, Feature extraction, K-mean clustering, Python programming, Standardizing and scaling.

INTRODUCTION

The greenhouse gas emissions mostly include carbon-dioxide as a major component. The CO_2 level is increasing day-by-day which is a great cause of worry for the future existence of the world's environment. The reason why green-

* **Corresponding author Nitin Jaglal Untwal:** Maharashtra Institute of Technology, Aurangabad, India; E-mail:nitinuntwal@gmail.com

Biswadip Basu Mallik, Kirti Verma, Rahul Kar, Ashok Kumar Shaw & Sardar M. N. Islam (Naz) (Eds.)

house gases' level increases in the environment is to be assessed and controlled. The greenhouse gages have heat-trapping capacity.

The reasons for the increase in GHG emissions are due to an increase in various activities like transportation, electricity generation, agriculture, commercial and residential which are the major contributors to the growth of GHG levels in the atmosphere. The GHG portfolio includes carbon dioxide, Methane, and Nitrous oxide. CO_2 is increasing because of deforestation, vehicles, and soil degradation. Methane levels are also rising because of urban waste, and biomass burning. Cholorofloro carbons are also increasing because of refrigeration and industrial processes hence keeping the above problem in mind, and the researcher decided to conduct a study titled Carbon Emission Assessment by Applying Clustering Technique to World Emission Datasets.

Machine learning includes unsupervised learning under which models are trained for unlabeled data sets and are allowed to act without any supervision. Unsupervised learning is applied to understand the meaningful patterns, a grouping inherent in data, and extracting the generative features. Unsupervised learning is an algorithm that learns patterns from untagged data or unlabelled data [1, 2, 3, 4].

Cluster analysis is used to determine similarities and dissimilarities in a given data set or objects. Data usually have some similarities, which enable us to categorize or group them into clusters. The k-mean clustering is non-hierarchical. The reason for the popularity of k-means clustering is its simplicity. K means clustering is a type of partitioning method having objects as data observations with the nearest location and distance from each other. The nearest objects form mutually exclusive clusters. Each cluster has its centroid which makes clusters distinctive [5, 6, 7, 8].

Clustering is one of the important machine learning algorithms. Clustering is a technique of grouping elements; it is an important method for classification and grouping. K-mean clustering is used to classify elements into different categories based on the nearest distance from the mean. The main objective of K-mean clustering is creating a partition of n objects into k-clusters. Objects belonging to different clusters are considered based on the nearest mean. The method produces exactly k different clusters of greatest possible difference, which is known as a priori. K-mean clustering reduces the total intra-cluster variance or the squared error function [9, 10].

It is represented by the equation:

$$J = \sum_{j=1}^{k} \sum_{i=1}^{n} \left\| x_i^{(j)} - c_j \right\|^2 \tag{1}$$

where J is the objective function, k is the number of clusters, n is the number of cases, x is the number of cases i, cj is the number of the centroid.

Research Methodology

Data source

Data taken for the study is from the Kaggle database

Study period

The study period commences in 1750 and ends in 2019. The data selected for analysis is yearly data country-wise.

Software used for Data Analysis

Python Programming

Model applied

For purpose of this study, we applied K-mean clustering

Limitations of the Study

The study is restricted to only cluster analysis for Green House Gases country-wise.

Future scope

A similar kind of cluster analysis can be done for different continents.

Research is carried out in Five steps:

• Feature extraction and engineering

• Data extraction

• Standardizing and Scaling

• Identification of Clusters

• Cluster formation

Feature Extraction and Engineering

Feature engineering is the process of preparing the raw data ready for the program to utilize as per the requirement of the model. The data frame is the first step in making the data which is easy to understand. Once the data frame is created it is ready to be used by the algorithm.

Data Extraction

It is the process of fetching the data from an external source to a program and making it readable. The purpose of this study's raw data is to fetch from Kaggle (website) in the form of (CSV) file, as shown in Fig. (1). The CSV file named emission data is fetched to a Python program by using the code below. Before starting the feature extraction and cluster analysis in Python programming we need to import different libraries in python, such as Panda, matplotlib, and sklearn.

Fig. (1). Showing data fetching in Python Environment. Data is cleaned by removing the countries column from the data frame by applying the python code as shown below on Fig. **2**.

```
In [3]:  # Remove DISTRICT columns
         data.drop(['Country'], axis=1, inplace=True)
         data.shape
Out[3]:  (231, 267)
```

Fig. (2). Showing data cleaning by dropping the countries column from Data frame.

Standardizing and Scaling

When there is a good amount of variation in the data set, it needs to be converted to equal magnitude, as shown in Fig. (3). The difference in magnitude can create difficulty since the K-means algorithm is a distance-based algorithm. Scaling can be done by applying standardizing method. Standardizing is the method where we bring down the standard deviation and mean of features to 1 and 0.

By applying python code as:

```
In [5]:  # standardizing the data
         from sklearn.preprocessing import StandardScaler
         scaler = StandardScaler()
         data_scaled = scaler.fit_transform(data)

         # statistics of scaled data
         pd.DataFrame(data_scaled).describe()
Out[5]:
```

	0	1	2	3	4	5	2.
count	2.310000e+02	2.310000e+02	2.310000e+02	2.310000e+02	2.310000e+02	2.310000e+02	2.
mean	1.902038e-16	1.898433e-16	2.053432e-16	1.902038e-16	1.902038e-16	2.053432e-16	1
std	1.002172e+00	1.002172e+00	1.002172e+00	1.002172e+00	1.002172e+00	1.002172e+00	1.
min	-1.147079e-01	-1.147079e-01	-1.147079e-01	-1.147079e-01	-1.147079e-01	-1.147079e-01	
25%	-1.147079e-01	-1.147079e-01	-1.147079e-01	-1.147079e-01	-1.147079e-01	-1.147079e-01	
50%	-1.147079e-01	-1.147079e-01	-1.147079e-01	-1.147079e-01	-1.147079e-01	-1.147079e-01	
75%	-1.147079e-01	-1.147079e-01	-1.147079e-01	-1.147079e-01	-1.147079e-01	-1.147079e-01	
max	8.717798e+00	8.717798e+00	8.717798e+00	8.717798e+00	8.717798e+00	8.717798e+00	8.

8 rows × 267 columns

Fig. (3). Showing Descriptive statistics for scaled data.

Identification of Clusters by Elbow Method

The Elbow method is used to define several clusters in a given data set. In this method, we plot the explained variation as a function of clusters. The elbow of the curves defines the number of clusters. This indicates the definite number of clusters further adding more clusters which does not give better modeling data.

There are various tools to measure explained variation. Explained variation measures the ratio to which a given model accounts for dispersion. Variation is measured by variance. Increasing the number of clusters improves the fit (Explained Variation) as more parameters (clusters) are used, but this is overfitting and the elbow method removes this constraint. In clustering identification, the number of k identification is a difficult task. The optimum number of k can be defined by applying the Elbow method.

Inertia is the measure of how well defined the clusters in a data set by applying the k mean. It is calculated by measuring the distance between the data points and their centroid, calculating the square of the distance, and further adding these squares across one cluster. An optimum model is one having lower inertia and less number of clusters.

The calculation of within-cluster inertia is equivalent to:

$$Inertia\ (k) = \sum\nolimits_{i\ \in\ C\_k} (y\_{ik} - \mu\_k)\ ^2 \tag{2}$$

where μ_k is the mean of cluster k and C_k corresponds to the set of indices of genes attributed to cluster k.

Now, we will carry out the process of cluster identification by creating an Elbow plot and further by calculating in inertia.

Before identifying the number of clusters we assume that 6 clusters exist, but after applying the Elbow technique we get to know the exact number of clusters existing in a given data set. Further, we will calculate inertia. Inertia is the sum of square error for each cluster hence lowering the inertia denser of the clusters, by applying the Python code as shown below in Fig. (**4**).

```
In [6]:  # defining the kmeans function with initialization as k-means++
         kmeans = KMeans(n_clusters=6, init='k-means++')

         # fitting the k means algorithm on scaled data
         kmeans.fit(data_scaled)
Out[6]:  KMeans(n_clusters=6)


In [7]:  # inertia on the fitted data
         kmeans.inertia_
Out[7]:  355.20251840695227
```

Fig. (4). Showing clusters formation for scaled data.

Cluster Formation

As we apply the python code below and we get the results for clusters 1 to 6 for different districts of Maharashtra according to their characteristics and features as shown in Fig. (**5**).

```
In [10]: frame = pd.DataFrame(data_scaled)
         frame['cluster'] = pred
         frame['cluster'].value_counts()

Out[10]: 0    220
         5      7
         4      1
         3      1
         2      1
         1      1
         Name: cluster, dtype: int64
```

Fig. (**5**). Showing clusters formation results with classification for scaled data.

RESULTS AND ANALYSIS

We categorized the data selected for analysis country-wise into 6 clusters as:

Cluster One – High Rainfall

In a cluster, one includes 220 countries of the world, as shown in Table **1**.

Table 1. Showing Average Minimum and Maximum for cluster one.

Country	Average	Max	Min
Afghanistan	48640263.39	178502925	190528
Africa	15424054532	43117573841	1839368304
Albania	125090653.1	277278189	7866608
Algeria	1232397342	4107869896	15220256
Andorra	2872681.567	13717377	0
Angola	141287658.7	623762311	436016
Anguilla	538643.4627	3040078	0
AntarcticFisheries	50475.70149	153888	0
Antigua and Barbuda	8906638.597	21756717	0
Argentina	3382765251	7977373398	591036176
Armenia	117205490.4	273731872	0
Aruba	25684172.48	74231827	0

(Table 1) cont.....

Country	Average	Max	Min
Australia	7185392708	17360810555	1399142368
Austria	3227602030	5303713347	1688876832
Azerbaijan	1120545647	2471780322	0
Bahamas	77385624.18	157456745	120912
Bahrain	258139238.6	826530054	48654256
Bangladesh	289532561.7	1361147180	0
Barbados	17537478.4	51506565	227168
Belarus	1787402913	4058119852	0
Belgium	8432282841	12257548524	4791826832
Belize	5448613.925	17162217	43968
Benin	18544419.94	98792204	0
Bermuda	10635821.93	27146704	102592
Bhutan	2306267.791	13762670	0
Bolivia	130441775.2	461310418	3088752
Bonaire SintEustatius and Saba	11296979.84	20786824	0
Bosnia and Herzegovina	314323014.4	839470358	0
Botswana	28845393.01	131552447	0
Brazil	4649995936	14190905220	276833520
The British Virgin Islands	1095475.388	4416724	0
Brunei	141464915.3	335970645	33221488
Bulgaria	1789305975	3703285889	127529184
Burkina Faso	11156487.6	50218081	0
Burundi	3383465.448	10728250	0
Cambodia	21512688.97	105225247	0
Cameroon	59507514.22	194766284	322432
Canada	15753180623	31913521876	4669035200
Cape Verde	2905798.433	11572647	179536
Cayman Islands	3955643.463	14062432	0
The central AfricanRepublic	4150215.955	11448062	0
Chad	4192662.239	14410061	0
Chile	1031784561	2657499285	213263120
Christmas Island	823087.5224	1330032	0
Colombia	1196570262	3110040939	83594160
Comoros	1149194.284	4221082	0

(Table 1) cont.....

Country	Average	Max	Min
Congo	21822783.34	70573384	0
Cook Islands	569644.7313	2044872	0
Costa Rica	67709690.1	231692589	597232
Cote d'Ivoire	98780128.16	303413163	0
Croatia	373610348.9	981746998	0
Cuba	700121832.9	1656996984	13245360
Curacao	218679091.4	416123737	0
Cyprus	86555228.63	270926137	549600
CzechRepublic	3853435529	8321584468	0
Czechoslovakia	8599259909	11241448784	3714618160
DemocraticRepublic of Congo	101586608.4	186868045	8394224
Denmark	2263967931	3991753370	717528448
Djibouti	6256741.299	19174274	36640
Dominica	1117027.806	3921840	3664
DominicanRepublic	193002001.4	666238638	762112
Ecuador	327751273.1	1100685365	22819392
Egypt	1604694653	5561231356	85294256
El Salvador	66046051.34	213279980	589904
EquatorialGuinea	13085603.27	92146727	21984
Eritrea	3233702.433	16336483	69616
Estonia	499974016.1	1147762306	304112
Ethiopia	52827353.84	207190474	190528
Faeroe Islands	10313468.46	28545340	80608
Falkland Islands	3446511.522	4785184	630208
Fiji	16878236.36	45160830	252816
Finland	1320036972	3065528408	131654848
French Guiana	7302570.746	21361120	18320
French Polynesia	8302980.761	27182548	0
Gabon	93017901.43	245703654	0
The Gambia	3325453.955	12030971	29312
Georgia	286244345.7	593121176	0
Germany	60132477436	90565630028	29766640112
Ghana	93889485.82	316321491	1513232
Gibraltar	3714421.015	11380384	219840

(Table 1) cont.....

Country	Average	Max	Min
Greece	1345758085	3884493460	66838688
Greenland	13010167.15	30246493	197856
Grenada	2042662.761	7332340	18320
Guadeloupe	20558157.13	66083904	128240
Guatemala	114947853	404420205	1377664
Guinea	25476584.43	77269714	0
Guinea-Bissau	3101859.015	9228086	10992
Guyana	38610107.1	89660737	545936
Haiti	20492869.96	69042835	245488
Honduras	62040407.76	229623078	648528
Hong Kong	465663345.7	1508760365	3114400
Hungary	2800532117	4870991390	795674240
Iceland	55604787.1	141492956	1557200
India	14075209270	48557863281	2264300704
Indonesia	3596735618	12430271016	592208656
Iran	5167970368	16580287145	878279120
Iraq	1232223960	3983988823	133175408
Ireland	961788327.8	2112667064	245000688
Israel	695886001	2221239489	6195824
Italy	10613133653	23645999964	1740649152
Jamaica	165892631.5	424398054	791424
Japan	26367358885	62304608199	4240841840
Jordan	160565256.8	614829331	333424
Kazakhstan	5249129493	12300616894	0
Kenya	141043910.6	410113224	2300992
Kiribati	632024.6269	1913895	0
Kuwait	803631868.2	2626874527	10618272
Kyrgyzstan	0	0	0
Kyrgyzstan	33564941.84	181734180	0
Laos	9434792.209	36077735	0
Latvia	285777434.1	618492628	494640
Lebanon	200576409.6	634652476	4242912
Lesotho	11094372.19	56424722	0
Liberia	22727420.46	47905144	91600

(Table 1) cont.....

Country	Average	Max	Min
Libya	628066206.7	1951955718	311440
Liechtenstein	189092	2000665	0
Lithuania	458956262.2	1015509983	0
Luxembourg	378070167	725159607	16645552
Macao	15024980.4	51947913	0
Macedonia	233544221.8	561863099	0
Madagascar	29557681.22	83638600	582576
Malaysia	1206384803	5181419717	65717504
Maldives	3125403.657	19836857	0
Mali	9563898.209	33149434	0
Malta	33354831.7	97461275	501968
Marshall Islands	404816.1045	2266040	0
Martinique	24476012.18	70172928	135568
Mauritania	18499666.13	63673149	0
Mauritius	26861838.61	102339737	340752
Mexico	7147538131	18971469004	1280604640
Micronesia (country)	636281.3284	3401355	0
Middle East	17245145100	60473230861	1404806912
Moldova	43394195.64	175514617	0
Mongolia	152202883.8	536837014	578912
Montenegro	42090710.31	109622459	0
Montserrat	472011.5821	1539754	0
Morocco	454786652.3	1589225046	13761984
Mozambique	69684032.6	163105098	2898224
Myanmar	193692137.9	484208427	47346208
Namibia	10740998.1	63941325	0
Nauru	2038801.582	4678403	0
Nepal	22668336.76	115699603	54960
Netherlands	5990344117	11308449554	1930253824
New Caledonia	50299593.22	133507792	501968
New Zealand	843140068.7	1779162164	262642848
Nicaragua	53380213.96	160721077	436016
Niger	12547398.63	44106013	0
Nigeria	1126557546	3372735176	33661168

(Table 1) cont.....

Country	Average	Max	Min
Niue	82684.98507	271579	0
NorthKorea	2269299139	4966052271	5173568
Norway	1292060975	2585216441	427566816
Oman	212905477.4	1071493410	0
Pakistan	1137921763	4360589827	0
Palau	3899581.791	11012245	0
Palestine	8484589.597	48304340	0
Panama	86239514.25	270033082	1117520
Papua New Guinea	41710705.85	152482152	117248
Paraguay	41867738.28	150098368	109920
Peru	766304329.8	1857299524	198768336
Philippines	931863994.2	2959759692	10369120
Poland	15451796116	26848816401	5688609152
Portugal	979237147.8	2476694776	215813264
Qatar	413810766.8	1878554596	1000272
Reunion	24599385.07	90324928	54960
Romania	4355364257	8323783409	740003424
Rwanda	7842080.343	25185419	0
Saint Helena	86457.98507	346309	0
Saint Kitts and Nevis	1215049.791	5660325	0
Saint Lucia	3307552.925	12036657	14656
Saint Pierre and Miquelon	1564736.403	3596642	36640
Saint Vincent and the Grenadines	1639147.075	6228123	7328
Samoa	2021469.045	6445614	7328
Sao Tome and Principe	881117.7761	2954820	3664
SaudiArabia	3625350197	13843097583	125649552
Senegal	60510169.31	203710385	0
Serbia	945517630.7	2381789224	0
Seychelles	3496951.537	14863511	0
Sierra Leone	15253512.09	35859969	252816
Singapore	635903835.3	1936584508	0
Sint Maarten (Dutch part)	25253211.81	46502953	0
Slovakia	1253003700	2730069466	0
Slovenia	286751695.1	756184328	0

(Table 1) cont.....

Country	Average	Max	Min
SolomonIslands	2309648.657	7165127	0
Somalia	11876049.45	31190568	95264
South Africa	8119581816	19787369762	1558163632
South Korea	4098370620	15786618228	10343472
South Sudan	9171044.582	29721727	0
Spain	5924525075	14136085452	1199732832
Sri Lanka	132203931.1	436284059	3173024
Sudan	117252820.6	353794293	1271408
Suriname	43163585.28	104379605	447008
Swaziland	10164756.93	35288300	7328
Sweden	2953971965	4858725461	966980896
Switzerland	1557025271	2918791195	485556944
Syria	551564514.7	1762385573	1337360
Taiwan	2326609877	8050965637	162798848
Tajikistan	137706228.2	287463210	0
Tanzania	49086459.19	203638082	0
Thailand	1592117818	7013231542	2627088
Timor	455619.5224	4729566	0
Togo	16890946.04	62673116	51296
Tonga	1189420.657	3965652	14656
Trinidad and Tobago	570146708.6	1455796378	194422832
Tunisia	241784296.7	808028626	4034064
Turkey	2746942592	9602486274	194041776
Turkmenistan	761403153.9	2183172085	0
Turks and CaicosIslands	492187.9701	3318276	0
Tuvalu	50474.59701	256923	0
Uganda	27328334.9	95059160	245488
Ukraine	12304318128	25796386297	0
United ArabEmirates	977201998.7	4154728973	0
Uruguay	165672998.6	353071942	6716112
Uzbekistan	2452899626	6034285830	0
Vanuatu	1503263.567	4315060	0
Venezuela	3109359641	7571193371	371405024
Vietnam	716991962.7	3016099138	134014464

(Table 1) cont.....

Country	Average	Max	Min
Wallis and Futuna	57528.0597	429573	0
World	7.47448E+11	1.58E+12	2.38E+11
Yemen	185811751.1	619432763	98928
Zambia	90185316.19	187368600	0
Zimbabwe	341188102.7	701987856	93593216

Cluster Two

Cluster two, as shown in Table **2**, includes Russia, France, Germany, China, Europe (others), America (others), and Asia Pacific countries. European countries contribute the highest emission of Greenhouse gases (GHG). The major reasons are Power emission and transportation emission. Russia's power emission is 52 percent and vehicle emission 13 percent, with industrial emission of 15 percent, which is the major contributor. In cluster two countries, Germany, Russia, and China, the power generation emission is 43 percent, 52 percent, and 40 percent which is the major contributor of Greenhouse gases. The industrial emission of China is fifty percent. Russia, France, and Germany industrial emission is fifteen percent, eighteen percent, and fourteen percent respectively. From the above discussion, it is clear that most of the greenhouse gases emission is caused by power, transportation, and industrial emission.

Table 2. Showing Average Minimum and Maximum Emission for cluster two.

District	Average	Max	Min
Russia	43283739552	101000000000	0
France	24403788678	37768075471	12113268272
Germany	60132477436	90565630028	29766640112
China	50340909256	200000000000	1973199568
Europe (others)	78590987795	158000000000	14178210736
America (others)	41735929420	98641159642	9266490496
Asia Pacific	65483786164	178000000000	7297387280

Cluster Three

Cluster three includes the United Kingdom. The reasons for a high level of Greenhouse gases emission are energy and industrial emission. The energy need is fulfilled by thermal power plant which is the major source of emission. As an industrial advanced country UK industrial emission is the second highest contributor of Greenhouse gases emission, as shown in Table **3**. Transportation emission is the third-largest contributor of Greenhouse gases emission in the UK.

Table 3. Showing Average Minimum and Maximum for Cluster Three.

District	Average	Max	Min
United Kingdom	58983558015	77071055648	39694281088

Cluster Four

Cluster four includes the United States as per the U.S Environment protection agency carbon dioxide is the major contributor in the portfolio of Greenhouse gases emission. The major source of Greenhouse gases emission in the U.S is transportation emission with twenty-nine percent, as shown in Table **4**. Industrial and power generation contributes to twenty-three percent and twenty-five percent. In cluster four, we can conclude that industry, power, and transportation are the major source of contribution to Greenhouse gases emission.

Table 4. Showing Average Minimum and Maximum for Cluster Four.

District	Average	Max	Min
United States	227984377680.478	399000000000	94419132896

Cluster Five

Cluster five includes EU-28 countries. The highest contributor to Greenhouse gases emission is power generation since these countries have more dependency on thermal power as shown in Table **5**. The second highest contributor to Greenhouse gases emission is transportation emission. The third-largest contributor to Greenhouse gases emission in EU-28 is industry.

Table 5. Showing Average Minimum and Maximum for Cluster Five.

District	Average	Max	Min
EU-28 countries	219462686567.164	353000000000	103000000000

Cluster Six

Cluster six includes Malawi. The highest contributor of Greenhouse gases emission is transportation emission with fifty-seven percent, as shown in Table **6**. The building and power emission contribute to seventeen percent. It is the cluster with the least average Greenhouse gases emission in the clusters understudy for the study period 1750 to 2018.

Table 6. Showing Average Minimum and Maximum for Cluster Six.

District	Average	Max	Min
Malawi	15433826.81	43051513	0

CONCLUSION

The study generates 6 clusters. Cluster one contains 220 countries, Cluster two includes Russia, France, Germany, China, Europe (others) and America (others), Asia Pacific. Cluster three includes the United Kingdom. Cluster four includes the United States. Cluster five includes EU-28 countries. Cluster six includes Malawi. The major contributors to greenhouse gases emission are caused by power generation emissions, transportation emissions, and industrial emissions.

REFERENCES

[1]   A.K. Jain, and R.C. Dubes, "Algorithms for clustering data", Prentice-Hall: Englewood Cliffs, NJ, USA, 1988.

[2]   L. Kaufman, and P.J. Rousseeuw, "Finding groups in data: An introduction to cluster analysis", Wiley: New York, NY, USA, 1990.
[http://dx.doi.org/10.1002/9780470316801]

[3]   G.J. McLachlan, and K.E. Basford, "Mixture models: Inference and appli-cations to clustering Marcel", Dekker: New York, NY, USA, 1988.

[4]   A. P. Dempster, N. M. Laird, and D. B. Rubin, "Maximum likelihood from incomplete data via the emalgorithm (with discussion)", *J. Roy. Stat. Soc., Ser. B, Methodol.,* vol. 39, no. 1, pp. 1-38, 1977.

[5]   J. Yu, C. Chaomurilige, and M.-S. Yang, "On convergence and parameter selection of the em and da-em algorithms for gaussian mixtures", *Patt.Recog.,* vol. 77, pp. 188-203, 2018.
[http://dx.doi.org/10.1016/j.patcog.2017.12.014]

[6]   A. K. Jain, "Data clustering: 50 years beyond K-means", *Patt. Recog. Let.,* vol. 31, no. 8, pp. 651-666, 2010.
[http://dx.doi.org/10.1016/j.patrec.2009.09.011]

[7]   M.-S. Yang, S.-J. Chang-Chien, and Y. Nataliani, "A fully-unsupervised possibilistic C-Means clustering algorithm", *IEEE Access,* vol. 6, pp. 78308-78320, 2018.
[http://dx.doi.org/10.1109/ACCESS.2018.2884956]

[8]   J. MacQueen, "Some methods for classi_cation and analysis of multivariate observations", *Proc. 5th Berkeley Symp. Math. Statist. Probab.,* vol. 1, p. 281, 1967.

[9]   M. Alhawarat, and M. Hegazi, "Revisiting K-Means and topic modeling, a comparison study to cluster arabic documents", *IEEE Access,* vol. 6, pp. 42740-42749, 2018.
[http://dx.doi.org/10.1109/ACCESS.2018.2852648]

[10]   Y. Meng, J. Liang, F. Cao, and Y. He, "A new distance with derivative information for functional k-means clustering algorithm", *Inform. Sci.,* vol. 463–464, pp. 166-185, 2018.
[http://dx.doi.org/10.1016/j.ins.2018.06.035]

A Machine Learning Application to Predict Customer Churn: A Case in Indonesian Telecommunication Company

Agus Tri Wibowo[1], Andi Chaerunisa Utami Putri[1], Muhammad Reza Tribosnia[1], Revalda Putawara[1] and M. Mujiya Ulkhaq[2,3,*]

[1] *Department of Consumer Service, PT Telekomunikasi Indonesia, Jakarta, Indonesia*

[2] *Department of Industrial Engineering, Diponegoro University, Kota Semarang, Indonesia*

[3] *Department of Economics and Management, University of Brescia, Brescia BS, Italy*

Abstract: This study aims to develop a churn prediction model which can assist telecommunication companies in predicting customers who are most likely subject to churn. The model is developed by employing machine learning techniques on big data platforms. Customer churn is one of the most critical issues, especially in high investment telecommunication companies. Accordingly, the companies are looking for ways to predict potential customers to churn and take necessary actions to reduce the churn. To accomplish the objective of the study, it first compares eight machine learning techniques, *i.e.*, ridge classifier, gradient booster, adaptive boosting, bagging classifier, *k*-nearest neighbour (kNN), decision tree, logistic regression, and random forest. By using five evaluation performance metrics (*i.e.*, accuracy, AUC score, precision score, recall score, and the F score), kNN is selected since it outperforms other techniques. Second, the selected technique is used to predict the likelihood of customers churning.

Keywords: Customer churn prediction, Churn, *k*-nearest neighbour, Machine learning, Telecommunication company.

INTRODUCTION

In the era of advanced technology, recent studies found that telecommunication sector has evolved and emerged as one of the brightest businesses due to the current needs of customers [1]. It has become one of the key sectors in the developed countries; hence, the level of competition increased as a result of technological advancement and growth in telecommunication providers [2].

---

* **Corresponding author M. Mujiya Ulkhaq:** Department of Industrial Engineering, Diponegoro University, Kota Semarang, Indonesia & Department of Economics and Management, University of Brescia, Brescia BS, Italy; E-mail: ulkhaq@live.undip.ac.id

Biswadip Basu Mallik, Kirti Verma, Rahul Kar, Ashok Kumar Shaw & Sardar M. N. Islam (Naz) (Eds.)

The telecommunication providers could perform several strategies to generate additional revenue, such as: upsell the current clients, obtain new clients, and lengthen customer retention [3]. Comparing these strategies based on return-on-investment value found that the last strategy is the most beneficial one [3]. It shows that keeping an existing customer is considerably less expensive than obtaining a new customer [4], and also is substantially more effortless than the upselling strategy [5]. This third strategy requires businesses to reduce possible customer churn, or the migration of clients from one service provider to another. Statistics showed that 53% of all causes of customer churn are due to three leading causes, *i.e.*, 23% of poor onboarding, 16% of weak relationship building, and 14% of poor customer service [6].

There are several telecommunication providers in Indonesia; hence, businesses are arranging measures to survive in this cutthroat market. The phenomenon of *churn* obviously affects telecommunication providers in Indonesia and enforces them to create a new business strategy focusing on customer orientation, which puts the needs of the customers over the needs of the business. These providers could implement customer relationship management (CRM) to study customer satisfaction, loyalty, profitability, and customer retention [7]. While CRM's objective is to make a strong engagement with the customers, this approach is widely acknowledged and applied in many industries. Regarding the telecommunication industry, CRM can be used as a tool to gather information on the organization's marketing efforts, customers, competitors, contracts, and agreements [8]. Subsequently, CRM can also be implemented in the telecommunication industry where customers might switch their providers due to a variety of reasons, such as more comprehensive services, better pricing plans and connections, and so forth [9]; hence, it is necessary to define adequate models to accurately forecast the likelihood of customers to churn.

This study aims to develop a model to predict customers churn that can help telecommunication provider to forecast customers who are most likely to churn; and then predict the likelihood of customers to churn. To do so, it first compares several machine learning algorithms to predict customer churn, *i.e.*, gradient booster, ridge classifier, *k*-nearest neighbor (kNN), adaptive boosting (AdaBoost), bagging classifier, random forest algorithms, logistic regression, and decision tree. This is to show how each machine-learning technique can be implemented to model customer churn. The comparison is performed in five performance evaluation scores, including AUC score, accuracy, F score, recall score, and precision score. Second, the selected technique is employed to predict the likelihood of customers to churn.

The remaining parts of this work are structured as follows. In the next section, we present a literature review discussing previous studies about implementing machine learning in telecommunication company in Indonesia. It shows that this research area is under-studied, especially among scholars in Indonesia. The research design is discussed in Section 3. Section 4 discusses briefly machine learning techniques. Section 5 shows how to compare and evaluate the machine learning techniques used. Section 6 shows the results, while the last section is the concluding remarks.

LITERATURE REVIEW AND CONTRIBUTION

Literature about implementing the machine learning (or data mining) technique in telecommunication companies in Indonesia is quite limited. To formally verify this claim, we conduct a literature review in the Scopus database (https://www.scopus.com/), following Mongeon and Paul-Hus [10] who mentioned, "Scopus includes most of the journals indexed in WoS [Web of Science]." This database provided access to scientific articles and a wide-ranging of journals from various fields. First, we used the following search terms: TITLE-ABS-KEY(("machine learning" OR "data mining" OR "knowledge discovery") AND ("customer*" OR "client") AND ("churn*" OR "evasion" OR "dropout") AND "telecom*").[1] It means that the articles which contained those search terms in the title, abstract, or keywords were extracted. The period of time was not limited. From a pragmatic point of view, only articles published in English were included. This search yielded 359 articles. In the second refinement, we added the term "Indonesia" into the previous search terms. This second search yielded only three articles. This low yield indicated that this research area was under-studied especially among scholars in Indonesia. All these three articles are discussed as follows.

Hartati *et al.* [11] investigated how to handle imbalanced data problem using a combination of synthetic minority over-sampling (SMOTE) and random under-sampling (RUS); and how to assess the performance of the model using only one classifier (*i.e.*, C4.5 classifier) with bagging approach. Result showed that a higher performance was obtained by implementing the SMOTE and RUS sampling methods. SMOTE was used to generate the synthetic data from the churn class to upsurge the probability of drawing the churn data; while RUS was employed to decrease the probability of an overfitting problem. Next, the authors also showed that the implementation of bagging approach (with number of bags equals to 7) in the classification was able to improve the F score.

Alamsyah and Salma [12] attempted to search for the best model for employee churn prediction using three widespread prediction models, *i.e.*, decision tree, naïve bayes and random forest. Result suggested that the best prediction model is random forest, while the second-best is naïve bayes and the worst model is a decision tree.

Ulkhaq *et al.* [13] presented a comparison among several machine learning algorithms for predicting customer churn, namely, gradient booster, bagging classifier, adaptive boosting (AdaBoost), ridge classifier, decision tree, logistic regression, random forest, and *k*-nearest neighbor (kNN). According to five performance evaluation scores (*i.e.*, the AUC score, accuracy, recall score, precision score, and the F score), the relatively best machine learning technique is kNN.

According to the insight of the literature review, it is apparent that previous studies did not attempt to predict the likelihood to churn (Alamsyah and Salma [12] and Ulkhaq *et al.* [13] only compared several models to predict the churn with several performance evaluation scores, while Hartati *et al.* [11] only used one classification model after showing how to handle imbalanced data problem). Therefore, to close the gap in the literature, this study tries to predict the likelihood to churn using the actual data. To do so, first, we compare eight machine learning techniques to look for the relatively best model to predict the churn; second, the selected technique is used to predict the likelihood to churn.

RESEARCH DESIGN

The research design framework is depicted in Fig. (**1**).

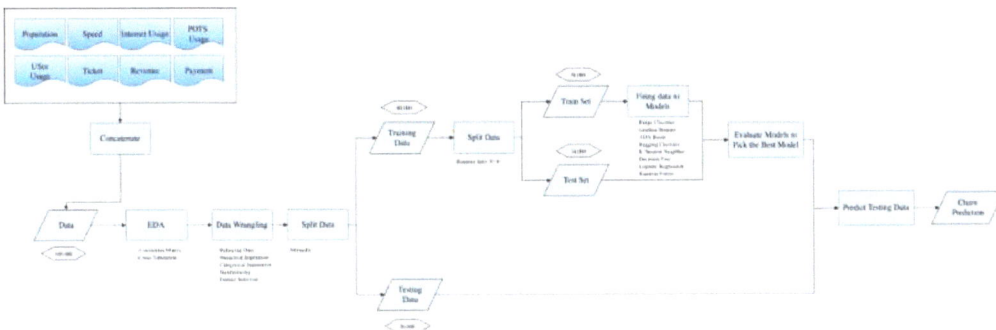

Fig. (1). Research design framework.

Dataset

The dataset is obtained from a large Indonesian telecommunication company. The dataset has a particularly skewed distribution, which shows an unsatisfactory result in predicting customer churn. Thus, in this study, we address this issue by using a suitably coordinated technique to create a classifier that can improve the performance.

The number of samples for this study is about 100,000 customers (active and disconnected). The dataset is split into training data (about 80%) as well as testing data (about 20%). The customers are classified by a dichotomous classification called status *active* (labeled by 0) and *churn* (labeled by 1). A particular customer is categorized as *active* if s/he continues using the service, else, when the customer decides to terminate the contract with the provider or no longer uses the service, s/he is classified as *churn*.

Data Preparation

As most machine learning algorithms demand structured data, the dataset generally requires some preprocessing steps before it may provide valuable insights. The dataset comprising values that are incomplete and invalid is difficult to be processed [14]. When the data is incomplete, the algorithm could produce less accurate or misleading results. Since the algorithm cannot treat missing data appropriately, it is critical to eliminate or *fill* the missing values in the dataset as well as to check for imbalanced class distributions which has been a concern in data preprocessing. Some data are clean but need to be manipulated; in addition, many data lack essential business context (*e.g.*, poorly defined ID values). Clean and well-curated data can be produced through good data preparation, resulting in more practical and accurate model findings [9, 14].

Exploratory Data Analysis

Exploratory data analysis (EDA) is an important step in which the data is simply presented, plotted, and modified without any assumptions to help in establishing data quality and creating predictions. The primary focus of EDA is to find distributions, outliers, and irregularities in the data. It also provides tools for hypothesis formulation through the display of data, generally in a graphical form. The rationale for the emphasis on the graphical form is that the major function of EDA is to explore; and visuals could give the researcher unparalleled power to do so while also being ready to get insight into the data.

We use correlation matrix and cross-tabulation in this study. A correlation matrix is a table that shows the correlation coefficients for variables under investigation. The matrix depicts the correlation values among all possible value pairs in a table. It is a useful tool for summarizing large datasets as well as discovering and showing patterns. Cross-tabulation is the primary non-graphical bivariate in the EDA technique. It is a tabulation enhancement for categorical and numerical data with a few variables. It generates a two-way table with column headings corresponding to one variable's levels and row headings corresponding to the other variable's levels, then fills in the counts of all subjects as a pair of levels [9]. In this study, we compare all variables with customers' length of stay (*los_inet*) that represent the customer's timespan of using the service and is considered one of the most critical factors in deciding whether a customer is churn or active. Result of the correlation analysis is shown in Fig. (**2**) while cross-tabulation analysis is shown in Fig. (**3**).

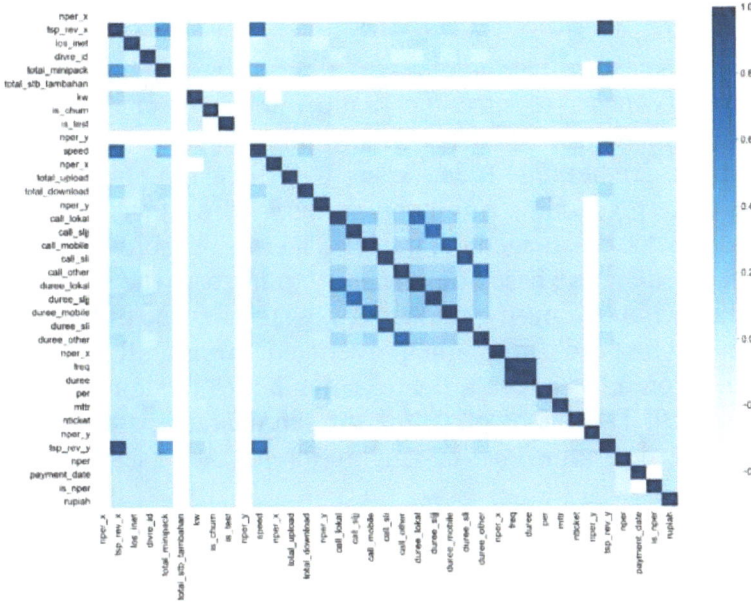

Fig. (2). Correlation matrix.

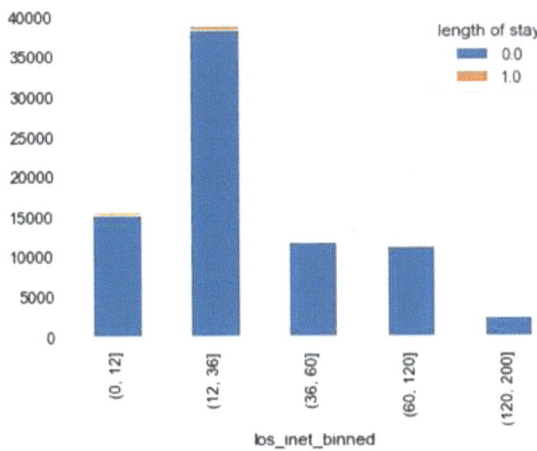

Fig. (3). Cross-tabulations analysis.

Features Selection

Defining the proper collection of features as predictors is a critical step before analyzing the information using machine learning techniques. This is a critical step since the major goal of the feature selection is to remove the non-significant characteristics that remain constant or have no significance for all occurrences. In brief, feature selection helps to minimize the dimensions of a dataset and remove irrelevant variables. As a result, the excluded characteristics are either invalid or have a low probability of predicting the model.

To determine if a feature has predictive value in the model, the random forest feature selection is chosen to select the 10 most important predictive features. It is a quantitative numerical method for determining how much each characteristic contributes to the predictions. It can assist with focusing on the most important components, either expanding or changing them, as well as deleting extraneous elements that may have damaged the model. The random forest's trees may assess the importance of a feature based on its ability to increase the purity of the leaves. The bigger the rise in leaf purity, the larger the significance of the feature. This is done separately for each tree, then averaged across all trees, and finally normalized to 1 (one). As a result, the total number of random forest significance ratings is one [15]. Table **1** displays the top ten characteristics with the highest relevance value as determined by the random forest feature selection.

Table 1. Top ten random forest features.

Feature	Description	Score
los_inet	Length of stay	0.17062
total_download	Total monthly download	0.10032
total_upload	Total monthly upload	0.09860
payment_date	Payment date	0.07448
kw	Customer classification	0.06904
rupiah	Total payment	0.05441
tsp_rev_x	Last billing amount	0.05256
tsp_rev_y	Up to the last 6 months billing amount	0.05044
call_lokal	Freq outgoing call lokal	0.04965
duree_lokal	Duration of outgoing call local	0.03517

MACHINE LEARNING APPLICATION

In this section, a brief summary of eight well-established machine learning approaches used for churn prediction is provided, taking into account factors such as efficiency, reliability, and popularity in the research community.

Ridge Classifier

The ridge classifier, which is based on the ridge regression methodology, converts the label data into the range (-1, 1) and addresses the problem using the regression method. For multiclass data, multiple output regression is performed, and the class with the greatest prediction value is selected as the target class. The predicted class is determined by the regressor's prediction sign. To address the issue, multi-output regression for multiclass classification is utilized, and the predicted class corresponds to the output with the greatest value [16].

Gradient Booster

Gradient boosting machines (GBMs) are machine-learning algorithms that may be tailored to the demands of the application. This technique is very adaptive, with the learning mechanism fitting new models sequentially to offer a more accurate estimate of the response variable. The basic idea behind this strategy is to create new base-learns with the highest correlation with the ensemble's overall negative gradient of the loss function. If the error function is the standard squared-error loss, the learning process will result in sequential error-fitting. However, in order to offer a greater perception, the loss functions used might be random.

GBMs may be easily adjusted to any given data-driven activity because of their considerable versatility. It gives the model a lot of leeway in terms of design, making choosing the best loss function a question of trial and error. Nonetheless, boosting algorithms are simple to implement, allowing for experimentation with various model designs. Furthermore, GBMs have shown remarkable efficacy in a number of machine-learning and data-mining challenges [17].

Adaptive Boosting

Adaptive Boosting (AdaBoost) is a sort of boosted decision tree that operates on the same premise as boosting and retraining difficult-to-classify data [18]. This approach produces stump-shaped decision trees with just one node and two leaves. In other words, the AdaBoost approach is a forest of stumps that contains all of the trees and applies an iterative methodology in which each training item is assigned a weight at each prediction level except the first. AdaBoost is simple to grasp and comprehend. It simply has a few hyper-parameters that need to be tuned. Although it is also particularly sensitive to noisy data and is not optimized for speed, in low noise datasets, this approach is somewhat resilient to overfitting and may be utilized in both regression and classification problems [19, 20].

Bagging Classifier

Bagging, also known as bootstrap aggregating classifier, is an ensemble meta-estimator that fits base classifiers on random subsets of the original dataset, then aggregates the individual predictions to generate a final prediction through voting or averaging. To minimize variance in a noisy dataset, the ensemble learning approach is often used [21]. Weak learners are instructed concurrently in bagging. It produces several bootstrap training sets from the initial training set (through sampling with replacements) and uses each to generate a classifier for the ensemble [21].

There are three basic steps used by this algorithm, *i.e.*, bootstrapping, parallel training, and aggregation [22]. In the last step, an average or a majority of the predictions are picked depending on the task (*i.e.*, regression or classification) to produce a more accurate estimate. Regression, which is referred to as soft voting involves averaging every output predicted by each classifier. Classification, on the other hand, which is known as a hard voting, accepts the class with the most votes.

k-Nearest Neighbor

k-nearest neighbor (kNN) is an effective and simple machine learning technique for classification and regression. Because it is non-parametric, it makes no assumptions about the underlying dataset. kNN is well-known for its effectiveness and simplicity. kNN is a supervised learning algorithm [23]. A training dataset divides data points into various groups, allowing the class of the unlabeled data to be predicted. Different criteria are employed in classification to determine which class the unlabeled data belongs to. When working with continuous data, kNN uses the Euclidean distance to find its nearest neighbors.

When a new input is considered, the kNN is computed, and the classification for the new input is determined by the majority of the nearby data. Despite the simplicity of the classifier, the value of "*k*" is critical in categorizing the unlabeled input. There are other ways to pick the *k* values, but we can just run the classifier several times with different values to see which one gets the best results [24]. The computation cost is slightly greater since all computations are performed while categorizing the training data rather than when it occurs in the dataset.

Decision Tree

Decision tree is a non-parametric classification technique with a basic structure that may govern nonlinear relationships between data and classes. Decision tree is a tree-based rule hierarchy that may be seen as a mechanism that recursively splits incoming data into progressively smaller groups. However, there are certain disadvantages to using the decision tree. The most significant ones are overfitting and providing a poor solution [18]. The decision tree may not provide the finest final model since it only utilizes one tree. Overfitting is another big concern that should be considered. On the other hand, the decision tree offers various advantages, including the ability to generate rules that are simple to grasp and interpret without any statistical understanding. Furthermore, this approach is capable of categorizing data using both numerical and categorical factors. It also minimizes the computational complexity necessary to categorize [18].

Logistic Regression

Logistic regression is commonly employed to model a binary variable according to one or more predictors. The dependent variable is the term used to describe the binary variable that is being modelled. Given that fitted model predictions are probabilities with a range of values limited to (0, 1), logistic regression is particularly useful. Exponentiation is typically used to interpret logistic model coefficients so that odds ratios can be understood. Whether in a grouped structure or an observation-based format, the class of logistic models is the only one with this ability. The primary reason a logistic model has enjoyed such popularity in the statistical community for the past several decades is that it can be used to evaluate the odds ratio of predictors as well as to calculate the probability of the response based on specific predictor values.

Random Forest

Random forest is a well-known and widely utilized bagging algorithm for remote sensing image categorization in a wide range of applications [25]. Random forest is a resilient ensemble learning approach built of numerous decision tree classifiers that overcomes the inadequacies of a single classifier in delivering the best solution. To circumvent this limitation, a random forest algorithm employs many trees rather than just one and assigns a final class label using the majority vote approach [15]. Even though a tiny change in the data might cause a significant change, it can handle overfitting and aid in increasing accuracy. Furthermore, it supports both categorical and continuous values, as well as big data sets with higher dimensionality.

MODEL PERFORMANCE AND EVALUATION

This study attempts to predict customer churn by first comparing eight different aforementioned machine learning techniques. Five evaluation performance metrics (*i.e.*, the AUC score, accuracy, precision score, the F score, and recall score) are employed to compare those machine learning techniques. Table **2** shows the confusion matrix, which is used to assess the predictive algorithms' ability to properly forecast churning clients. True positive and false positive are characterized by the letters A and B, respectively, whilst true negative and false negative are represented by the letters C and D, respectively. Each criterion is explained as follows:

- True positive (A): The number of customers who are actually in positive category (churn) and the model accurately predicts this.
- True negative (B): The number of customers who are actually in negative category (active) and the model accurately predicts this.
- False positive (C): The number of customers who are actually in negative category (active), however, the model inaccurately predicts this.
- False negative (D): The number of customers who are actually in positive category (churn), however the model inaccurately predicts this.

Table 2. The confusion matrix.

-	-	Predicted Class	
-	-	*Churn*	*Active*
Actual Class	*Churn*	A	D
	Active	C	B

Precision is described as the percentage of anticipated positive or negative (churn and active) categories that are changed, and it is determined using equations (1) and (2) as follows:

$$Precision_{churn} = \frac{A}{A+C}, \tag{1}$$

$$Precision_{active} = \frac{B}{B+D}. \tag{2}$$

The fragment of correctly predicted positive (churn) and negative (active) cases is called *recall*, and it is computed as follows:

$$Recall_{churn} = \frac{A}{A+B},\qquad(3)$$

$$Recall_{active} = \frac{C}{C+D}.\qquad(4)$$

Accuracy is the fraction of all numbers correctly predicted positive (churn) and negative (active), and it is calculated using equation (5) as follows:

$$Accuracy = \frac{A+C}{A+B+C+D}.\qquad(5)$$

F score is a harmonic average of accuracy and recall scores that is frequently used as a single performance measure. A score closer to 1 indicates that a particular approach obtains a higher combination of precision and recall, implying that it performs well in predicting the model. It is calculated as follows:

$$F\ score = \frac{(2 \times Precision \times Recall)}{Precision+Recall}.\qquad(6)$$

Another performance evaluation method used in this study is the AUC score. It is a performance statistic that considers all classification criteria. AUC score can be calculated by comparing the likelihood that the model would rate a random negative example lower than a random positive example. The AUC score of zero denotes a model with 100% incorrect predictions, whereas the AUC score of one denotes a model with 100% right predictions [14].

RESULT

Result of the comparison among eight different machine learning techniques using five predefined performance evaluation metrics is shown in Table **3**. The scores vary from 0 to 1 that can be translated as a proportion representing the measurement to select which algorithm is more effective for detecting relationships and patterns among parameters of the dataset. Accordingly, a score of 0 (0%) implies a technique is not error-free, whilst a score of 1 (100%) indicates flawless accuracy.

Table 3. A comparison among eight machine learning techniques.

Machine Learning Techniques	Evaluation Performance Metrics				
	Accuracy	F Score	Recall Score	Precision Score	AUC Score
Gradient booster	0.595	0.610	0.638	0.585	0.639
Ridge classifier	0.588	0.625	0.691	0.571	0.589
Adaptive boosting	0.578	0.587	0.603	0.572	0.587
Bagging classifier	0.771	0.702	0.543	0.992	0.989
Logistic regression	0.589	0.627	0.694	0.571	0.636
Decision tree	0.635	0.667	0.736	0.610	0.700
Random forest	0.809	0.764	0.619	0.996	0.994
k-nearest neighbor	0.976	0.976	0.996	0.957	0.988

Overall, kNN surpasses other machine learning techniques and offers the best comprehensive assessment result by correctly predicting data with 97.6%, 98.8%, 95.7%, 99.6%, and 97.6% for accuracy, AUC score, precision score, recall score, and F score, respectively. Despite kNN having moderately lower results in the precision score and AUC score, kNN stands strong with the highest score for the rest of the parameters. Furthermore, the proportion for the churn customer is 35.57% while the non-churn customer is 64.43% using this algorithm.

In comparison to kNN, decision tree approach gets the second-best performance with 73.6% of recall score and 70.00% of AUC score. Next, the bagging classifier and random forest have somewhat better AUC scores than kNN, with 98.9% and 99.4% for the bagging classifier and random forest, respectively. The remaining machine learning techniques get scores ranging from 50% to 70%.

kNN is then chosen as the best machine learning technique to predict customer churn using this particular dataset. Subsequently, we apply this technique with ten neighbors ($k = 10$) to differentiate the minority (0, 0.1, …, 0.4) and majority class (0.5, 0.6, …, 1.0) [26]. The cut-off is usually set to 0.5 by default. This means that any data with a probability of more than 0.5 is predicted to churn. This rationale follows the logistic regression procedure [27]. The prediction result is depicted in Table **4**. Note that the result is divided into two groups, namely, *churn* with the probability of equal and more than 0.5; and *non-churn* with a probability of less than 0.5.

Table 4. kNN's prediction result.

Non-churn		Churn	
Probability	**Percentage of Customers**	**Probability**	**Percentage of Customers**
0.0	29.93%	0.5	10.38%
0.1	15.65%	0.6	9.66%
0.2	5.19%	0.7	8.78%
0.3	5.07%	0.8	4.28%
0.4	858%	0.9	2.20%
-	-	1.0	0.28%
Total	**64.43%**	**Total**	**35.57%**

The percentage of customers which is likely to churn is forecasted to be around 35.57%, while the non-churner is 64.43%. Among the non-churner, the proportion of customers with zero likelihood to churn is the greatest, with 29.93%. On the other hand, for churn category, the probability of 0.5 has the highest value of the percentage of customers with 10.38%; while customers with 100% certainty to churn are the least predicted, with only 0.28% of the total customers.

After categorizing the result into two groups, more information about customers' attributes is extracted, such as service, payment habits, and duration of stay, see Table **5**.

Table 5. Classification of the different groups according to customers' attributes.

Variables	Categories	Group 1	Group 2	Total
		Non-churned	Churned	
Billing amount (IDR)	Under 100K	3.41%	4.36%	3.88%
	100K – 300K	33.87%	29.32%	31.59%
	300K – 500K	50.75%	53.82%	52.29%
	500K – 1.000K	11.16%	11.52%	11.34%
	> 1.000K	0.82%	0.99%	0.90%
Length of stay (month)	< 12	15.86%	1.81%	8.84%
	12-18	46.24%	32.07%	39.16%
	18-24	19.87%	48.34%	34.11%
	> 24	18.02%	17.78%	17.90%
-	10-30	4.71%	56.96%	30.84%

(Table 5) cont.....

Variables	Categories	Group 1 Non-churned	Group 2 Churned	Total
Speed (Mbps)	30-50	25.01%	34.69%	29.85%
	50-100	51.59%	4.62%	28.10%
	> 100	18.70%	3.72%	11.21%
Payment date	Late	38.12%	72.86%	55.49%
	Not late	61.88%	27.14%	44.51%
Number of problems tickets per person	< 10	95.20%	7.75%	51.48%
	10-20	4.80%	53.14%	28.97%
	> 20	0.00%	39.11%	39.11%

Group 1 is labeled as non-churned customers. They are customers which have the likelihood to stay using the existing service by the company. This group has a proportion of 64.43% of total customers from the dataset. More than half of the group (50.75%) have billing amount between IDR 300K to 500K monthly; 95.20% have no trouble experience; and 51.59% use an internet speed of 50 to 100 Mbps. A larger part of the group (*i.e.*, 61.88%) do not have payment issues and have stayed with the company for around 12 to 18 months (46.24%).

Group 2 is labeled as churned customers. They are customers which are likely to leave the company by terminating the service. Based on the billing amount, this group has a similarity to Group 1. Most of the churners (53.82%) must pay IDR 300K – 500K monthly for Wi-Fi service, while customers who pay more than IDR 1,000K monthly have the least proportion (0.99%). It can be concluded that the amount of money paid by the customers does not affect whether the customers will churn or not. According to Table **5**, we can see that among the churners, customers with a length of stay between 18 to 24 months have a greater number than the others (48.34%). This is a result of the fact that the company applies a minimum of a twelve-month subscription contract for the "Terms of Service". If a customer terminates the service and breaches the contract, they have to pay IDR 1,000K penalty. The highest portion of the internet speed from this group is 10 Mbps to 30 Mbps (56.96%). Speaking of the service quality, the majority of the churners have reported an issue/problem regarding their internet connection 10 to 20 times in the last six months (53.14%); and have experienced more than 20 times issues in the past six months (39.11%). This leads to the fact that the company no longer offers low-speed packages for existing customers, or they are switching to other internet service providers due to price competition. In addition, customers with 10 Mbps to 30 Mbps are not provided with premium modem or optical network terminal; thus, the connection is less stable than the higher speeds provided with premium optical network terminal. About 72.86% of the group have experienced payment problems. Based on the company's statement, late payment could be one of the greatest symptoms of customer churn. The company's billing cycle ends in the starts from the fifth and ends every 21st of each month. If the customers do not pay their bills by that time, the internet will be temporarily disabled. The customers often get angry, and this could lead to a more severe problem which is a problem ticket raised by the customers, and/or they will likely want to terminate their service permanently.

CONCLUDING REMARKS

This study aims to predict the likelihood of the customer to churn according to the dataset from Indonesian telecommunication company. This study is expected to give such contributions to the related literature of machine learning applications for prediction, specifically in predicting customer churn in the telecommunication company. The findings of this study showed that kNN algorithm has the best result among other machine learning techniques, which is evaluated using the AUC score, recall, accuracy, precision, and the F score. The algorithm predicts 64.43% as the percentage of non-churned customers and 35.57% as the percentage of churned customers. The non-churned customers are the customers who are likely to stay with the company and keep using the service. They have the following characteristics: billing amount between IDR 300K to 500K, have been using the service for 12 to 18 months, do not have any payment issues, have less connection trouble, and rarely face payment difficulty. On the other hand, the churned customers are those who have the likelihood to terminate the service. The characteristics of this group are: billing amount between IDR 300K to 500K, have stayed with the company for more than 12 months, subscribe low-speed packages (10 to 30 Mbps), frequently face connection issues, and often pay late.

Several recommendations could be addressed for the particular company as well as other telecommunication companies as follows. Establishing a decent churn prediction system could be a proactive solution to prevent churning customers. A good strategical plan and after-sales strategy are a great way to boost customer experience for reactive solution for existing customers.

Finally, for future research, a smart recommendation based on a machine learning approach may be included for broader and expanded results and analysis. Furthermore, the data used in this study is restricted to a single organization. A larger, more diverse, and complete database from other telecommunication companies should be included to increase the significance and provide a generalized conclusion.

NOTES:

[1] The asterisk sign (*) is used to look for a root word as well as all the words constructed by adding letters to the end (or beginning) of it.

REFERENCES

[1] M. Stone, "The evolution of the telecommunications industry : What can we learn from it?", *J. Direct. Data. Digit. Mark. Pract.,* vol. 16, no. 3, pp. 157-165, 2015.
[http://dx.doi.org/10.1057/dddmp.2014.80]

[2] H. Chen, R.H.L. Chiang, and V.C. Storey, "Business intelligence and analytics: From big data to big impact", *Manage. Inf. Syst. Q.,* vol. 36, no. 4, pp. 1165-1188, 2012.
[http://dx.doi.org/10.2307/41703503]

[3] C.P. Wei, and I.T. Chiu, "Turning telecommunications call details to churn prediction: A data mining approach", *Expert Syst. Appl.,* vol. 23, no. 2, pp. 103-112, 2002.
[http://dx.doi.org/10.1016/S0957-4174(02)00030-1]

[4] S.A. Qureshi, A.S. Rehman, A.M. Qamar, A. Kamal, and A. Rehman, "Telecommunication subscribers' churn prediction model using machine learning", *Eighth Int. Conf.Dig. Inform. Manag.,* pp. 131-136, 2013.
[http://dx.doi.org/10.1109/ICDIM.2013.6693977]

[5] E. Ascarza, R. Iyengar, and M. Schleicher, "The perils of proactive churn prevention using plan recommendations: Evidence from a field experiment", *J. Mark. Res.,* vol. 53, no. 1, pp. 46-60, 2016.
[http://dx.doi.org/10.1509/jmr.13.0483]

[6] D. Radosavljevik, P. van der Putten, and K.K. Larsen, "The impact of experimental setup in prepaid churn prediction for mobile telecommunications: What to predict, for whom and does the customer experience matter?", *Trans. Mach. Learn. Data. Min.,* vol. 3, no. 2, pp. 80-99, 2010.

[7] A. Idzikowski, P. Kuryło, J. Cyganiuk, and M. Ryczko, "Customer relationship management (CRM) : Philosophy and its significance for ehe enterprise", *System Safety: Human : Technical facility : Environment.,* vol. 1, no. 1, pp. 1004-1011, 2019.

[8] J. Stasieńko, "Information models of customers in CRM And E-CRM Systems", Information and Engineering Systems, 2007, pp. 182-189.

[9] M. Komorowski, D.C. Marshall, J.D. Salciccioli, and Y. Crutain, "Exploratory data analysis". *Analy. Electr. Health. Rec.* Springer: Cham, 2016, pp. 185-203.
[http://dx.doi.org/10.1007/978-3-319-43742-2_15]

[10] P. Mongeon, and A. Paul-Hus, "The journal coverage of web of science and scopus: A comparative analysis", *Scientometrics,* vol. 106, no. 1, pp. 213-228, 2016.
[http://dx.doi.org/10.1007/s11192-015-1765-5]

[11] E.P. Hartati, Adiwijaya, and M.A. Bijaksana, "Handling imbalance data in churn prediction using combined smote and rus with bagging method", *J. Phys. Conf. Ser.,* vol. 971, no. 1, p. 012007, 2018.
[http://dx.doi.org/10.1088/1742-6596/971/1/012007]

[12] A. Alamsyah, and N. Salma, "A comparative study of employee churn prediction model", *Proc. 4th Int. Conf. Sci. Tech.,* pp. 1-4, 2018.
[http://dx.doi.org/10.1109/ICSTC.2018.8528586]

[13] M.M. Ulkhaq, A.T. Wibowo, M.R. Tribosnia, R. Putawara, and A.B. Firdauz, "Predicting customer churn: A comparison of eight machine learning techniques: A case study in an indonesian telecommunication company", *Proc. Int. Conf. Data. Analy. Busin. Ind.,* pp. 42-46, 2021.
[http://dx.doi.org/10.1109/ICDABI53623.2021.9655790]

[14] B. Huang, M.T. Kechadi, and B. Buckley, "Customer churn prediction in telecommunications", *Exp.*

Syst. Appl., vol. 39, no. 1, pp. 1414-1425, 2012.
[http://dx.doi.org/10.1016/j.eswa.2011.08.024]

[15]   L. Breiman, "Random forests", *Mach. Learn.,* vol. 45, no. 1, pp. 5-32, 2001.
[http://dx.doi.org/10.1023/A:1010933404324]

[16]   C. Tirink, S.H. Abaci, and H. Önder, "Comparison of ridge regression and least squares methods in the presence of multicollinearity for body measurements in saanen kids", *J. Ins. Sci. Tech.,* vol. 10, no. 2, pp. 1429-1437, 2020.
[http://dx.doi.org/10.21597/jist.671662]

[17]   A. Natekin, and A. Knoll, "Gradient boosting machines, a tutorial", *Front. Neurorobot.,* vol. 7, no. 21, p. 21, 2013.
[PMID: 24409142]

[18]   M.A. Friedl, and C.E. Brodley, "Decision tree classification of land cover from remotely sensed data", *Remote Sens. Environ.,* vol. 61, no. 3, pp. 399-409, 1997.
[http://dx.doi.org/10.1016/S0034-4257(97)00049-7]

[19]   G.J. Briem, J.A. Benediktsson, and J.R. Sveinsson, "Multiple classifiers applied to multisource remote sensing data", *IEEE Trans. Geosci. Remote Sens.,* vol. 40, no. 10, pp. 2291-2299, 2002.
[http://dx.doi.org/10.1109/TGRS.2002.802476]

[20]   T. Vafeiadis, K.I. Diamantaras, G. Sarigiannidis, and K.C. Chatzisavvas, "A comparison of machine learning techniques for customer churn prediction", *Simul. Model. Pract. Theory,* vol. 55, pp. 1-9, 2015.
[http://dx.doi.org/10.1016/j.simpat.2015.03.003]

[21]   S.B. Kotsiantis, G.E. Tsekouras, and P.E. Pintelas, Bagging model trees for classification problems.*Adv. Inform.,* P. Bozanis, E.N. Houstis, Eds., Springer: Berlin, 2005, pp. 328-337.
[http://dx.doi.org/10.1007/11573036_31]

[22]   L. Breiman, "Bagging predictors", *Mach. Learn.,* vol. 24, no. 2, pp. 123-140, 1996.
[http://dx.doi.org/10.1007/BF00058655]

[23]   M. Pal, and P.M. Mather, "An assessment of the effectiveness of decision tree methods for land cover classification", *Remote Sens. Environ.,* vol. 86, no. 4, pp. 554-565, 2003.
[http://dx.doi.org/10.1016/S0034-4257(03)00132-9]

[24]   J. Liang, Q. Liu, N. Nie, B. Zeng, and Z. Zhang, "An improved algorithm based on KNN and random forest", *Proc. 3rd Int. Conf. Comp. Sci. Appl. Eng.,* pp. 1-6, 2019.
[http://dx.doi.org/10.1145/3331453.3360963]

[25]   M. Mahdianpari, H. Jafarzadeh, J.E. Granger, F. Mohammadimanesh, B. Brisco, B. Salehi, S. Homayouni, and Q. Weng, "A large-scale change monitoring of wetlands using time series landsat imagery on google earth engine: A case study in newfoundland", *GIsci. Remote Sens.,* vol. 57, no. 8, pp. 1102-1124, 2020.
[http://dx.doi.org/10.1080/15481603.2020.1846948]

[26]   N. Verbiest, C. Cornelis, and R. Jensen, "Fuzzy rough positive region based nearest neighbour classification", *Proc. 2012 IEEE Int. Conf. Fuzzy. Sys.,* pp. 1-7, 2012.
[http://dx.doi.org/10.1109/FUZZ-IEEE.2012.6251337]

[27]   M.M. Ulkhaq, A.K. Widodo, M F A. Yulianto, Widhiyaningrum, A. Mustikasari, and P.Y. Akshinta, "A logistic regression approach to model the willingness of consumers to adopt renewable energy sources", *IOP Conf. Ser. Earth Environ. Sci.,* vol. 127, no. 1, p. 012007, 2018.
[http://dx.doi.org/10.1088/1755-1315/127/1/012007]

A State-Wise Assessment of Greenhouse Gases Emission in India by Applying K-mean Clustering Technique

Nitin Jaglal Untwal[1,*]

[1] Maharashtra Institute of Technology, Aurangabad, India

Abstract: India is a vast country with variations in geography as well as in population density. The pollution in India is increasing day by day. The Greenhouse gas emission is on the rise due to various activities like agriculture, industry, power generation, transportation, *etc.* Carbon dioxide (CO_2), Carbon Monoxide (CO), and Methane (CH_4) are the major elements in greenhouse gases. The emission of greenhouse gases causes various threats to the environment and health. The states in India have been under development since independence. Various activities are on the rise. The states are not having balanced growth as far as the industrial and agriculture sectors are concerned. The powerhouse of industrial growth is the state of Maharashtra and Gujarat. The population density is also scattered in India. The states contribute differently to greenhouse gases emission and it is difficult for the government to make policy category-wise for the control of greenhouse gases emissions. The classification of states into different categories will help in the strategic formulation of policy and strategy for different states depending on their greenhouse gases emission and per capita analysis of these emissions. The per capita greenhouse gas emission is calculated by dividing the total emissions by the total population. After analyzing the above problem, the researchers have decided to conduct the study titled A state-wise Assessment of greenhouse gas emission in India by applying the K-mean Clustering Technique using Python Programming. Research is carried out in Five steps -Feature extraction and engineering, Data extraction, Standardizing and Scaling, Identification of Clusters, Cluster formation. The study period is 2020. The data selected for analysis is yearly data state-wise of different Indian states. Data taken for the study is from the Kaggle database. Findings - The k- mean algorithm (cluster analysis using Python Programming) classifies the states of India into three clusters. Cluster one includes 16 states of India *viz.* Arunachal, Assam, Bihar, Himachal Pradesh, Jammu & Kashmir, Jharkhand, Madhya Pradesh, Manipur, Meghalaya, Mizoram, Odisha, Rajasthan, Sikkim, Tripura, Uttar Pradesh, Uttarakhand. Cluster two includes 8 states of the India. *Viz* Andhra Pradesh, Goa, Gujarat, Karnataka, Kerala, Maharashtra, Tamilnadu, West Bengal. Cluster three includes 4 states of India *Viz* Haryana, Nagaland, Punjab, Chhattisgarh. The major contributors to greenhouse gase emission are in cluster three.

[*] **Corresponding author Nitin Jaglal Untwal:** Maharashtar Institute of Technology, Aurangabad, India;
E-mail: nitinuntwal@gmail.com

Biswadip Basu Mallik, Kirti Verma, Rahul Kar, Ashok Kumar Shaw & Sardar M. N. Islam (Naz) (Eds.)

The medium-range emission for greenhouse gases emission are grouped in cluster two and Minimum Range greenhouse gase emission states are included in cluster one.

Keywords: Carbon emission, Data extraction, Feature extraction and engineering, K-mean clustering, Python programming, Standardizing and scaling.

INTRODUCTION

India is a vast country with variations in geography as well as in population density. The pollution in India is increasing day by day. The Greenhouse gase emission is on a rise due to various activities like agriculture, industry, power generation, transportation, *etc.* Carbon dioxide (CO_2), Carbon Monoxide (CO), and Methane (CH_4) are the major elements in greenhouse gases. The emission of greenhouse gases causes various threats to the environment and health. The states in India have been under development since independence. Various activities are on the rise. The states are not having balanced growth as far as the industrial and agriculture sectors are concerned. The powerhouse of industrial growth is the state of Maharashtra and Gujarat. The population density is also scattered in India. The contribution of states contributes differently to greenhouse gases emission and it is difficult for the government to make policy category-wise for the control of greenhouse gase emissions. The classification of states in different categories will help in the strategic formulation of policy and strategy for different states depending on their greenhouse gase emission and per capita analysis of greenhouse gase emissions. The per capita greenhouse gase emission is calculated by dividing the total emissions by the total population. After analyzing the above problem the researcher hat decided to conduct the study titled A state-wise Assessment of greenhouse gases emission by Applying the Clustering Technique to different states of India. Research is carried out in Five steps -Feature extraction and engineering, Data extraction, Standardizing and Scaling, Identification of Clusters, Cluster formation.

Introduction to Cluster Analysis

Machine learning includes unsupervised learning under for which models are trained for unlabeled data sets and are allowed to act without any supervision. Unsupervised learning is applied to understand the meaningful patterns, the grouping inherent in data, and extraction of the generative features. Unsupervised learning is an algorithm that learns patterns from untagged data or unlabelled data.

Cluster analysis is used to determine similarities and dissimilarities in a given data set or objects. Data usually have some similarities which enable us to categorize or group them into clusters. The k-mean clustering is non-hierarchical. The reason for the popularity of k-means clustering is its simplicity. K means clustering is a type of partitioning method having objects as data observations with the nearest location and distance from each other. The nearest objects form mutually exclusive clusters. Each cluster has its centroid which makes clusters distinctive [1, 2].

Clustering is one of the important machine learning algorithms. Clustering is a technique of grouping elements; it is an important method for classification and grouping. K-mean clustering is used to classify elements into different categories based on the nearest distance from the mean. The main objective of K-mean clustering is creating a partition of n objects into k-clusters [3, 4, 5, 6]. Objects belonging to different clusters are considered based on the nearest mean. The method produces exactly k different clusters of greatest possible difference which is known as a priori. K-mean clustering reduces the total intra-cluster variance or the squared error function [7, 8, 9, 10].

It is represented by the equation:

$$J = \sum_{j=1}^{k} \sum_{i=1}^{n} \left\| x_i^{(j)} - c_j \right\|^2 \qquad (1)$$

Where J is the objective function, k is the number of clusters, n is a number of cases, x is a number of cases i, c_j is a number of the centroid.

Drawbacks of k mean clustering:

a. The early-stage clusters affect the overall results.
b. When dataset size is small clustering is not accurate.
c. As we give variables the same weightage we do not know which variable occupies more relevance in the clustering process.
d. The noise can reduce the accuracy of the mean which further pulls the centroid away from its original position.

How to overcome the above drawbacks:

a. To increase the accuracy data set should also be increased
b. Use median to prevent outlier (Noise)

Research Methodology

Data Source

Data taken for the study is from the Kaggle database

Period of Study

The study period is 2020. The data selected for analysis is yearly data state-wise of different Indian states.

Software used for Data Analysis

Python Programming

Model Applied

For purpose of this study, we had applied K-mean clustering

Limitations of the Study

The study is restricted to only cluster analysis for Green House Gases state-wise (India).

Future Scope

A similar kind of cluster analysis can be done for the different districts at the micro-level.

Research is Carried Out in Five Steps

- Feature extraction and engineering

- Data extraction

- Standardizing and Scaling

- Identification of Clusters

- Cluster formation

Feature Extraction and Engineering

Feature engineering is an important element of the machine learning pipeline. For the suitable representation of data, we need to craft the given raw data. The raw data need to be evaluated by applying domain knowledge, mathematical transformations, *etc* to get good features. It also needs to process and wrangler for making it ready to be used for machine learning models or algorithms. It is very difficult to create a good machine learning model unless we have an in-depth idea about feature engineering.Frames consist of a collection of slots and slot values.

The slot contains information about the entities which are as follows:

a. Frame identification
b. Relationship with other frames
c. The descriptor of the requirement for frame
d. Procedural information
e. New instance information

Data Extraction

It is the procedure of obtaining data from an external source and making it usable for a programme, as depicted in Fig. (**1**). The Government of Maharashtra's website will provide the raw data for this study in the form of an Excel file. Maha is the name of the Excel file. The Python programme uses the code below to retrieve Excel. Before starting the feature extraction and cluster analysis in python programming we need to import different libraries in python such as Panda, matplotlib, sklearn.clusterimport KMeans.

Standardizing and Scaling

The machine learning algorithm can work efficiently only when the input variables are standardized and scaled properly to a given range since the data had a huge variation that needs to be converted into scaling as shown in Fig. (**3**). When there is a good amount of variation in the data set it needs to be converted to equal magnitude. The difference in magnitude can create difficulty since the K-means algorithm is a distance-based algorithm. Scaling can be done by applying standardizing method. Standardizing is the method where we bring down the standard deviation and mean of features to 1 and 0.

By applying python code as shown in Fig. (**3**).

Identification of Clusters by Elbow Method

The Elbow method is used to define several clusters in a given data set. In this method, we plot the explained variation as a function of clusters. The elbow of the curves defines the number of clusters. This indicates the definite number of clusters and adding more clusters does not give much better modeling data.

```
In [1]:  # importing required libraries
         import pandas as pd
         import numpy as np
         import matplotlib.pyplot as plt
         %matplotlib inline
         from sklearn.cluster import KMeans
```

```
In [2]:  import pandas as pd

         data = pd.read_csv (r'C:\Users\nitin\Desktop\CarbonEmissionIndia.csv
         print (data)
                        States   per capita CO2 (kg per person)   \
         0        Andhra Pradesh                          974.17
         1             Arunachal                          405.90
         2                 Assam                          340.91
         3                 Bihar                          179.01
         4            Chattisgarh                         1963.88
         5                   Goa                          2682.51
         6               Gujarat                          1310.58
         7               Haryana                          1381.86
         8      Himachal Pradesh                           784.16
         9      Jammu & Kashmir                            509.03
         10            Jharkhand                          1403.43
         11            Karnataka                           888.86
         12               Kerala                           780.12
         13       Madhya Pradesh                           656.37
         14          Maharashtra                           936.70
         15              Manipur                           379.20
         16            Meghalaya                           691.53
         17              Mizoram                           754.71
         18             Nagaland                          1275.27
         19              Odhisha                           700.13
         20               Punjab                          1618.08
         21            Rajasthan                           793.69
         22               Sikkim                           711.39
         23            Tamilnadu                           985.70
         24              Tripura                           295.64
         25        Uttar Pradesh                           404.26
         26          Uttarakhand                           493.01
         27          West Bengal                           763.13

              per capita CO (kg per person)   per capita CH4 (kg per person)
         0                            27.18                            16.97
         1                            17.43                            25.82
         2                            16.63                            21.29
         3                             8.83                             9.59
         4                            17.56                            22.37
         5                            23.12                             7.62
         6                            24.01                            12.26
         7                            17.90                            21.57
         8                            16.98                            18.28
         9                            15.59                            14.42
         10                           15.02                            15.39
         11                           24.93                            12.20
         12                           18.29                             4.52
         13                           16.14                            15.15
         14                           23.58                             9.80
         15                           10.80                            22.63
         16                           12.65                            19.80
         17                           15.40                            10.72
         18                           24.13                            29.08
         19                           18.40                            19.88
         20                           27.90                            33.38
```

Fig. (1). Showing data fetching in Python Environment.

Data is cleaned by removing the States column from the data frame by applying python code below Fig. (**2**):

```
In [3]:  # Remove DISTRICT columns
         data.drop(['Country'], axis=1, inplace=True)
         data.shape

Out[3]:  (231, 267)
```

Fig. (2). Showing data cleaning by dropping the countries column from the Data frame.

```
In [5]:  # standardizing the data
         from sklearn.preprocessing import StandardScaler
         scaler = StandardScaler()
         data_scaled = scaler.fit_transform(data)

         # statistics of scaled data
         pd.DataFrame(data_scaled).describe()
```

Out[5]:

	0	1	2	3	4	5
count	2.310000e+02	2.310000e+02	2.310000e+02	2.310000e+02	2.310000e+02	2.310000e+02	2.
mean	1.902038e-16	1.898433e-16	2.053432e-16	1.902038e-16	1.902038e-16	2.053432e-16	1
std	1.002172e+00	1.002172e+00	1.002172e+00	1.002172e+00	1.002172e+00	1.002172e+00	1
min	-1.147079e-01	-1.147079e-01	-1.147079e-01	-1.147079e-01	-1.147079e-01	-1.147079e-01	
25%	-1.147079e-01	-1.147079e-01	-1.147079e-01	-1.147079e-01	-1.147079e-01	-1.147079e-01	
50%	-1.147079e-01	-1.147079e-01	-1.147079e-01	-1.147079e-01	-1.147079e-01	-1.147079e-01	
75%	-1.147079e-01	-1.147079e-01	-1.147079e-01	-1.147079e-01	-1.147079e-01	-1.147079e-01	
max	8.717798e+00	8.717798e+00	8.717798e+00	8.717798e+00	8.717798e+00	8.717798e+00	8

8 rows × 267 columns

Fig. (3). Showing Descriptive statistics for scaled data.

There are various tools to measure explained variation. Explained variation measures the ratio to which a given model accounts for dispersion. Variation is measured by variance. Increasing the number of clusters improves the fit (Explained Variation) as more parameters (clusters) are used but this is overfitting and the elbow method removes this constraint. In clustering identification, the number of k identification is a difficult task. The optimum number of k can be defined by applying the Elbow method.

Inertia is the measure of how well defined are the clusters in a data set by applying the k mean. It is calculated by measuring the distance between the data points and their centroid, calculating the square of the distance, and further adding these squares across one cluster. An optimum model is one having lower inertia and less number of clusters.

The equation below demonstrates how to calculate the equivalent of the within-cluster inertia:

$$Inertia\ (k) = \sum_{i \in C\_k} (y_{ik} - \mu\_k)^2 \qquad (2)$$

where μ_k is the mean of cluster k and C_k corresponds to the set of indices of genes attributed to cluster k.

Now, we will carry out the process of cluster identification by creating an Elbow plot and further by calculating Inertia. In Fig. (**4**), we will calculate Inertia. Inertia is the sum of square error for each cluster hence lowering the inertia denser of the clusters. By applying the Python code below:

```
In [6]:  # defining the kmeans function with initialization as k-means++
         kmeans = KMeans(n_clusters=6, init='k-means++')

         # fitting the k means algorithm on scaled data
         kmeans.fit(data_scaled)
Out[6]:  KMeans(n_clusters=6)


In [7]:  # inertia on the fitted data
         kmeans.inertia_
Out[7]:  355.20251840695227
```

Fig. (4). Showing clusters formation for scaled data.

Cluster formation

As we apply the python code below and we get the results for clusters 1 to 3 for different states of India according to their characteristics and features (Fig. **5**).

RESULTS AND ANALYSIS

We categorized the data selected for analysis state-wise into 3 clusters (Fig. **6**) in Python.

The k- mean algorithm (cluster analysis using Python Programming) classifies the states of India into three clusters. Cluster one includes 16 states of India *viz.* Arunachal, Assam, Bihar, Himachal Pradesh, Jammu & Kashmir, Jharkhand, Madhya Pradesh, Manipur, Meghalaya, Mizoram, Odisha, Rajasthan, Sikkim, Tripura, Uttar Pradesh, Uttarakhand. Cluster two includes 8 states of the India *Viz* Andhra Pradesh, Goa, Gujarat, Karnataka, Kerala, Maharashtra, Tamilnadu, West Bengal. Cluster three includes 4 states of the India *Viz* Haryana, Nagaland, Punjab, Chhattisgarh.

```
In [9]:  # k means using 5 clusters and k-means++ initialization
         kmeans = KMeans(n_jobs = -1, n_clusters = 3, init='k-means++')
         kmeans.fit(data_scaled)
         pred = kmeans.predict(data_scaled)

         C:\Users\nitin\anaconda3\lib\site-packages\sklearn\cluster\_kmeans.py:938: Futu
         reWarning: 'n_jobs' was deprecated in version 0.23 and will be removed in 0.25.
           warnings.warn("'n_jobs' was deprecated in version 0.23 and will be"


In [10]:  frame = pd.DataFrame(data_scaled)
          frame['cluster'] = pred
          frame['cluster'].value_counts()

Out[10]:  0    16
          1     8
          2     4
          Name: cluster, dtype: int64
```

Fig. (5). Showing clusters formation results with classification for scaled data.

```
In [24]:  print(frame)

                      0         1         2  cluster
          0    0.148338  1.720856  0.064920        1
          1   -0.908414 -0.167155  1.430563        0
          2   -1.029269 -0.322068  0.731539        0
          3   -1.330337 -1.832477 -1.073887        0
          4    1.988797 -0.141981  0.898194        2
          5    3.287966  0.934669 -1.377877        1
          6    0.773924  1.107011 -0.661879        1
          7    0.906476 -0.076143  0.774746        2
          8   -0.205004 -0.254294  0.267066        0
          9   -0.716634 -0.523456 -0.328570        0
          10   0.946588 -0.633832 -0.178889        0
          11  -0.010304  1.285162 -0.671138        1
          12  -0.212516 -0.000622 -1.856238        1
          13  -0.442641 -0.416953 -0.215924        0
          14   0.078659  1.023745 -1.041482        1
          15  -0.958065 -1.451002  0.938314        0
          16  -0.377258 -1.092764  0.501617        0
          17  -0.259769 -0.560248 -0.899516        0
          18   0.708262  1.130248  1.933613        2
          19  -0.361265  0.020678  0.513962        0
          20   1.345750  1.860279  2.597146        2
          21  -0.187282 -0.767445 -0.365604        0
          22  -0.340326 -1.280597 -1.004447        0
          23   0.169779  1.608544 -0.948896        1
          24  -1.113453 -0.103253  0.413661        0
          25  -0.911464 -1.141175 -0.567750        0
          26  -0.746425 -0.777128  0.213058        0
          27  -0.244111  0.851403 -0.086303        1
```

Fig. (6). Showing different clusters.

Cluster One

Cluster one includes 16 states of India *viz*. Arunachal, Assam, Bihar, Himachal Pradesh, Jammu & Kashmir, Jharkhand, Madhya Pradesh, Manipur, Meghalaya, Mizoram, Odisha, Rajasthan, Sikkim, Tripura, Uttar Pradesh, Uttarakhand. In cluster one the highest carbon dioxide per capita is observed in Jharkhand state with 1043.43 per kg per person which is way above the national average of 894.40 per kg per person (Table **1**). Cluster one average carbon dioxide is 593.89 per capita CO_2. The electricity generation plants are the major source of CO_2.> emission in Jharkhand, besides transportation and industrial process emission. The lowest CO_2 emission was observed in the state of Bihar with 179.01, which is below the national average and cluster one average.

Table 1. Showing greenhouse gases per capita and different cluster classifications.

State	Per Capita CO_2 (Kg Per Person)	Per Capita CO (Kg Per Person)	Per Capita CH_4 (Kg Per Person)	Cluster
Andhra Pradesh	974.17	27.18	16.97	1
Arunachal	405.9	17.43	25.82	0
Assam	340.91	16.63	21.29	0
Bihar	179.01	8.83	9.59	0
Chattisgarh	1963.88	17.56	22.37	2
Goa	2662.51	23.12	7.62	1
Gujarat	1310.58	24.01	12.26	1
Haryana	1381.86	17.9	21.57	2
HimachalPradesh	784.16	16.98	18.28	0
Jammu &Kashmir	509.03	15.59	14.42	0
Jharkhand	1403.43	15.02	15.39	0
Karnataka	888.86	24.93	12.2	1
Kerala	780.12	18.29	4.52	1
MadhyaPradesh	656.37	16.14	15.15	0
Maharashtra	936.7	23.58	9.8	1
Manipur	379.2	10.8	22.63	0
Meghalaya	691.53	12.65	19.8	0
Mizoram	754.71	15.4	10.72	0
Nagaland	1275.27	24.13	29.08	2
Odisha	700.13	18.4	19.88	0
Punjab	1618.08	27.9	33.38	2

(Table 1) cont.....

State	Per Capita CO_2 (Kg Per Person)	Per Capita CO (Kg Per Person)	Per Capita CH_4 (Kg Per Person)	Cluster
Rajasthan	793.69	14.33	14.18	0
Sikkim	711.39	11.68	10.04	0
Tamilnadu	985.7	26.6	10.4	1
Tripura	295.64	17.76	19.23	0
UttarPradesh	404.26	12.4	12.87	0
Uttarakhand	493.01	14.28	17.93	0
West Bengal	763.13	22.69	15.99	1
Average	894.4010714	18.29321429	16.54928571	-
Max	2662.51	27.9	33.38	-
Min	179.01	8.83	4.52	-

The highest CO_2 emission in cluster one is registered in the state of Odisha which is slightly above the national average of 18.29 per capita CO. The average per capita CO_2 is 14.64 kg per person for cluster one which is below the national average of 27.9 per capita CO. The CO_2 level in Odhisha is higher because of petrol and diesel emission by vehicles which played a havoc role. The minimum CO_2 per capita is registered with Bihar 9.59 per capita CO.

The highest CH_4 is measured in Arunachal Pradesh with 25.82 kg per person which is way above the national average of 16.54 per capita CH_4. The livestock rearing and agriculture activities are the reason responsible for a high level of CH_4. in the state (Table 2). The state ranked third in CH_4 emission after Nagaland and Punjab. The minimum CH_4 is registered with Bihar 9.59 per capita CH_4.

Table 2. Showing average, minimum, and maximum greenhouse gases for cluster one.

State	Per Capita CO_2 (kg per person)	Per Capita CO (kg per person)	Per Capita CH_4 (kg per person)	Cluster
Arunachal	405.9	17.43	25.82	1
Assam	340.91	16.63	21.29	1
Bihar	179.01	8.83	9.59	1
HimachalPradesh	784.16	16.98	18.28	1
Jammu &Kashmir	509.03	15.59	14.42	1
Jharkhand	1403.43	15.02	15.39	1
MadhyaPradesh	656.37	16.14	15.15	1
Manipur	379.2	10.8	22.63	1
Meghalaya	691.53	12.65	19.8	1

(Table 2) cont.....

State	Per Capita CO$_2$ (kg per person)	Per Capita CO (kg per person)	Per Capita CH$_4$ (kg per person)	Cluster
Mizoram	754.71	15.4	10.72	1
Odisha	700.13	18.4	19.88	1
Rajasthan	793.69	14.33	14.18	1
Sikkim	711.39	11.68	10.04	1
Tripura	295.64	17.76	19.23	1
UttarPradesh	404.26	12.4	12.87	1
Uttarakhand	493.01	14.28	17.93	1
Average	593.898125	14.645	16.70125	-
MAX	1403.43	18.4	25.82	-
MIN	179.01	8.83	9.59	-

Cluster Two

Cluster two includes 8 states of India, *Viz* Andhra Pradesh, Goa, Gujarat, Karnataka, Kerala, Maharashtra, Tamilnadu, West Bengal. In cluster two, the state of Goa registered the highest CO$_2$ per capita of 2662.52 which is above the cluster two average of 1162 per capita CO$_2$ (Table **2**). The CO$_2$ per capita in the state of Goa is above the national average of 894.40 per capita CO$_2$. The CO$_2$. per capita in Goa ranks number one in the overall national ranking of CO$_2$ per capita. The reason for high per capita CO$_2$ is energy emission which contributes to ninety percent.

The highest CO$_2$ per capita is measured in the state of Andra Pradesh with 27.18 per capita CO$_2$ which is above the cluster average of 23.8 per capita CO. The reason for high CO$_2$ per capita is transportation emission (Table **3**).

Table 3. Showing Average Minimum and Maximum GHG Emission for cluster two.

State	per Capita CO$_2$ (kg per person)	Per Capita CO (kg per person)	Per Capita CH$_4$ (kg per person)	Cluster
Andhra Pradesh	974.17	27.18	16.97	2
Goa	2662.51	23.12	7.62	2
Gujarat	1310.58	24.01	12.26	2
Karnataka	888.86	24.93	12.2	2
Kerala	780.12	18.29	4.52	2
Maharashtra	936.7	23.58	9.8	2
Tamilnadu	985.7	26.6	10.4	2

(Table 3) cont.....

State	per Capita CO_2 (kg per person)	Per Capita CO (kg per person)	Per Capita CH_4 (kg per person)	Cluster
West Bengal	763.13	22.69	15.99	2
Average	1162.72125	23.8	11.22	-
MAX	2662.51	27.18	16.97	-
MIN	763.13	18.29	4.52	-

The CH_4 is highest in the state of Andra Pradesh because of the agriculture activities. The CH_4 per capita for Andra Pradesh is 16.92 per capita CH_4 which is higher than the average of cluster two of 11.22 per capita CH_4. The CH_4. of Andra Pradesh is almost equal to the national average of 16.52 per capita CH_4. The lowest CH_4. per capita is registered with 4.52 per capita CH_4 emission with the state of Kerala being the lowest in all three clusters.

Cluster Three

Cluster three includes 4 states of India *Viz* Haryana, Nagaland, Punjab, Chhattisgarh (Table 3). In cluster three, the highest CO_2 per capita is observed in Chhattisgarh state with 1963.88 per capita CO_2 which is above the cluster three average of 1559.77 per capita CO_2 and way above the national average of 894.40 per capita CO_2. The reason for high per capita CO_2.> is power plant emission. The lowest CO_2 per capita in cluster three is 1275 registered with Nagaland since the emission of CO_2 is lowest with the lowest CO_2 emission activities and high land coverage with dense forest.

For cluster three the highest CO_2 per capita is measured for the state of Punjab with 27.9 per capita CO_2 which is above the cluster 3 average per capita CO_2 and way above the national average of 18.29 per capita CO. The reason for high CO_2 per capita is due to transportation emissions. The minimum CO_2 per capita is 17.56 kg per person for the state of Haryana (Table 4).

Table 4. Showing Average Minimum and Maximum for Cluster Three.

State	Per Capita CO_2 (kg per person)	Per Capita CO_2 (kg per person)	Per Capita CH_4 (kg per person)	Cluster
Haryana	1381.86	17.9	21.57	3
Nagaland	1275.27	24.13	29.08	3
Punjab	1618.08	27.9	33.38	3
Chhattisgarh	1963.88	17.56	22.37	3
Average	1559.7725	21.8725	26.6	-

(Table 4) cont.....

State	Per Capita CO$_2$ (kg per person)	Per Capita CO$_2$ (kg per person)	Per Capita CH$_4$ (kg per person)	Cluster
MAX	1963.88	27.9	33.38	-
MIN	1275.27	17.56	21.57	-

In cluster three the highest CH$_4$ is registered with the state of Punjab with 33.38 per capita CH$_4$ which is way above the national average of 16.54 per capita CH$_4$. In clusterthree the average per capita CH$_4$. is 26.6 per capita CH$_4$. The reason for a high level of CH$_4$. emissionis agriculture emission.

CONCLUSION

The k- mean algorithm (cluster analysis using Python Programming) classifies the states of India into three clusters. Cluster one includes 16 states of India *viz.* Arunachal, Assam, Bihar, Himachal Pradesh, Jammu & Kashmir, Jharkhand, Madhya Pradesh, Manipur, Meghalaya, Mizoram, Odisha, Rajasthan, Sikkim, Tripura, Uttar Pradesh, Uttarakhand. Cluster two includes 8 states of India *Viz* Andhra Pradesh, Goa, Gujarat, Karnataka, Kerala, Maharashtra, Tamilnadu, West Bengal. Cluster three includes 4 states of India *Viz* Haryana, Nagaland, Punjab, and Chhattisgarh. The major contributors to greenhouse gases emission are in cluster three. The medium-range emission for greenhouse gases emission are grouped in cluster two and Minimum Range greenhouse gases emission states are included in cluster one.

REFERENCES

[1]   A.K. Jain, and R.C. Dubes, "Algorithms for Clustering Data", Prentice-Hall: Englewood Cliffs, NJ, USA, 1988.

[2]   L. Kaufman, and P.J. Rousseeuw, "Finding Groups in Data: An Introduction to Cluster Analysis" Wiley: New York, NY, USA, 1990.
[http://dx.doi.org/10.1002/9780470316801]

[3]   G.J. McLachlan, and K.E. Basford, "Mixture Models: Inference and Appli- cations to Clustering" Marcel Dekker: New York, NY, USA, 1988.

[4]   A. P. Dempster, N. M. Laird, and D. B. Rubin, Maximum likelihood from incomplete data *via* theEMalgorithm (with discussion)., *J. Roy. Stat. Soc., Ser. B, Methodol.,* vol. 39, no. 1, pp. 1-38, 1977.

[5]   J. Yu, C. Chaomurilige, and M.-S. Yang, "On convergence and parameter selection of the EM and DA-EM algorithms for gaussian mixtures", *Pattern Recognit.,* vol. 77, p. 188, 2018.
[http://dx.doi.org/10.1016/j.patcog.2017.12.014]

[6]   A. K. Jain, "Data clustering: 50 years beyond K-means", *Pattern Recognit. Lett.,* vol. 31, no. 8, pp. 651-666, 2010.
[http://dx.doi.org/10.1016/j.patrec.2009.09.011]

[7]   M.-S. Yang, S.-J. Chang-Chien, and Y. Nataliani, "A fully-unsupervised possibilistic C-Means clustering algorithm", *IEEE Access,* vol. 6, pp. 78308-789320, 2018.
[http://dx.doi.org/10.1109/ACCESS.2018.2884956]

[8]   J. MacQueen, "Some methods for classi_cation and analysis of multivariate observations", *Proc. 5th Berkeley Symp. Math. Statist. Probab.,* vol. 1, pp. 281-297, 1967.

[9]   M. Alhawarat, and M. Hegazi, "Revisiting K-Means and topic modeling, a comparison study to cluster arabic documents", *IEEE Access,* vol. 6, pp. 42740-42749, 2018.
[http://dx.doi.org/10.1109/ACCESS.2018.2852648]

[10]   Y. Meng, J. Liang, F. Cao, and Y. He, "A new distance with derivative information for functional k-means clustering algorithm", *Inf. Sci.,* vol. 463, no. C, pp. 166-185, 2018.
[http://dx.doi.org/10.1016/j.ins.2018.06.035]

CHAPTER 12

Data Mining Techniques: New Avenues for Heart Disease Prediction

Soma Das[1,2,*]

[1] *Life Science, B.Ed. Department, Syamaprasad Institute of Education and Training, Kolkata, India*

[2] *Honorary Guest Faculty, Sports Science Department, University of Calcutta, Kolkata, India*

Abstract: The medical management sector assembles a large volume of unexposed data on the health status of patients. At times this hidden data could be useful in diagnosing diseases and making effective decisions. For providing an appropriate way out and planning a diagnostic system based on this information, now-a-days, the newest data mining strategies are in use. In this study, a thorough review has been done on the identification of an effective heart disease prediction system (EHDPS) designed by neural network for the prediction of the risk level of cardiovascular diseases. The study focused on the observation of various medical parameters, namely, age, height, weight, BMI, sex, blood pressure, cholesterol, and obesity. Based on this study, a concept map has been designed on the prediction ways for individuals with heart disease with the help of EHDPS. The study assembled considerable information about the multilayer perceptron neural network with rear proliferation as the algorithm for data analysis. The current review work may be significant in establishing knowledge of the association between health factors related to the risk level of heart disease. The study also suggests means of early intervention and prevention of medical emergencies posed by the late detection of cardiovascular diseases, especially in the context of post COVID 19 complications.

Keywords: Data mining, Disease detection, Heart diseases, Neural network, Risk factors.

INTRODUCTION

The noncommunicable diseases (NCDs) generally include various types of cancers, chronic respiratory diseases, diabetes, cardiovascular diseases (CVD) and so on. These diseases together contribute to 60% of all deaths. CVDs are the leading cause among NCDs which account for 17.7 million deaths [1]. According to the World Health Organization (WHO), CVD related death in India contributes

* **Corresponding author Soma Das:** Life Science, B.Ed. Department, Syamaprasad Institute of Education and Training, Kolkata, India; & Honorary Guest Faculty, Sports Science Department, University of Calcutta, Kolkata, India; E-mail: somad.cal@gmail.com

Biswadip Basu Mallik, Kirti Verma, Rahul Kar, Ashok Kumar Shaw & Sardar M. N. Islam (Naz) (Eds.)

to one-fifth of global mortality specifically in immature age groups. The Global Burden of Diseases reported that nearly a quarter (24.8%) of all deaths in India are associated with CVD [2]. The global average age-specific mortality rate on account of CVDs is 235 out of 100 000 population, whereas it is much higher (272 out of 100 000 population) in India [2]. The disease burden due to CVDs in ratio expression at India and Global level is shown below in Fig. (**1**). The age-adjusted CVD mortality rate is found more in males (255–525 out of 100 000 population) than their females (225–299 out of 100 000 population) counterparts. The sharp rise in CVD cases has brought a profound change in the disease profile in India within a span of the last two decades. It is marked by the epidemiological transition from diseases caused by poor nutrition, maternal - childhood diseases and infectious diseases to noncommunicable diseases (NCDs) across the country [3]. Literature revealed that the disease overload contributed by undernutrition (like marasmus, kwashiorkor), diarrhoea, cholera, measles, maternal - childhood diseases decreased by 50% in the last two decades. In addition, there is a rise in the average life expectancy of individuals at 65.2 years which earlier was 58.3 years and slow pace of getting old of large number of people in the same time frame [3]. The NCDs specially CVDs have a direct association with aged people. Increased life expectancy is leading to rapid growth in NCDs burden, more specifically a sharp rise in CVD overload among the general population [3]. Presently, in India, around 66% of the total mortality cases are attributed to health issues linked with cardiovascular system [4]. The CVD-mediated severity has risen considerably in developing countries like India than in developed countries of the world [5, 6]. In comparison to the Western world, people in India got affected by CVD a decade earlier which unfortunately resulted in the appearance of moderate to severe health complications in the most productive Middle Ages of Indian population [4]. A recent study indicated the mortality cases due to CVD fall within 23% in Western populations below the age of 70 years whereas the similar cases in India rise up to 52% [7].

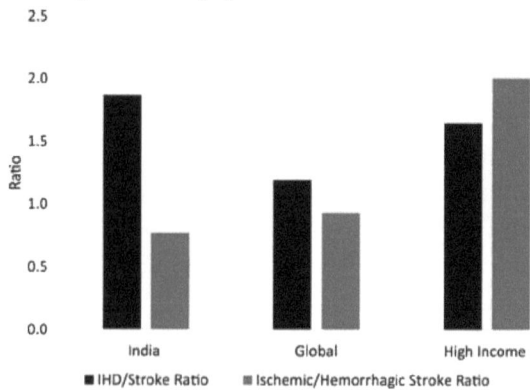

Fig. (1). Ratio Expression of CVDs at India and Global Level [2].

The World Health Organization (WHO) reported that India would pass through a huge economic burden of $237 billion due to massive spending on treatment and medical facilities for CVD patients in coming 10 years [7]. Prospective relevant studies reported myocardial infarction (MI) and cardiac arrest (CA) are the most common (83%) causes of CVD mediated complications which account for above one-fifth (21.1%) of mortality cases in India [2]. In this connection, these CVDs contribute to 1/10th of the premature death of the younger generation over the deaths of the older Indian population [8], and the value has risen by 59% from 1990 to 2010 [3].

ADVERSE IMPACT OF CARDIOVASCULAR DISEASES IN INDIA

A wide range of risk factors (RFs) having vast biological and social heterogeneity includes hypertension, diabetes mellitus, metabolic diseases, poor physical fitness, obesity, and other related risk factors like smoking, sedentary lifestyles, unbalanced food habits, poor dietary intake of fiber, mental stress, *etc.* as key players in the faster progression of CVDs, the high rate of fatalities, and the advanced propensity to develop CVD as the profound source of mortality across the country. Some of the prominent risk factors that must be addressed to improve awareness among common Indians are listed below:

Smoking

Presently, India surpasses China in the consumption of tobacco [9]. According to the Global Adult Tobacco Survey report, there has been a 6% decline in the consumption of tobacco among adult males in India [9]. However, the cases of tobacco smoking among Indian males (23.6%) are still higher than the cases worldwide (22%). The consumption of tobacco is a common threat to cardiorespiratory diseases; it can, however, be modified or detached from CVD.

Hyperglycaemia

Hyperglycemia, commonly known as diabetes, is one of the most common lifestyle diseases in India. It is so prevalent nowadays that it occurs in 1 out of 10 individuals within the age group of 18 years. The number of potent hyperglycemic patients is rising sharply in urban as well as rural Indian communities and is estimated to reach up to 8.8% between the age groups of 20 and 70 years in the near future [10].

Hypertension

Hypertension, or an increased blood pressure level, is another very common risk factor for CVD. One in every four Indians over the age of 18 has hypertension.

There is a sharp rise in CVD cases related to hypertension in both urban and rural India. It is expected to rise to 213.5 million by 2025 [10].

Obesity

Obesity, with its threefold rise, has become a worldwide risk factor for various health issues. A study revealed that urban Indians have a greater body mass index, or BMI (about 24–25), and a greater waist-to-hip ratio, or WHR (0.99) than their rural counterparts (BMI: 20; WHR: 0.95). Contrary to the Caucasian population, Asian adults, specifically Indians, are more susceptible to obesity in the abdominal region than general obesity [6]. From a medical point of view, abdominal obesity is a more serious concern than a high BMI. It is reported that serious health issues like myocardial ischemia, high blood pressure, cardiac arrest, osteoarthritis, diabetes (type II), and cancers are directly linked with the rapid rise in obesity among Asian-Indian communities [3].

Dyslipidaemia

Studies revealed a rise in a noticeable type of atherogenic dyslipidaemia in the Asian Indian population. This unique pattern is characterized by the dominance of low high-density lipoproteins (HDL) (11.8%), high triglycerides (29.5%), and high low-density lipoprotein (LDL) (72.3%) particles [11]. The study done by the Indian Council of Medical Research (ICMR) in 2014 reported that these factors are strongly associated with the risk of CVDs.

Dietary Habits and Exercise

In reality, around 50% of Indians are vegetarians, yet their cases of diabetes and CVDs are not less than those of the Western population, which has been nonvegetarian all along. Probably, high consumption of carbohydrates, dairy fats, vegetable oils (coconut oil, vanaspati, *etc.*), irregular dietary habits, and re-use of cooking oil (rich in trans fatty acids) are prominent sources of cardiovascular diseases in the Indian subcontinent. Other risks of CVD mortality may incorporate a lack of physical exercise and a sedentary urbanized lifestyle [3].

Genetic Risk Factors

The genome-based studies and meta-analysis indicated a significant connection between genetic inheritance and mutation in cardiac diseases [4]. Gene mapping studies found that 109 loci are linked with cardiac dysfunction. This finding perhaps goes strongly in favor of the genetic connection between CVDs. The impact of environmental factors such as smoking on cardiorespiratory diseases has also been studied [11].

Recent findings revealed some emerging risk factors like high homocysteine levels, temperature fluctuation, ambient air pollution, psychological and social factors, mental health problems, and high levels of chronic infection and inflammation indicator, highly sensitive C-reactive protein (hsCRP) levels, in connection to the high prevalence of CAD at present.

Treatment Gaps

Observation of urban and rural epidemiological studies revealed the major reasons for the higher rate of CVD-related morbidity and mortality in India, including the unfollowing of guideline-recommended basic therapeutic medicines for CVD, ignorance about CVDs, and prevalence of the above-mentioned risk factors among commoners in urban as well as rural India [5].

In this context, dependable and effective medical diagnostic systems are of the utmost importance to increase accuracy in the diagnosis of cardiovascular diseases with less time and cost [12]. These decision-backup systems are based on statistical algorithms involving complex artificial neural networks. The data mining tools are being widely used now in the clinical diagnosis of diseases, including CVDs [12]. These techniques have evolved the disease prediction strategy faster and more effectively. An array of data mining techniques have been mentioned in the following section:

The Multilayer Perceptron (MLP)

It is a decision support system. Its input layer contains 40 input variables. The variables are classified into four types before coding. The number of nodes is calculated in the hidden layer based on learning [13]. There are five nodes in the output layer, each of which represents a specific type of cardiovascular ailment. The multilayer perceptron system is based on the rear proliferation algorithm. The concealed nodes are set as number 15 by means of the sequential learning process. The database on cardiac ailments was gathered from 352 patients from two hospitals in China and was used to test and tune the system in the study. In order to evaluate the efficiency of the clinical decision support system grounded in MLP, three types of assessment techniques were used. The cross-validation classification accuracy measured was high, *i.e.*, 91.5%. The process accuracy for every individual process also came in high, *i.e.*, above 90%. Based on the findings, the system was reported to have a high capacity (>90%) to accurately diagnose all five cardiac diseases with short intervals (5%) that can be compared.

Coactive Neuro-Fuzzy Inference System (CANFIS)

This system applied the Coactive Neuro-Fuzzy Inference System and Genetic Algorithm technique based on genetic arrangement [13]. This system works by assembling the adjustable neural network with the fuzzy logic mechanism. The assembled form is then combined with an algorithm based on gene sequencing to diagnose cardiac abnormalities. This set-up runs with a neural network having a tri-layer feed-forward mechanism where the first layer shows input variables, the hidden layer depicts fuzzy rules, and the third layer presents the product. A significant component is a modular network, where functional rules are applied at the entry point. In this case, two fuzzy systems are introduced, namely the Sugano (TSK) model and the Tsukamoto model. After that, the MF outputs are applied to the modular network products with the help of a combiner. A genetic algorithm (GA) is set for the purpose of best performance. The GA connects choice, crossover, and modification operators to fully fulfill the target of getting the effective result to overcome an issue by finding the precise criterion. The Neuro Solution software was used for the implementation of the simulation of the model. The database used in this prediction analysis was based on four types of Cleveland heart disease cases from 303 patients. The outcomes obtained by this system have the desired standard and precision.

Aptamer Biochip-based CDSS –ensemble (Apta CDSS-E)

This clinical decision-making approach is classifier ensemble-based to predict the level of heart disease [14]. This system is grounded in a multiple classifier-based system instead of the conventional monoclassifier technique. Here, a group of four various classifiers is assembled to run the system. The group of four classifiers includes neural networks (ANN), support vector machines (SVM), Bayesian networks (BN), and decision trees (DT). These different classifiers are utilised for the analysis of serum and microarray chip information for diagnosis. This system proves very effective in providing data on biomarkers for fast detection and treatment of CVDs. The techniques used in this system are as follows: 1. Collection of blood from the CVD patient 2. Use of serum after separating it from the collected blood sample to create an Aptamer biochip 3. Scanning of the blood protein expression level 4. Creation of a work list by scanner interface 5. Production of a new work list by scanner interface 5. Analysis and decisions are taken by the decision engine of AptaCDS. The system is found to produce an accuracy of more than 94%.

Intelligent Heart Disease Prediction System (IHDPS)

This diagnostic tool uses decision trees, Nave Bayes, and the neural network method [15]. The content of this approach is judged using the Data Mining

Extension (DMX) strategy. The system was authenticated using a sample dataset and the life chart and classification matrix techniques. The interpretation of results in IHDPS is being done efficiently with the help of tabular and graphical visualization techniques. This model provides the most accurate prediction of cardiovascular diseases.

Intelligent and Effective Heart Attack Prediction System (IEHPS)

This system runs by applying data mining and artificial neural networks to the extraction of significant data from warehouses in connection with the detection of cardiac ailment [16]. At the beginning, the data is pre-processed and classified by applying the K-means clustering design. Frequent Itemset Mining (FIM) is carried out using the Maximal Frequent Itemset Algorithm (MAFIA) to derive linkage patterns from the clustered data pool. The patterns are then given a weight based on their vitality in disease prediction. The system shows high efficiency and effectiveness in disease prediction.

Decision Tree Fuzzy System (DTFS)

The system uses fuzzy decision trees for the detection of CVDs. This technique uses fuzzy rules for prediction on the designed fuzzy-based CDSS [17]. The information used for prediction is classified into two categories and labeled as "0," referring to cardiac abnormalities that are less than 50%, and "1," referring to alarming states that are greater than 50%. Here, data mining is done by getting the frequency of the attribute and categorizing it. The fixed type is then separated into two vectors, with the highest and lowest levels for each type. The deviation scale is marked for the two maximum vectors of two classes. Based on the two changing vectors, automatically generated rules are generated. These fuzzy rules act as an entry point for a non-fuzzification technique. This approach has less uncertainty as a decision tree is employed. However, this system has very limited classes and therefore incorporates vagueness.

CONCLUDING REMARKS

Based on the present study, it can be concluded that, despite the availability of a considerable volume of health facts, the quality and completeness of data prediction and diagnosis of CVDs are dependent on advanced data mining techniques in order to develop an efficient medical support system. However, the overall authenticity and universal capability of these modern techniques are not yet beyond question. It is necessary to upgrade the data mining techniques by supplying a complete medical data set for more accuracy and precision in the system. These technology-based prediction techniques could be an effective means for early detection of CVDs and action for proper health care to avoid huge economic and medical burdens in a vastly populated country like India.

REFERENCES

[1]   K. Srinath Reddy, B. Shah, C. Varghese, and A. Ramadoss, "Responding to the threat of chronic diseases in India", *Lancet,* vol. 366, no. 9498, pp. 1744-1749, 2005.
[http://dx.doi.org/10.1016/S0140-6736(05)67343-6] [PMID: 16291069]

[2]   S. Yusuf, S. Rangarajan, K. Teo, S. Islam, W. Li, L. Liu, J. Bo, Q. Lou, F. Lu, T. Liu, L. Yu, S. Zhang, P. Mony, S. Swaminathan, V. Mohan, R. Gupta, R. Kumar, K. Vijayakumar, S. Lear, S. Anand, A. Wielgosz, R. Diaz, A. Avezum, P. Lopez-Jaramillo, F. Lanas, K. Yusoff, N. Ismail, R. Iqbal, O. Rahman, A. Rosengren, A. Yusufali, R. Kelishadi, A. Kruger, T. Puoane, A. Szuba, J. Chifamba, A. Oguz, M. McQueen, M. McKee, and G. Dagenais, "Cardiovascular risk and events in 17 low-, middle-, and high-income countries", *N. Engl. J. Med.,* vol. 371, no. 9, pp. 818-827, 2014.
[http://dx.doi.org/10.1056/NEJMoa1311890] [PMID: 25162888]

[3]   A. Ramachandran, C. Snehalatha, J. Ram, S. Selvam, M. Simon, A. Nanditha, A.S. Shetty, I.F. Godsland, N. Chaturvedi, A. Majeed, N. Oliver, C. Toumazou, K.G. Alberti, and D.G. Johnston, "Effectiveness of mobile phone messaging in prevention of type 2 diabetes by lifestyle modification in men in India: A prospective, parallel-group, randomised controlled trial", *Lancet. Diab. Endocrinol.,* vol. 1, no. 3, pp. 191-198, 2013.
[http://dx.doi.org/10.1016/S2213-8587(13)70067-6] [PMID: 24622367]

[4]   P. Joshi, S. Islam, P. Pais, S. Reddy, P. Dorairaj, K. Kazmi, M.R. Pandey, S. Haque, S. Mendis, S. Rangarajan, and S. Yusuf, "Risk factors for early myocardial infarction in south asians compared with individuals in other countries", *JAMA,* vol. 297, no. 3, pp. 286-294, 2007.
[http://dx.doi.org/10.1001/jama.297.3.286] [PMID: 17227980]

[5]   D. Xavier, P. Pais, P.J. Devereaux, C. Xie, D. Prabhakaran, K.S. Reddy, R. Gupta, P. Joshi, P. Kerkar, S. Thanikachalam, K.K. Haridas, T.M. Jaison, S. Naik, A.K. Maity, and S. Yusuf, "Treatment and outcomes of acute coronary syndromes in India (CREATE): A prospective analysis of registry data", *Lancet,* vol. 371, no. 9622, pp. 1435-1442, 2008.
[http://dx.doi.org/10.1016/S0140-6736(08)60623-6] [PMID: 18440425]

[6]   S.S. Kar, J.S. Thakur, N.K. Virdi, S. Jain, and R. Kumar, "Risk factors for cardiovascular diseases: is the social gradient reversing in northern India?", *Natl. Med. J. India,* vol. 23, no. 4, pp. 206-209, 2010.
[PMID: 21192513]

[7]   V. Patel, S. Chatterji, D. Chisholm, S. Ebrahim, G. Gopalakrishna, C. Mathers, V. Mohan, D. Prabhakaran, R.D. Ravindran, and K.S. Reddy, "Chronic diseases and injuries in India", *Lancet,* vol. 377, no. 9763, pp. 413-428, 2011.
[http://dx.doi.org/10.1016/S0140-6736(10)61188-9] [PMID: 21227486]

[8]   D. Prabhakaran, P. Jeemon, and A. Roy, "Cardiovascular diseases in india", *Circulation,* vol. 133, no. 16, pp. 1605-1620, 2016.
[http://dx.doi.org/10.1161/CIRCULATIONAHA.114.008729] [PMID: 27142605]

[9]   M.S. Pednekar, R. Gupta, and P.C. Gupta, "Illiteracy, low educational status, and cardiovascular mortality in India", *BMC Pub. Heal.,* vol. 11, no. 1, p. 567, 2011.
[http://dx.doi.org/10.1186/1471-2458-11-567] [PMID: 21756367]

[10]   E. Parva, R. Boostani, Z. Ghahramani, and S. Paydar, "The necessity of data mining in clinical emergency medicine: A narrative review of the current literatrue", *Bull. Emerg. Trauma,* vol. 5, no. 2, pp. 90-95, 2017.
[PMID: 28507995]

[11]   M. Preuss, I.R. König, J.R. Thompson, J. Erdmann, D. Absher, T.L. Assimes, S. Blankenberg, E. Boerwinkle, L. Chen, L.A. Cupples, A.S. Hall, E. Halperin, C. Hengstenberg, H. Holm, R. Laaksonen, M. Li, W. März, R. McPherson, K. Musunuru, C.P. Nelson, M. Susan Burnett, S.E. Epstein, C.J.

O'Donnell, T. Quertermous, D.J. Rader, R. Roberts, A. Schillert, K. Stefansson, A.F.R. Stewart, G. Thorleifsson, B.F. Voight, G.A. Wells, A. Ziegler, S. Kathiresan, M.P. Reilly, N.J. Samani, and H. Schunkert, "Design of the coronary artery disease genome-wide replication and meta-analysis (CARDIoGRAM) Study: A Genome-wide association meta-analysis involving more than 22000 cases and 60000 controls", *Circ. Cardiovasc. Genet.,* vol. 3, no. 5, pp. 475-483, 2010.
[http://dx.doi.org/10.1161/CIRCGENETICS.109.899443] [PMID: 20923989]

[12]   R. Das, I. Turkoglu, and A. Sengur, "Effective diagnosis of heart disease through neural networks ensembles. expert systems with applications", In: *Elsevier* vol. 36. , 2009, pp. 7675-7680.

[13]   K. Srinivas, B.K. Rani, and A. Govrdhan, "Applications of data mining techniques in healthcare and prediction of heart attacks", *Int. J. Comput. Sci. Eng.,* vol. 2, pp. 250-255, 2010.

[14]   D.E. Rumelhart, G.E. Hinton, and R.J. Williams, "Learning representations by back-propagating errors", *Nature,* vol. 323, no. 6088, pp. 533-536, 1986.
[http://dx.doi.org/10.1038/323533a0]

[15]   D. Ferreira, S. Silva, A. Abelha, and J. Machado, "Recommendation system using autoencoders", *Appl. Sci.,* vol. 10, no. 16, p. 5510, 2020.
[http://dx.doi.org/10.3390/app10165510]

[16]   S. Palaniappan, and R. Awang, "Intelligent heart disease prediction system using data mining techniques", *Int. J. Comput. Sci. Net. Secur.,* vol. 8, pp. 108-115, 2008.
[http://dx.doi.org/10.1109/AICCSA.2008.4493524]

[17]   A.T. Sayad, and P.P. Halkarnikar, "Diagnosis of heart disease using neural network approach", *Int. J. Adv. Sci. Eng. Technol.,* vol. 2, pp. 88-92, 2014.

CHAPTER 13

Data Science and Healthcare

Armel Djangone[1,*]

[1] *Dakota State University, Business Analytics and Decision Support, Washington Ave N, Madison, United States*

Abstract: Data science is often used as an umbrella term to include various techniques for extracting insights and knowledge from complex structured and unstructured data. It often relies on a large amount of data (big data) and the application of different mathematical methods, including computer vision, NLP (or natural language processing), and data mining techniques. Advances in data science have resulted in a wider variety of algorithms, specialized for different applications and industries, such as healthcare, finance, marketing, supply chain, management, and general administration. Specifically, data science methods have shown promise in addressing key healthcare challenges and helping healthcare practitioners and leaders make data-driven decision-making. This chapter focuses on healthcare issues and how data science can help solve these issues. The chapter will survey different approaches to defining data science and why any organization should use data science. This chapter will also present different skills required for an effective healthcare data scientist and discusses healthcare leaders' behaviors that in impacting their organizational processes.

Keywords: Data science, Healthcare, Mathematical models, Machine learning, Natural language processing.

INTRODUCTION

So, What is Data Science?

Data Science is a crucial component of today's growing world. The reason is that data scientists have been reading and compiling data for a long time now. On average, data scientist spends 80% of their time collecting and cleaning data.

Therefore, the trends that an assembled data sets, the facts it produces, and all the new information gathered help develop organizations, healthcare, understanding a pattern, and overall building the world. Data science refers to the study of data. Data science allows the development of methods of collecting, storing, and analy-

---

* **Corresponding author Armel Djangone:** Dakota State University, Business Analytics and Decision Support, Washington Ave N, Madison, United States; E-mail: djangonearmel17@gmail.com

Biswadip Basu Mallik, Kirti Verma, Rahul Kar, Ashok Kumar Shaw & Sardar M. N. Islam (Naz) (Eds.)

zing data to find insightful information. Data science is essential for extracting knowledge and information from any type of structured or unstructured data.

Data science and computer science are two separate fields. Computer science is an area where algorithms and programs are developed to record and process data, while data science is about the analysis of data, with or without computers. However, fields of mathematics such as Statistics are related to data science as they can be applied for data collection, organization, analysis, and presentation.

Data science is not a building block for the IT industry, as modern companies and institutions deal with a massive amount of data. For example, someone with a massive amount of data would need to use data science so they can create useful approaches to collect, organize, and analyze the data.

Data Science Techniques *vs.* Data Mining

Data science and Data mining are often confused and used for one another. Although, data mining is actually a subset of the field of data science. Data mining is particularly aimed at analyzing large data (such as Big Data) to identify patterns, among other useful information. Data science, on the other hand, exclusively focuses on data collection and analysis.

Data science finds patterns within a set of data. With data extraction, we can record history, predict future possibilities, and understand our behavior. These closely similar interests are why users often may not accurately distinguish the role of a data scientist.

Now, Why is Data Essential?

Data is an essential facet of every industry and organization, including healthcare. According to the internet, just about 2TB of data is generated daily by users. This data comes in several types that may be either structured or unstructured. The proper use of data can allow companies to make the best decisions.

Data Science turns raw data into meaningful insights. Thus, businesses should integrate data science approaches. Data science has helped big companies in obtaining great heights. It helps in better marketing, and a company needs to understand its customers as the market grows. Data science helps understand the pattern a customer follows, what is more, liked and disliked. This way, data science has helped the commercial sector and the whole world with its innovation and discoveries. The marks of data acquired from several sources have led to the most significant age of innovation. Data Science is allowing us to discover the greatest of secrets hidden within the data. Data Science is the play-acting mechanism behind our current evolution, and it is growing at a petrifying pace.

What is an Ideal Data Scientist?

A Data Scientist works extensively with Big Data applications. The routine roles and responsibilities of a Data Scientist can be predictable sometimes, and sometimes they deal with extraordinary data challenges. There are several requirements to fulfill to become a Data Scientist. If someone is keen to be a data scientist, in that case, they must have the skills for munching data, making new assumptions, and the ability to look at the same problem from different angles, and so on.

A Data Scientist's job is to make the most of collected data by analyzing and deriving actionable insights. Some of those tasks may include:

- Identifying the data analytics issues that can unlock the most outstanding value for the organization.
- Learning about the most suitable datasets and variables.
- Working with different unstructured data forms like video or images.
- Exploring the latest opportunities and solutions through data analysis.
- Collecting massive structured and/or unstructured data from various sources.
- Reviewing, filtering, and validating data to gain the highest accuracy and completeness.
- Mining big data by evaluating and applying various algorithms.
- Analyzing the data set to identify underlying patterns and trends.
- Communicating different findings to relevant stakeholders through visualizations.

Technical and Soft Skills for Healthcare Data Scientists

The U.S. Bureau of Labor Statistics expects a massive job expansion in the field of data science by 2026, along with an estimation of 11.5 million new jobs within just the next six years. But there is a possibility of an even larger gap between the number of job opportunities and the number of job seekers in the healthcare industry particularly.

Furthermore, a HIMSS survey covers that only 38% of healthcare organizations are adequately staffed in their IT departments. These departments consist of data science, analysis, and data management professionals. Therefore, for any aspirant healthcare data worker, the following soft and technical skills need to be an integral part of your profile and portfolio.

Technical Skills

• **Advanced Math and Statistical Analysis and Modelling:** Applied maths are required skills in a career in data science to effectively gather, organize, explore, understand and represent data. It can help form hypotheses and create models. From the educational perspective, the user may need to polish algebra, and trigonometry. User also may consider learning calculus. The role of a Data scientist includes being a statistician and a computer scientist; it consists of scrubbing and modeling available data for predicting future occurrences, actions, and prospects.

• **Programming Knowledge:** Programming is not a primary part of every data scientist's responsibility, but they can get a competitive advantage if they are experienced with programming languages and frameworks such as Java, Python, Apache, and SQL. Data analysts can also benefit from these technology tools that can help with data mining, warehousing, and modeling, such as SQL, SAS, and R.

• **Data Visualization & Storytelling:** Data Visualization & Storytelling: Data can be a great help for decision-makers as they can make evidence-based, insightful, and highly probable decisions. From healthcare to business growth, companies can invest their time and money in the best strategies by building data science capabilities. Therefore, presenting visually intuitive insights and recommendations is essential for data workers. Some of the most common tools and approaches include Power Bi, Python (Matplotlib, Plotly), and R (ggplot2).

Soft Skills

• **Curiosity:** One of the crucial skills for a data scientist is curiosity. Data professional utilize massive data to answer business questions every single day. Critical or exciting questions, or even problems that no one has yet demanded. Data scientists must experiment, analyze, and discover new scenarios instinctively.

• **Problem-solving skills:** The ability to decode problems with data, what data to look at, how to look at it, how to extract meaning, make forecasts, *etc.*

• **Communication skills:** Data science skills involve the ability to convey difficult knowledge easily. In addition, communication skills become even more critical if you are at an executive level. As an executive leader, you need to be able to explain how you want the work to be accomplished. You also want to be able to share the results of your finding with non-technical leaders as well.

• **Scientific Method Expertise:** The process of objectively establishing facts through testing and experimentation. In this process, the scientists state a hypothesis and then investigate to prove or disprove the hypothesis. A Data worker is a scientist that employs the scientific processes thoroughly around every single task to accomplish increasing degrees of reliability and certainty through discipline.

• **Healthcare Industry Knowledge:** One of the top skills of an effective data scientist is their ability to provide suggestions or predictions to leaders that enhance decision-making, effectiveness, or efficiency. A detailed understanding of the functions of healthcare providers, including health systems leadership, delivery of care, outcomes, strategic planning, and management, is crucial. This helps identify the proper questions and share understandings in a pertinent manner.

Why is Data Science so Crucial for Organizations?

Applications of data science can be versatile for various parts of a business. It can help on several different fronts, such as customer insights, personalized marketing inputs, and highly targeted advertising campaigns for more sales. In industrial setups, data science can help manage financial risks, find fraudulent operations, and predict possible machine breakdowns for prevention. Moreover, data science can play a key role against cyber-attacks and similar security threats in the IT industry.

Businesses need data scientists more and more as the amount of data they produce and gather grows. Due to the strong demand for people with data science experience or training, several businesses are having trouble filling open positions. People in other positions can pursue an alternative career path by retraining to become data scientists, which is a popular choice for businesses that are having problems hiring experienced candidates.

Big Data is useless without the knowledge of experts who can transform cutting-edge technology into useful insights. The importance of data scientists who knows how to wring relevant insights out of petabytes of data is soaring as more and more firms try to harness the power of big data.

Here are some advantages of leveraging data science

• **Eliminating fraud and risk:** Data scientists are taught to spot data that is particularly noteworthy. Then, in order to build warnings that help assure prompt responses when unexpected data is noticed, they utilize statistical, link, path, and comprehensive data procedures for predicting fraud propensity models.

• **They are offering relevant products:** The ability for businesses to determine when and where particular items sell best is one of the benefits of data science. By doing so, businesses can create new items to satisfy the demands of their customers and deliver the correct product right when it is needed.

• **They tailor the customer interactions:** The ability of the marketing team to intimately understand their customer is one of the most talked-about advantages of data science. An organization may design the finest customer experiences by using this information.

• Businesses use data to examine their marketing plans and develop more effective campaigns. Companies regularly spend enormous sums of money promoting their offerings. Sometimes, this might not produce the desired outcomes. Therefore, businesses may need to produce better marketing by studying and evaluating customer feedback. Companies accomplish this by carefully examining user behavior through data.

• With a wealth of data, Organizations develop ideas that are better. By examining and developing insights into conventional designs, data scientists contribute to product innovation. They help businesses create products that perfectly fit client comments and reviews by analyzing online customer reviews. Companies undertake the following appropriate action by using the information from client feedback.

Data-intensive businesses rely heavily on data scientists. Data scientists are employed to extract, prepare, and analyze data. This enables businesses to make wiser judgments. Various companies use data in accordance with their own requirements. A data scientist's ultimate objective is to improve corporate growth. With the choices and information offered, the enterprises can tailor their approaches and adopt methods that will optimize the consumer experience.

HEALTHCARE DATA: CHALLENGES AND OPPORTUNITIES

Opportunities

A vital aspect of our lives is healthcare. Patients want competent care from sympathetic individuals, so healthcare organizations should hire the best candidates to fill such positions. The Bureau of Labor Statistics of the United States of America (USA) projects that from 2020 to 2030, employment in healthcare professions will increase by 16%. This suggests that the sector will generate around 16.97 million new employment in the healthcare sector. This indicates that more jobs are expected to be added in the healthcare sector than in any other occupational category. The main cause of this anticipated growth is an aging population, which raises the healthcare service demands.

In May 2021, the median annual wage for all jobs in the economy was $45,760, but the median annual wage for healthcare professionals and technical occupations (including registered nurses, surgeons, and dental hygienists) was $75,040.

At the same time, in May 2021, the average annual pay for occupations supporting the healthcare industry comes about $29,880, which is a lesser number than the median yearly income among each profession in the financial system.

The healthcare industry produces, gathers, and manages large amounts of data. This undoubtedly has a rising impact on the sector. According to a survey from RBC Capital Markets, the healthcare sector currently generates about 30% of the aggregate volume of data around the globe. The cumulative yearly increase rate of data will be 36% by 2025 in the healthcare industry see Fig. (**1**) below. This is roughly 6% quicker than the manufacturing sector, about 10% more rapidly than the financial sector, and 11% quicker than the mass media & entertainment sector.

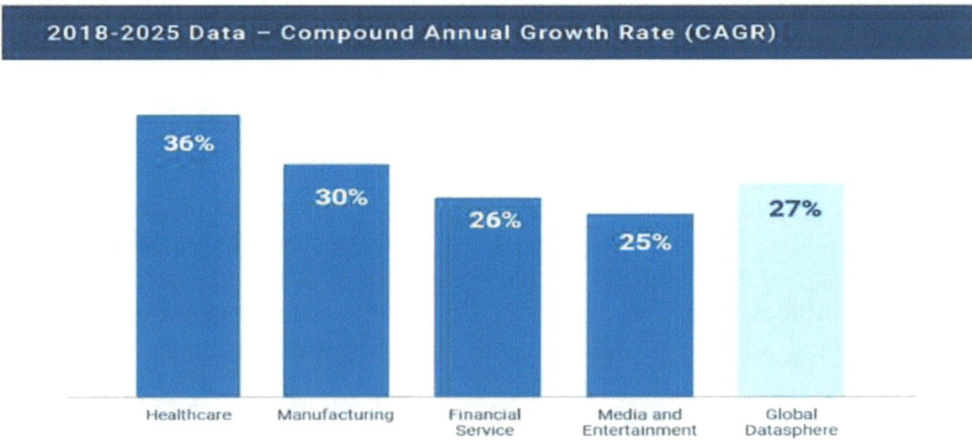

2018-2025 Data – Compound Annual Growth Rate (CAGR)

Source: Coughlin et al Internal Medicine Journal article "Looking to tomorrow's healthcare today: a participatory health perspective". IDC White Paper, Doc# US44413318, November 2018: The Digitization of the World – From Edge to Core".

Fig. (1). goes here healthcare data annual growth (source: IDC).

The International Data Corporation (IDC) did another report to corroborate the healthcare data's explosive expansion. According to the study, the data generation rate in the healthcare industry will outpace that of all other industries by 2025. As a result, the size of data that the healthcare industry generates is practically incomprehensible.

Data difficulties in healthcare are unavoidable when maintaining this vast amount of data primarily derived through insurance, imaging, telehealth, electronic health records, and other sources. To obtain important insights to raise the quality and effectiveness of healthcare, it is necessary to manage this enormous amount and velocity of data. This section will examine the issues with everyday data production in the healthcare industry and outline potential opportunities for data science.

The development of the numerical age took the lead to the convergence of information technology and health care. This fact has generated a large amount of data in the healthcare industry. Data science through big data analytics offers support to the process, management, and analysis and embraces the large quantities of data created by healthcare organizations. This section will describe some of the challenges of healthcare data and how healthcare practitioners use various data science techniques to help in these matters.

Defining Big Data

The term "big data" addresses data that is so massive, quick, or complex that it is challenging, if not impossible, to process it using standard computer software or web-based platforms. Large-scale data access and storage for analysis have been used for a very long time. But in the early 2000s, industry analyst Doug Laney coined the now-accepted definition of big data with the three V's: volume, velocity, and variety, which gave the idea of big data a boost.

Big data's vast volume is indicated by the word "big" in the phrase. We see data collected in all distinct types of formats, from unstructured text, emails, videos, audios, documentation, and financial transactions to structured, quantitative values in traditional databases, according to the big data definition, which also includes velocity and variety. Velocity describes how quickly information is gathered and made available for further analysis.

Big Data technologies are already having an impact on the healthcare sector. For example, medical diagnosis using imaging data in medicine and quantifying lifestyle statistics in the fitness sector. Big Data will unquestionably create new possibilities and enable developments in healthcare data analytics that address several perceptions:

1. Descriptive to describe what transpired.
2. Diagnostic to explain why it occurred.
3. Predictive to comprehend what will occur.
4. Prescriptive to identify the steps we may take to ensure that it occurs (Fig. **2**).

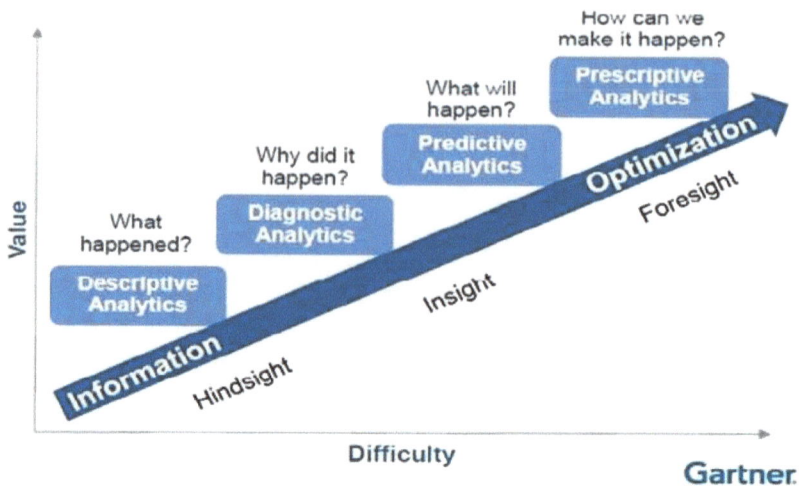

Fig. (2). Descriptive, diagnostic, predictive, prescriptive analytics (source: Gartner).

Challenges

There are numerous issues in healthcare data. From electronic health records (EHR), administrative data, claims data, patient / disease registries, healthcare practitioners, and leaders are facing unprecedented challenges.

• Inaccuracies abound in healthcare data. Healthcare professionals and leaders are confronting unintelligible difficulties in areas such as electronic health records (EHR), administrative data, insurance claims, and patient / disease registries. For instance, the distribution of medical data is subject to privacy restrictions established by federal legislation. Due to data protection regulations, it is challenging to combine data from many healthcare services. A very important issue that needs to be resolved is privacy concerns.

• There are more opportunities to access and merge information from many sources in today's evolving digital world, as data can be collected from nearly everything that can be connected. This suggests that other parties could acquire access to and abuse the knowledge gleaned from this enormous collection. In this line, most people's opinions are rather ambiguous about "where the data travels to," "by whom it is utilized," and "for what reason."

• The difficulties in getting healthcare data go hand in hand with privacy concerns. The industry is highly fragmented; acquired data is not shared between organizations and is not even shared within divisions. This contributes to the emergence and spread of numerous underutilized single data silos. Electronic health records (EHR), genomic and pharmaceutical data, clinical test results, imaging (such as x-ray), insurance claims, telemedicine, mobile apps, home monitoring, ongoing clinical trials, real-time sensors, and data on wellbeing, behavior, and socioeconomic indicators are just a few examples of the types of data in this category. Because this data may be of varying quality and is dispersed across numerous internal and external sites, gathering, integrating, and analyzing it can be challenging. Additionally, keeping up with constantly changing and updating data sources is quite complicated.

• The quality of healthcare data is a critical issue. The American healthcare system must be improved, and data quality is crucial for this. Extraction of value for patients, doctors, and payers is at the heart of data quality. Low-quality data, such as duplicate records, patient names missing from records, or outdated information, causes problems with invoicing and payment, while high-quality data are also both actionable and useable. The healthcare system suffers from financial gaps as a result of these deficiencies. The data gathered and used by healthcare organizations help scientists make data models that can enhance patient outcomes. Then, using this information, healthcare professionals can develop better treatment methods.

• The interoperability of health data is another problem. The ability of healthcare providers and different electronic health record (EHR) systems that digitally share health information is a complex technical task. There are many thousands of EHR systems available across the nation, each with its own set of functional needs, technological specifications, and medical jargon. Due to these variances, developing a uniform interoperability format for exchanging patient data is difficult. The molecular time and length scales are not sufficiently small compared to the characteristic macroscopic flow scales.

Data Science Opportunities for Healthcare

Big data analysis, or "data science," is the process of gathering, storing, cleaning, integrating, analyzing, and displaying data. It is now an essential part of many sectors, including the healthcare industry. For example, data science has made it feasible to discover genetic changes and the scope for new medicine development. It is now possible to find new trends in a variety of ailments, such as cardiovascular and neurological disorders, thanks to data science approaches like data mining and predictive modeling. The healthcare industry has undergone a revolution thanks to data science techniques. Clinics, hospitals, wellness centers, labs, and diagnostic centers are just a few examples of places where healthcare firms may find the big data they need. This section examines a few healthcare-related fields where data science and data analytics can produce impressive outcomes. Below are a few of these areas:

• Determines efficiency of therapies, procedures, and processes to identify cost-effective and efficient alternatives, and then suggests the replacement process to a better approach with an effective transition.

• Identifies environmental or lifestyle factors that raise risk or precipitate adverse outcomes and modifies treatment strategies as necessary to reduce readmissions.

• Enhances results by evaluating patients' vital signs through remote monitors and promptly getting in touch with patients when problems are found.

• Brings together multiple data types from many sources, such as clinical, financial, and operational data for analysis, to build a sustainable healthcare system.

• Decreases failure risk while treating patients.

The following paragraphs are taken from an IBM Software White Paper that describes how data science is utilized to enhance patient outcomes and decrease healthcare spending while gaining a fundamental understanding of the operational aspects of the healthcare industry.

• Premier Inc. is the biggest healthcare alliance in the USA (https://premierinc.com/). It consists of a network of 400,000 doctors, 90,000 non-acute care facilities, and over 2,700 partner hospitals and health systems. One in every four hospitals discharged patients in the US is included in the alliance's largest clinical, financial, supply chain, and operational database. The database gives members access to all available comparative clinical outcome indicators, data on resource usage, and transaction-level cost information required to make well-informed strategic decisions that improve procedures and results. Across one Premier performance improvement collaborative of more than 330 hospitals, more than 29,000 lives have been saved, and healthcare spending has been reduced by almost USD7 billion.

• North York General Hospital (https://www.nygh.on.ca/) - improved patient experience then developed a greater comprehension of the operating issues influencing its functions by utilizing real-time data. The hospital has implemented robust, real-time technology solutions that offer a comprehensive view of the therapeutic, operational, and financial activities of the facility. Administrators and physicians gain analytics-driven insights from the solution, which processes data from more than 50 independent collection points spread across 12 internal systems, improving business performance and patient success.

• Rizzoli Orthopaedic is healthcare institute located in Bologna, Italy (https://www.ior.it/), the first healthcare facility in the West to concentrate on orthopedic disorders, is enhancing care and lowering the cost of treating genetic bone illnesses. The institution is utilizing advanced analytics to get a new level of detail into the patterns of clinical variations in families where members demonstrate wide variances in the severity of their illnesses. More effective and affordable care has been observed as a result, with greater than 60% decreases in imagery tests and over 30% reductions in annual hospitalizations. The institute wants to learn more about the intricate interactions of genetic elements and find treatments.

• SickKids – is a hospital focusing on sick children in Toronto (https://www.sickkids.ca/) and is the foremost facility devoted to improving children's health in Toronto, CA. The hospital is increasing the results for kids who are at risk for nosocomial infections that could be fatal. SickKids employs cutting-edge analytics to analyze vital-sign data to identify probable infection signals up to 24 hours before compared to previous techniques. According to researchers and clinicians, it is anticipated that it will offer significant future benefits for various medical diagnostics.

HEALTHCARE LEADERSHIP

In an organization, leadership is essential. According to studies, a leader's honesty, team diversity management, capacity to develop and maximize the potential of their team, and ultimately organizational capability determine whether an organization succeeds or fails [1, 2].

Healthcare leaders must put in a lot of effort to provide the most effective, secure, and greatest care possible because this industry is dynamic and characterized by a constant. They must successfully manage resources while managing administrative and clinical teams. Leaders in the healthcare industry inspire people to perform their best to benefit patients, their coworkers, and the organization as a whole. They plan, direct, and organize healthcare services and establish goals and objectives. They may also be in charge of running a particular division or overseeing a whole building. Additionally, they are accountable for the following:

• Incorporating new technology.

• Ensuring that operations adhere to rules and legislation.

• Improving efficiency and standard.

Healthcare managers must constantly adapt and develop new ideas in this industry marked by shifting rules, advancing clinical and technical advances, and rising ethical issues. We will cover the most crucial qualities that a successful healthcare manager must possess in this part. We will talk specifically about the two well-known leadership qualities of transformative leadership and how they apply to the healthcare industry.

Healthcare practitioners may need to use a range of leadership philosophies to handle various tasks and respond to problems. The literature on the subject of leadership frequently discusses both transformational and transactional issues.

Transactional leader

The transactional way of thinking emphasizes rewards and penalties. The exchange-based method is built around the leader rewarding (or threatening to penalize) followers for engaging in desirable behaviors and finishing predetermined tasks. The manager sets the objectives under this management style, and the employees must follow them. For instance, a nursing facility may have a code forcing an employee to serve a shift the following weekend if they call in ill during a weekend shift. Without discussing the missed shift with the employee, the unit manager will appoint the worker for this make-up shift. This is the standard, and it must be adhered to. This leadership approach does not frequently foster innovation or problem-solving. However, it is very helpful in organizing and inspiring people to carry out their clearly defined jobs as quickly and accurately as possible. Respect for laws, regulations, and practices, as well as well-defined duties and close monitoring, are three characteristics of transactional leaders.

Management by exception (*e.g.,* monitoring performance and minimizing errors) and contingent reward behaviors (such as time off or bonuses in exchange for performance) are both necessary for transactional leadership.

Transformational leadership

The transformational leadership approach emphasizes giving employees the freedom to take the initiative in making changes that can improve an organization. The goal of a transformational leader is to communicate the leadership method with all employees, regardless of their status. The unit should operate according to the leader's vision for it. How this vision is realized is up to the team. The workforce is involved, they feel like they belong, and they accept responsibility for achieving the goals. Thus transformative thinking is more effort in the long run. Burns highlighted that transformational leadership involves a dedication to a vision and the empowerment of others to realize the vision [3]. Bujak contends that a leader can motivate followers and help them rediscover the primary goal of their job by getting rid of the consequences of pursuing a transcendent vision.

Employees of a healthcare company are inspired and motivated by transformational leaders to work for its success. They increase employee loyalty by fostering trust and a sense of purpose. Fig. (**3**) below illustrates the four specific types of behaviors that physician leaders, as well as other healthcare managers, must exhibit in order to be effective transformational leaders: idealized influence, inspirational motivation, customized consideration, and intellectual stimulation.

THE 4IS OF TRANSFORMATIONAL LEADERSHIP

Fig. (3). transformational leadership traits or the 4I.

The method by which transformative leaders wield their persuasion inside a group is known as Idealized Influence (II). It implies that a transformational leader sets an example by articulating a clear vision and creating a sense of community that inspires others to support the organization's long-term goals. They are motivated to accomplish their own objectives by this mindset. For example, leaders in the healthcare industry must set an example for their teams by acting in ways that they would want their coworkers and subordinates to (for example, reporting errors and patient-centered actions). Healthcare managers use their influence to establish a culture that encourages the quest for the true objective, even under pressure, by modeling the appropriate behaviors themselves.

Leaders in the field of Intellectual Stimulation (IS) foster a diverse and open environment in which they inspire others to develop and come up with fresh concepts for the company and for themselves. As a result, such leaders can significantly impact strategic planning and change.

By using motivating approaches to boost team morale and serving as an example for their followers, Inspirational Motivation (IM) leaders play a pivotal role in improving performance.

Individualized consideration (IC) actively works to create a welcoming environment that is diverse and where people are encouraged to embrace their own differences. Transformational pediatric leaders can increase the effectiveness of their teams by identifying the uniqueness of team members and capitalizing on these differences by changing motivational techniques and role distributions.

Healthcare management can benefit from a transformational leadership mentality in certain circumstances. For instance, transformational leadership functions better when team members are experts in the relevant field. However, the transformative leadership style might not be the best or most helpful in circumstances where staff members lack abilities and require close supervision.

CONCLUDING REMARKS

Data is a vital component of any industry, including healthcare. It aids healthcare organizations in enhancing results and delivery. Therefore, Healthcare executives must grasp data science for their businesses to successfully traverse the complexities of a data-driven environment and seize development possibilities. Additionally, like with any industry, healthcare must comprehend and adopt various leadership styles. For instance, transformational leaders excel when team members have specialized knowledge of the subject matter. However, the transformative leadership style might not be the best or most useful in circumstances where people lack competencies and need close supervision.

REFERENCES

[1]   C. Millar, K. Peters, and H. Millar, "Culture, the missing link in value creation and governance in knowledge-intensive institutions", In: *J. Pub. Aff.* vol. 18. John Wiley & Sons, Inc., 2018, no. 1, p. e170.
[http://dx.doi.org/10.1002/pa.1702]

[2]   Beverly. Robbins, and hizar David, "Transformation leadership in health care today", *Heal. Care. Manag.*, vol. 39, no. 3, pp. 117-121, 2020. Available from: https://journals.lww.com/healthcaremanagerjournal/Abstract/2020/07000/Transformational_Leadership_in_Health_Care_Today.2.aspx#JCL-P-4 (Accessed 28th July, 2022)

[3]   J.M. Burns, *Leadership* Harper & Row: New York, NY, 1978.

SUBJECT INDEX

A

Activation functions, sigmoid 124
Activities 66, 196
  economic 66
  financial 196
Age, numerical 193
Aggregate 69, 192
    occurrence 69
    volume 192
Agriculture 162, 163, 172, 174
    activities 172, 174
    sectors 162, 163
Air resistance 40
Algorithms 61, 132, 151, 166, 181
    action 61
    distance-based 132, 166
    machine-learning 151
    statistical 181
Analytics 56, 113, 197
    cutting-edge 197
    cyber security information 113
ANN cells 119
Applied math experiments 57
Applying 128, 129, 132, 162, 165, 166, 167, 183
    clustering technique 128, 129
    data mining 183
    domain knowledge 165
    K-mean clustering 162
    python code 132, 166, 167
Artificial neural network 120, 121
    constructing 120
    works 121
Atherogenic dyslipidaemia 180

B

Bayesian networks (BN) 182
Bayes' theorem 17, 51, 52, 61
Bernoulli distribution 57
Biases, algorithmic 90

Big data 24, 186, 187, 188, 190, 193, 195
    analysis 195
    applications 188
Binary classification problem 119
Biological neural network (BNN) 116, 117
Blood pressure 177
BMI, high 180
Boltzmann constant 37
Boosting algorithms 151
Business 55, 65, 92, 189
    environment 92
    growth 189
    planning 55
    sectors 65

C

Carbohydrates 180
Carbon 128, 162, 163
    emission assessment 128
    monoxide 162, 163
Carbon dioxide 128, 129, 142, 162, 163
    environment protection agency 142
Cardiac 94, 102, 179, 180, 197
    arrest (CA) 94, 102, 179, 180, 197
    diseases 180
    dysfunction 180
Cardiovascular system 178
Chronic infection 181
Churn prediction 151
Cloud storage systems 87
Cluster 129, 130, 131, 133, 134, 162, 163, 165, 166, 169, 175
    analysis 129, 130, 131, 162, 163, 165, 166, 169, 175
    formation 131, 133, 134, 162, 163, 165, 169
Clustering 128, 163, 164
    process 164
    technique 128, 163
Coactive neuro-fuzzy inference system (CANFIS) 182

Coconut oil 180
Cognitive learning factor 102
Computational algorithms 18
Cosine distances 68, 70, 77, 78
Customer 144, 145, 154, 156, 159
   churn 144, 145, 154, 156, 159
   relationship management (CRM) 145
Cyber security 111, 112, 113, 114, 115
   data analytics 111, 112, 113, 114, 115
   flexible 112
   systems 112, 115

D

Data 3, 12, 66, 86, 146, 177, 181, 182, 183,
   187, 188, 189, 195
   analytics issues 188
   mining 3, 146, 177, 182, 183, 187, 189, 195
   mining tools 181
   technology 66
   transformation 3, 12
   warehousing 3
   wrangling 3, 86
Data analysis 1, 2, 17, 24, 55, 81, 85, 105,
   114, 130, 165
  massive 114
  techniques 114
Data science 1, 3, 21, 53, 81, 82, 83, 84, 85,
   86, 89, 90, 186, 187, 189, 193, 195
   approaches 187, 195
   contemporary 89
   courses 81, 84, 85
   education 1, 83, 84, 89, 90
   industry 86
   methods 3, 186
   opportunities for healthcare 195
   position 82
   processes 53
   skills 189
   techniques 81, 187, 193, 195
   theory 21, 81
   training 83
Databases, traditional 193
Decision tree fuzzy system (DTFS) 183

Deterioration cost 95
   for own warehouse 95
   for rented warehouse 95
Development, business intelligence 1
Diabetes mellitus 179
Differential calculus 55
Diseases 177, 178, 179, 180, 181, 183
   cardiorespiratory 179, 180
   cardiovascular 177, 179, 180, 181, 183
   chronic respiratory 177
   infectious 178
   metabolic 179
   noncommunicable 177, 178
Dyslipidaemia 180

E

EDA technique 148
Educational framework, traditional 89
Effective heart disease prediction system
   (EHDPS) 177
Electronic health records (EHR) 193, 194, 195
Emission, industrial process 171
Encyclopedia Britannica 53
Energy emission 173
Ensemble learning approach 152
Environment(s) 94, 107
   fuzzy 94
   harsh 107
Epidemiological transition 178

F

Facility 179, 198
   medical 179
   nursing 198
Fatty acids 180
Financial 2, 193
   projections 2
   transactions 193
Functions 8, 9, 17, 21, 27, 28, 55, 119, 120,
   190, 196, 200
   probability density 8, 9
   transfer 119

transformational leadership 200

G

Game theory 21
Gaussian 9, 51, 52, 57, 63
    distribution 57, 63
    Naive Bayes 9
Gene sequencing 182
Genetic 64, 93, 180
    alogorithm 93
    mutations 64
    risk factors 180
Genetic algorithm (GA) 93, 94, 182
    based heuristic 94
    technique 182
GHG emissions 128, 129
Global positioning system 33
Gradient boosting machines (GBMs) 151
Greenhouse gases 128, 141, 142, 143, 162,
        163, 175
    emission 141, 142, 143, 162, 163, 175
Growth 129, 144, 162, 163, 191
    corporate 191
    industrial 162, 163

H

Healthcare 191, 192, 193, 194, 195, 198, 199
    data 191, 192, 193, 194, 195
    managers 198, 199
    system 195
Heart diseases 177, 182
High-density lipoproteins (HDL) 180
Hubble's 41, 43, 45
    constant 41, 43, 45
    law 41
Human-computer interaction (HCI) 90
Hyperglycemia 179
Hypertension 179, 180

I

IBM software white paper 196

Identification of clusters by elbow method
        132, 166
Illnesses, genetic bone 197
Image 4, 24, 33, 68, 69, 116, 124
    analysis 68, 69
    predictions 124
    processing 4, 24, 33, 68, 116
Imaging data 193
Imbalanced data problem 146, 147
Industries 82, 83, 88, 89, 90, 107, 108, 142,
        145, 162, 163, 186, 187, 197, 198, 200
    telecommunication 145
Inputs, transform data 121
Intelligence 20, 106, 112, 114, 116
    artificial 20, 106, 114, 116
    system 112
Intelligent heart disease prediction system
        (IHDPS) 182, 183
Inventory system 95
Iron calorimeter 46

K

Kaggle database 130, 162, 165
Kalman filter 32, 37, 40, 43, 45
    process 32, 40, 43
    technique 37, 45
Kalman filtering 24, 25, 35, 37, 43
    process 35
    technique 24
Kalman gain equation 32, 34
K-mean clustering 128, 129, 130, 162, 163,
        164, 165
    applied 130, 165
    technique 162

L

Leadership 82, 190, 197, 198
    health systems 190
    transactional 198
    transformative 198
Linear 5, 21, 26, 45, 47, 48, 53
    dynamic systems 26, 47, 48

regression problem 21
   systems 5, 45
   transformation 53
Logistic regression 9, 13, 16, 53, 60, 144, 145,
    147, 153, 156
Loss, standard squared-error 151
Low-density lipoprotein (LDL) 180

M

Machine learning 1, 4, 13, 20, 115, 144, 145,
    146, 147, 150, 154, 155, 156, 159, 166
   algorithms 1, 4, 13, 20, 145, 147, 166
   method 115
   techniques 144, 146, 147, 150, 154, 155,
    156, 159
Malformation 109
Mastercard transaction 109
Mathematical 1, 21, 51, 52, 56, 61, 68, 69,
    165, 186
   analysis 1, 56
   computation 69
   methods 21, 68, 186
   reasoning 51
Mathematics, applied 57, 59, 61, 84
MATLAB's matrices 3
Maximal frequent itemset algorithm (MAFIA)
    183
Mean 26, 27, 28, 53, 54
   absolute error (MAE) 54
   squared error (MSE) 26, 27, 28, 53, 54
Measured doppler 49
Mechanism 24, 25, 120, 153, 182
   computational 24
   fuzzy logic 182
Medical emergency 177
Mental 179, 181
   health problems 181
   stress 179
Microarray chip information 182
MNIST 116, 122, 124
   database 122, 124
   dataset 116
Multilayer perceptron (MLP) 177, 181

Myocardial 179, 180
   infarction (MI) 179
   ischemia 180

N

Network's life expectancy 120
Neural network method 182
Neurological disorders 195
Neurons, artificial 117
Neutral hydrogen 49
Noisy data 24, 152
Nonlinear 47, 153
   dynamics 47
   relationships 153
Non-linear systems 46, 47
Nonparametric statistical methods 58
Norm, vector's 6

O

Obesity, abdominal 180
Obtrusion, networks-based 112

P

PCA 14, 15
   algorithm 14
   transformation 14, 15
Power, thermal 142
Principal component analysis (PCA) 14, 15,
    112
Probability theory 3, 8, 12, 52
Problems 17, 18, 20, 56, 57, 60, 88, 90, 111,
    146, 162, 163, 188, 189, 195, 196
   decode 189
   informational 111
   overfitting 146
Process 2, 3, 10, 11, 25, 27, 28, 68, 69, 87, 89,
    90, 129, 131, 190, 193, 195, 196
   computational 89
   filtration 25
   industrial 129
   problem-solving 87

Programming 66, 67, 81, 83, 85, 86, 87, 90,
    128, 189
  computer 86, 87
  entry-level 85
  languages 87, 189
Properties, mapping 93
Python 69, 128, 130, 131, 162, 163, 165, 166,
    169, 175
  programme 166
  Programming 69, 128, 130, 131, 162, 163,
    165, 166, 169, 175
Python's NumPy arrays 3

R

Radial velocity 42, 43, 45, 47
Radio equipment 24
Random forest features 150
Regression 13, 60, 61, 151
  logistical 60, 61
  polynomial 13, 60
  method 151
Remarks- kalman filter 47
Restrictions 21, 85, 86
  credit 86
Russia's power emission 141

S

Scopus database 146
Sectors 144, 177, 193
  fitness 193
  medical management 177
  telecommunication 144
Security data 115
Service 87, 105, 111, 114, 115, 148, 149, 157,
    158, 159
  intelligence security 115
  virtual private network 111
  web 87
Sigmoid functions 9
Skew distribution 64
Skills 54, 81, 84, 87, 88, 115, 186, 188, 189
  communication 189

  computational 84
  problem-solving 189
Software 61, 84, 89, 105, 111, 130, 165
  algorithmic 61
  data reliability 111
Soil degradation 128, 129
Support vector machine (SVM) 5, 6, 7, 61,
    182

T

Techniques 10, 53, 145, 183
  deep learning 53
  machine-learning 145
  technology-based prediction 183
  transformation 10
Technology 12 ,67
  contemporary data 67
  data transformation 12
Telecommunication companies 144, 146, 159
Telemedicine 194
Test, chi-squared 59
Theory, chaos 21
Tobacco smoking 179

V

Vegetable oils 180
Virial theorem 49

www.ingramcontent.com/pod-product-compliance
Lightning Source LLC
Chambersburg PA
CBHW050839220326
41598CB00006B/407